The comparative analysis of terrorist financing will be of value to both practitioners and academics.

Dr Anthony Richard, Reader in Criminology University of East London

It has become somewhat twee to speak of the need to inform present day actions by referring to the historical past. However, as Dr Ridley ably demonstrates, through his comprehensive and lucid analysis of Michael Collins, there is clearly a great deal to learn about the characteristics and mitigation of modern day terrorist financing from an exploration of the life of arguably one of its earliest proponents.

Professor Rob McCusker, De Montfort University

The historical account is fascinating, the analysis of insurgency financing invaluable.

Professor Chizu Nakajima, Institute of Advanced Legal Studies, London

Michael Collins and the Financing of Violent Political Struggle

Michael Collins was a pivotal figure in the Irish struggle for independence and his legacy has resonated ever since. Whilst Collins' role as a guerrilla leader and intelligence operative is well documented, his actions as the clandestine Irish government Minister of Finance have been less studied. The book analyses how funds were raised and transferred in order that the IRA could initiate and sustain the military struggle, and lay the financial foundations of an Irish state.

Nicholas Ridley examines the legacy of these actions by comparing Collins' *modus operandi* for raising and transferring clandestine funds to those of more modern groups engaged in political violence, as well as the laying of foundations for Irish financial and fiscal regulation.

Nicholas Ridley is Senior Lecturer in Policing and Security at London Metropolitan University. He has previously worked as an Intelligence Analyst at New Scotland Yard, Criminal Intelligence Department and Anti-Terrorist Unit and at Europol. He has been a trainer in intelligence and anti-terrorism for police forces in Africa, and has lectured on combating terrorist financing on courses at NATO Centre of Excellence – Defence against Terrorism.

Routledge Studies in Modern History

www.routledge.com/history/series/MODHIST

Michael Collins and the Financing of Violent Political Struggle

Nicholas Ridley

Routledge
Taylor & Francis Group

LONDON AND NEW YORK

First published 2018 by Routledge

2 Park Square, Milton Park, Abingdon, Oxfordshire OX14 4RN
52 Vanderbilt Avenue, New York, NY 10017

Routledge is an imprint of the Taylor & Francis Group, an informa business

First issued in paperback 2019

British Library Cataloguing in Publication Data
A catalogue record for this book is available from the British Library

Library of Congress Cataloguing in Publication Data
Names: Ridley, Nicholas, author.
Title: Michael Collins and the financing of violent political struggle /
Nicholas Ridley.
Description: Abingdon, Oxon ; New York, NY : Routledge, 2018. |
Series: Routledge studies in modern history ; 34 | Includes
bibliographical references and index.
Identifiers: LCCN 2017036312| ISBN 9781138214897 (hardback :
alk. paper) | ISBN 9781315444925 (ebook)
Subjects: LCSH: Collins, Michael, 1890–1922–Influence. | Ireland–
History–War of Independence, 1919–1921. | Ireland–History–Civil
War, 1922–1923. | Ireland–Politics and government–1910–1921. |
Political violence–Ireland–History–20th century.
Classification: LCC DA965.C6 R53 2018 | DDC 941.5082/1–dc23
LC record available at https://lccn.loc.gov/2017036312

ISBN: 978-1-138-21489-7 (hbk)
ISBN: 978-0-367-34898-4 (pbk)

Typeset in Sabon
by Wearset Ltd, Boldon, Tyne and Wear

MIX
Paper from
responsible sources
FSC
www.fsc.org   FSC™ C013985

Printed in the United Kingdom
by Henry Ling Limited

Contents

Preface

This book is about a period of Irish history through an individual who was, and is, one of Ireland's greatest patriots and about funding of violent political struggle and insurgency. These latter activities have come to be termed, in a later era, terrorist financing.

The individual, Michael Collins, is rightly revered for his patriotism, integrity and focussed dedication to obtaining freedom for Ireland, and for his brilliant activities as a guerrilla insurgent leader, as a leader of intelligence operatives and as a sincere and far-seeing Irish statesman. This book focusses more on his financial activities. In concentrating on these financial aspects and activities it reinforces and enhances the place of Michael Collins in Irish and modern history. As such the book makes a modest contribution to the many works already devoted to Collins.

The author has been guided by distinguished historians of Irish history, particularly Tim Pat Coogan, and gratefully draws upon their authoritative opinions and works in several parts of the book. The author also extends grateful thanks to the staff of the National Library of Ireland and the staff of University College Dublin Archives, whose patient, friendly, efficient and speedy help is much appreciated.

Certain terminology has been chosen carefully, to be as neutral as possible. In describing the conflict period of 1919–1921, the epithets "Tan War" and "War of Independence" have both been avoided. It is suggested that the first is too emotive and omits the vital component of the intelligence war, and the second is not strictly accurate as the result of the conflict was to bring both sides to agree to discuss "Articles of Agreement etc". The de facto independence was arguably gained by the skill of the Irish negotiating team. The author has been guided by the works of one of the doyens of Irish history, Tim Pat Coogan, in keeping the term of "Volunteers" up to and including the early stages of the conflict, and following the transition to more intense conflict using the term "IRA". In the period of the debate consuming Ireland after the Treaty was signed and the period of the Civil War period, i.e. the years 1921–1923, the author has used the terms "pro-Treaty IRA" and "anti-Treaty IRA" to emphasise the all too real and tragic division amongst former comrades in arms. In the conflict itself the term "Irregulars" has been avoided and the terms "Free State" and "Republicans" used to denote the opposing forces.

The fourth part of the book is a form of placing Collins' funding of violent political struggle in a long-term context. Whilst historical parallels and analogies are very much *falsos amigos* to historians and rightly regarded with caution, there may be some germ of lessons learned from the Collins era for modern efforts against terrorism and terrorist financing. (It is the author's fervent-and-vain hope that eventually such efforts will no longer be necessary.) This fourth part also further emphasises Collins' innovations and ability in clandestine financing.

As amounts of monies are often cited, it is suggested that the reader to bear in mind that £1.00 in 1917 is estimated to be the equivalent modern value, as at 2017, of £79.40. This makes Collin's achievement in the raising of the Dail Loan within Ireland all the more remarkable. But then Collins was a remarkable individual. This book makes a modest contribution to knowledge about him and adds – unequivocally and without apology – to the tributes to him.

Part I
Violent undercurrents
Pre-1914 Europe

1 Violence in pre-1914 Europe

It has been held that the attacks of 9/11 heralded in a new era of terrorism. However, in the late nineteenth and early twentieth century Europe experienced political turbulence and violence from clandestine liberationist and ideological groups.[1] The main groups were the anarchists and the revolutionaries.

The anarchists were ideologically spawned from the various revolutions of 1848, and the writings of the French socialist thinker Proudhon and his admirer the Russian Mikhael Bakhunin. At the core of their political philosophy was the minimum – and indeed near absence – of government and the abolition of all private property. Abolish all property ownership, the political logic ran, and no-one could exist due to the labour and travail of someone else and the role of the state would wither away. It would be replaced by voluntary cooperation between groups of individuals and the rule of law would be replaced by collective and communal common sense.

The idea was encapsulated by Proudhon's twin maxims of, "All property is theft" and "Government of Man by Man is slavery". To Proudhon and his followers, the way forward was the somewhat vague and esoteric abstract idea of rights which, when propounded and explained enough, would galvanise the human race to the ideal statelessness, through reason. Bakunin and his flowers shared this ultimate goal. However, from his upbringing and experience of Czarist Russia, Bakunin held that only violent revolution would achieve this.

The long-term revolutionary philosophy to emerge from Proudhon was Marxism, which developed and adapted into revolution through the industrial proletariat. This, it was held, would take time whilst the industrial masses trained and – in contradiction to anarchism – became organised and disciplined. Bakunin, whilst sympathetic to Marx' long-term goal, was implacable in his doctrine of immediate revolution by immediate and constant violent attacks. If these attacks were perpetuated enough against countries which were at a certain stage of their economic development – Italy, Spain or Russia – then there would be large-scale risings by the poor masses who had nothing to lose.

Bakunin died disappointed that by the time of his death no substantial violence had erupted, but his cause was taken up by an unlikely figure. This was a former Russian Army officer and a distinguished explorer and geographer, Prince Peter Kuropatkin. Kuropatkin joined a secret revolutionary anarchist committee. Together with a group of French anarchists they produced the inflammatory publication *La Revolte*, issued from underground printing presses in Paris. By the late 1870s anarchist groups in the Russian Empire emerged through action. There was an attempted assassination of the St Petersburg police chief and the assailant, a 26-year-old female revolutionary, stood meekly by awaiting arrest. At her trial the prosecution evidence of intent to murder was overwhelming, but the jury insisted upon acquitting. Indulgent leniency was possible and common in this, the early days of the cycle of terror in imperial Russia.

In fact, the idealistic youth of Russia had not at this stage embraced violence, but rather sought to reach out and enhance awareness amongst the perceived exploited poor. Their guiding spirit was Lavrov, who formed from exile "Land and Liberty" and who wrote that the educated and privileged classes should go out to the poorer class and galvanise them into a reforming movement. Hundreds of well born and highly educated youths turned their backs on privilege and career paths and moved out to Russia's vast countryside, educating the peasants of their "true situation" and their plight and persuaded them to concerted action and reforming movements and if necessary, eventual revolution.

They suffered a robust and often violent rejection by the peasants who were suspicious, sly and the most active of them, aggressive entrepreneurs who wished to increase their holdings at the expense of their neighbours. The peasants even reported them to the police, the very source of authority against whom the idealistic youths were attempting to turn the peasantry. The idealistic youths, rejected by the very strata they were trying to help, became bitter and looked to themselves as uncompromising. By this time, "Land and Liberty" had been taken over by a group of neo-anarchists, who adopted the more strident title for the movement, "The People's Will". Revolutionary acts followed.

In February 1878, a police spy who had infiltrated the St Petersburg anarchist group was murdered. Then in St Petersburg in broad daylight the head of the Third Section (Secret Service), General Metzensev, was killed by an anarchist who slowly shadowed his victim in a horse-drawn carriage then jumped down and inflicted several fatal stab wounds. In 1880 there was an attack which though unsuccessful caused extreme concern as the imperial Winter Palace had been penetrated and the target was the Czar's brother. Ten palace guards were killed in the attack. There had already been three attempts to blow up the imperial railway carriage whilst the imperial train was transporting the Czar and his family from St Petersburg to the royal holiday in the Crimea. Now, with the Winter Palace itself penetrated, intensive anti-terror measures were implemented.

The government dispensed with jury trial in all cases of offences against imperial officials, and later all attacks against such officials were tried before military court martial. A strategic assessment was made, intelligence reports were studied, and the three most subversive areas identified and their centres – St Petersburg, Kharkov and Odessa – were placed under military rule. In the first two the military governors acted with harsh repression, whilst in the third, Odessa, there was a policy of firmness, restrain and moderation with even some measures of attempted relief to the population in times of hardship.

The Governor of Odessa, Loris-Melikov, was efficient. When initially engaged in anti-terrorism he himself was the target of an attempted assassination and he arrested the would-be assassin with his own hands. He was industrious and reflective and realised the folly of rigid repression and reprisal. His success in Odessa led to his being appointed as overall commander for internal security of Russia (including the protection of the imperial family) and part of his remit was to formulate a more effective way of dealing with subversion and countering attacks. His methods and his enlightened approach placed him ahead of his time, and arguably would have been instructive to the British authorities in in Ireland in the post-1916 period. Loris-Melikov's approach, as fully in keeping with the Czar Alexander II himself who was attempting reforms, included the radical reform of freeing the entire serf population and turning Russian agriculture into various levels of landowning by the peasantry. Loris-Melikov was no ardent Liberal but saw the value of reform and any measures which alleviated the cause of subversion and violence. He cultivated the Liberal politicians and even had dialogue with some of the less extreme revolutionaries. The more extreme revolutionaries and anarchists accordingly felt threatened at that time, as reforms would alleviate and reduce the rebelliousness of the mass of the population, essential for revolution. Continuation and escalation of extreme action was necessary.

A group of determined conspirators planned a multiple attack on the Czar, involving mining the route of his carriage, together with individuals armed with bombs ready to throw and detonate if the mines did not succeed. The bombing attack was carried out, disabling the Czar's carriage. Alexander, instead of being bundled into another carriage and driven away at speed, remained at the scene and another conspirator in the crowd stepped forward and threw his bomb on target; Alexander died shortly afterwards. Ironically, this was the same day in which he had signed the imperial *ukase* which freed all the serfs throughout imperial Russia. The anarchists in Europe had claimed their first head of state victim.

Alexander II was succeeded by Alexander III, a giant of a man and determined to confront terrorism, whilst presiding over significant, sweeping developments in the industrialisation of Russia, and a bullish foreign policy expanding Russia's Asian territories. His reactionary Ministers eventually persuaded him to turn against Loris-Melikov who was obliged to resign and retire in April 1881. Loris-Melikov's legacy was nullified in Russia, but in the post 1989 period, with the emergence of new states from the break up of the former Soviet Union, his example and his general principles are venerated by the Armenian Police. (His statue stands in a prominent place in the Armenian Central Police Academy.)

Alexander III's reign saw industrial development, alleviating in some aspects the lot of the peasantry, who migrated to work in the towns, but there remained much poverty and squalor amongst large numbers of industrial workers, which proved to be fertile recruiting ground for extremist groups. However, the repressive counter-terrorism measures were generally effective and there were comparatively few attacks and isolated acts of terrorism. The Peoples Will movement had splintered and one group emerged which was to dominate; this was the Social Revolutionaries.

An unsuccessful attempt to kill Alexander III resulted in several of the perpetrators, including one Alexander Ulyanov, being hanged. Retribution also fell on his brother who was expelled from his law studies at university. His mother lobbied and appealed for several years for her son to be allowed to resume his studies. Finally her persistence paid off, and her son was allowed to re-enrol, study at home, sit his exams, which he passed and he gained his law degree. However, the damage had been done. The new graduate changed his name and joined the revolutionary movement. The world was to hear more of Nicoli Ulyanovic Lenin.

In the final years of Alexander III and the first years of Nicholas I, Russian industrial development intensified and expanded, with increasing numbers of industrial workers living in harsh conditions. The expansionist foreign policy continued, resulting in disastrous war and defeat by Japan. In January 1905, there occurred the infamous "Bloody Sunday" massacre when a large crowd of industrial workers, peacefully demonstrating in St Petersburg were fired on by troops. This then sparked off a mutiny of the Black Sea fleet in Odessa, and mass industrial unrest.

However, during this period Russia produced two outstanding statesmen Count Sergei Witte and Peter Stolypin. Their wisdom and far-sightedness ensured a period of relative stability. By the early 1900s the country, whilst still extremely autocratic, had taken on a new dimension in societal terms. The 97 million agrarian peasants also worked seasonally in the factories or in cottage industries. There was now a small bourgeoisie of 13 million small shopkeepers, tradesmen and skilled artisans.[2] Order was maintained by provincial governors being given increased powers of arrest and punishment, and the police were given increased resources, whilst the Secret Service had been given wide powers to infiltrate agents provocateurs, investigate, gather intelligence and carry out preemptive operations.

Nonetheless subversion and evolutionary activity advanced in stages. Though opposed by Lenin and the Bolshevik group the Social Revolutionaries continued their individual attacks. In the early years of Nicholas II's reign the Minister of Education, Nicoli Bogolapev, was assassinated followed by the assassinations of Minister of Interior, Sipyagan, in 1902 and then in 1904 Sipyagan's successor as Minister of the Interior, Plehve, was assassinated. The following year the Czar's brother Grand Duke Sergei was killed.

In the same period of 1905–1906 there was an outbreak of mass insurgency in Moscow which lasted three weeks when whole suburbs rose up in revolt. Individuals armed with smuggled rifles and home-made bombs fought police detachments and troops until being suppressed with much bloodshed. Russian troops returning from the disastrous Russo-Japanese War mutinied and took possession of large stretches of the Trans-Siberian Railway and had to be quelled by two loyal Army corps advancing from either end of the long railway, gradually restoring order and taking back possession of this communications artery so vital to the Russian Empire.

Between 1906 and the beginning of 1908 there were over 35,000 murders of provincial governors, police, civil servants and imperial officials. All were carried out by another group of the Social Revolutionaries, the Maximalists. The Maximalist doctrine was that all those in uniform, or serving the régime in any sort of official capacity, were "excluded from the human race"[3] and it was an obligation and a duty to exterminate them.

The new Prime Minister, Peter Stolypin, met violence with violence, sanctioning court martials and executions. He continued and expanded proactive police operations, infiltration of revolutionary groups and full use of agents provocateurs. However, this was also accompanied by a period of economic and political reform. A Russian parliament or Duma, based on a limited electoral franchise, was established and met. A series of five enactments completed the transformation of the peasant from being indebted to the state to a small-scale landowner, and replacing poverty-stricken and inefficiently run farming communities into more advanced agricultural practice, giving more scope for individual effort and enterprise. The economic benefits were enormous, and combined with Russia's increasing industrialisation and growth of the railway network, significantly advanced the Russian economy.

The Social Revolutionaries, alarmed at the possibility of the populace becoming more prosperous and therefore more contented under the régime, were implacable and in 1911 Stolypin was murdered whilst attending the Kiev Opera house. The Czar and his family were present in the royal boxes, whilst the murder took place below.

Thus there was continuous subversion and assassination in pre-1914 Russia by the Social Revolutionaries, rounding off a generation of sporadic terrorism in Russia. The murders of a Minister of Education, the murders of two Ministers of Interior, the assassination of a member of the imperial family, the brother of the Czar, a disastrous mishandling of a mass peaceful demonstration and the murder of a chief Minister, had all occurred and the Social Revolutionaries were responsible. Yet there was a further aspect of concern.

The peaceful demonstration of 1905 which ended so bloodily was organised and led by an Orthodox priest, Father Gapon; he was also a police agent and had links to revolutionary groups. It is unclear where his true loyalties lay – Gapon himself was torn by self-doubts – but after "Bloody Sunday" he fled into exile, and was eventually murdered by a revolutionary group.

Also, the murders of Plehve and the Grand Duke Sergei were planned organised and facilitated by a Social Revolutionary who was also a police agent. The agent, Yevna Azev, had been embedded into the Social Revolutionaries by Plehve's reorganised police. Enjoying a wide licence to act as agent provocateur, Azev facilitated and masterminded many plots, then ensured by intrigue and timely informing, that the perpetrators would be intercepted and the attacks thwarted. However, in these two attacks Azev may have become too involved, or by his location(s) and activities and role as a Social Revolutionary have been prevented from ensuring the attacks failed. The undercover policing had become ill-managed and too complex.

The same occurred in the murder of Stolypin in 1911. His assassin, Bogov, was a Social Revolutionary turned police agent. Bogov arrived at the theatre and reported direct to Stolypin, giving a verbal report purporting to be an update of what was a fictitious plot. Stolypin acknowledged and dismissed Bogov, who remained waiting, lingering in the aisles during the performance. When the interval came he stepped forward and shot Stolypin, who died several hours later, Bogov was arrested, quickly tried and speedily executed, preventing any further inquiries. The police undercover system appeared out of control. In Russia, the doctrine of terrorism developed by Bukanin and Koropatkin appeared to have come full circle.

In Italy one of Kropotkin's disciples was a middle class young student who had been expelled from the University of Naples for participating in a student riot. He devoted himself to the anarchist cause. He travelled to Belgium and attempted to turn a general strike into revolutionary activity, and was excelled from Belgium, and then expelled from other European countries. He fled to Argentina, returning in and out of Europe to foment revolution. By his writings and example he inspired other Italians to anarchistic violence.

In 1897, Luigi Luchini, ex-NCO of the Italian Army, turned anarchist. He attended meetings of Italian groups of anarchists who were plotting to assassinate King Humbert. Frustrated with the endless talk and delays, he travelled to Switzerland and stayed in cheap lodgings. Empress Elizabeth, the wife of the Austrian Emperor had travelled to Switzerland. In September 1898 whilst walking near Lake Geneva she was stabbed to death by Lucini, who had been following her movements. Lucini, as a self-proclaimed anarchist, made a full confession and was sentenced to 12 years' imprisonment. At his trial he stated that it was a war against the rich and powerful and, "Humbert's turn will be next".

A year earlier there had been an attempted stabbing of King Humbert, but the monarch had displayed surprising agility, dodged the blade, and stolidly ordered his coachman to drive on. The following year, in 1989, the Italian government convened and hosted an international conference of police and interior ministry security specialists to deal with international violence. Common objectives were identified but little else was agreed upon, with Belgium, UK and Switzerland refusing to give up anarchist individuals if requested by another country, and confirmed within their respective countries political fugitives' rights of asylum.

Two years later in 1900, during a period of bad harvests, rising prices, riots in Milan and other cities, King Humbert travelled to Monza in the north to attend a ceremony. During the ceremony he was shot, and died shortly afterwards. The assassin was an Italian anarchist, Gaeto Bresci, who had travelled all the way from New York with the specific aim of assassinating the King. Investigating officers believed that his travel expenses from New York had been paid for by his fellow anarchists in the New Jersey cell. He was sentenced to life imprisonment. During his trial and in prison he received congratulatory telegrams from his comrades in New Jersey.

United States newspaper accounts of Bresci's actions and his trial inspired a young Polish-American, Lois Golgosc. Golgosc had been made redundant from his job and then suffered illness. He embraced radicalism, then turned to anarchism. Obsessed by Bresci, Gologosc joined various anarchist circles in the United States. Anxious to prove himself, he travelled to Buffalo, where President McKinley was due to visit a trade exhibition. Waiting patiently at the exhibition, Golgosc positioned himself near the official entrance, and when the President and his aides arrived he stepped forward and shot McKinley dead.

Italian anarchist influence on radicalising individuals was not confined to the United States. An Italian anarchist was to commit the final act of political violence in France which would round off a particularly turbulent period of political violence in that country. In the country of Proudhon, a revolution deposing the monarchy had occurred, followed by a brief republic, overthrown by a coup d'état leading to a régime of an Empire under Napoleon III, the nephew of Napoleon, then a disastrous foreign war resulting in the deposition of the emperor and eventually in re-establishing a republic. An exhausted political establishment had wearily decided that, in the words of the elder statesman Thiers, "a republic divides us least".

Economic and industrial development and progress had dramatically advanced, but like other countries in Europe, at a cost of widespread social deprivation and poverty in the conditions of the industrial workers. In such changing political and economic times, anarchist cells flourished and it would only be a matter of time before political violence broke out in France.

A two-year period, 1982 to 1989, of political violence started with two explosions in the Paris homes of a judge and a prosecutor, who, in the previous year, had tried and prosecuted a group of anarchist demonstrators. The perpetrator of the explosions, the anarchist Ravaillac was sentenced to life imprisonment. However further inquiries revealed that Ravaillac had also committed at least two murders, and he was re-tried and eventually executed, becoming a martyr to anarchists and the poorer masses. At his trial and execution he constantly asserted that he would be revenged. He was. Four months later a bomb exploded within the precincts of a Paris police station in the Opera district of Paris, killing six police officers. Police investigations produced little result, and for a time the perpetrators remained undetected.

The following year an individual, Vaillant, driven to distraction by various business failures, and in poverty, turned to anarchism. He resolved to make a gesture, a demonstration which would stop short of killing. He made an explosive device from home-made materials, with a limited explosive charge and impact. He then attended the public gallery of the Chambre des Deputes, activated the detonator and threw the device onto the floor of the Chamber. It exploded, showering the members with metal fragments, but killing none.

The anarchist press made much of the "gesture" or "noble deed" of Vaillant. The French government, tense with the previous anarchist attacks and furious over the violation of the very centre of the republic's law-making, ensured that Vaillant went on trial for intent to kill. Although the evidence was overwhelming, that there was no intention to kill, and that this evidence was ably presented by his defending lawyer, Vaillant was found guilty. He was sentenced to death and eventually guillotined in 1894.

A week later, bombs exploded in a bar in a Paris mainline railway station, and in the following, three more bombs exploded in Paris. Police investigations tracked down the perpetrator, whose apartment was found to be a veritable bomb making factory. The individual was arrested and further inquiries found that he was the same anarchist responsible for the Paris police station bombing two years previously. The individual, Emile Henry, was a former outstanding university student who had been expelled for abusive conduct to teaching staff. Bitter, and driven to poverty, he had embraced anarchism and all its doctrines. He made a full confession, claiming responsibility for the police station bombings, his motivation being revenge for Vaillant and that "there are no innocent bourgeoisie".

Revenge for Vaillant motivated the next attack, this time carried out by an Italian. Santo Cesario was from an anarchist group from Milan. Following closely newspaper coverage of Vaillant's trial over a two-year period, and forming an incandescent obsession with the eventual death sentence and execution, he also read in the same newspaper of President Sadi Carnot's visit to a trade exhibition in Lyons. Travelling to Lyons he waited amongst the crowds for Carnot's open carriage to pass through Lyons and, running close to it, leant over and stabbed the President to death. The cycle of political violence in France had ended with the assassination of the head of state, one of several such assassinations at the hands of anarchists in pre-1914 Europe.

Across the Pyrenees in Spain, political violence also occurred with the anarchists, against a background of a society tightly held by a powerful church, a backward agrarian system favouring large landowners and efficient forces of law and order. Parliamentary democracy was rudimentary, with the elected legislature, the Cortes, having a limited franchise which excluded lower sections of Spanish society. An outbreak of political violence occurred in 1893, the same decade as the Italian anarchist stalked and killed the Empress Elizabeth in Switzerland, and the violent explosions against the judge, prosecutor and the Paris police station. In this outbreak, a bomb was thrown at the Prime Minister, General Martinez de Campes whilst he reviewed a military parade in Barcelona. The attempt was a reprisal attack for the suppression by military force of peasants in Andalusia rioting against starvation wages the previous year. The bomb thrower and would-be assassin was executed, shouting for vengeance as the firing squad took aim. Vengeance arrived in the form of two bomb attacks in Barcelona, followed in turn by the authorities making mass arrests, intense interrogations and tortures of suspects, and then the arrest of an individual anarchist who proclaimed himself fully committed to anarchy and freely admitted the Opera bombings. Another anarchist cell then carried out another two bombings.

The government in their turn immediately took from custody six individuals from the mass arrests, tried and executed them.

Two years later in 1896, during a religious procession in Barcelona, a bomb was thrown. The intended targets were a bishop and a general; the bomb missed the targets but killed 11 spectators. Prime Minister Canovas then authorised a mass arrest of 400 suspects of whom 84 appeared before hastily convened military courts. Of the 84 hailed before the tribunals, 4 were executed and 76 sentenced to various terms of imprisonment. A year later, Canovas was assassinated. The perpetrator was an Italian national and a printer of anarchist broadsheets. He had been imprisoned in Italy several times for sedition, and on his latest release had travelled around Europe until finally deciding to avenge his fellow anarchists in Spain.

Before leaving pre-1914 violence in Europe and focussing upon Ireland, it is suggested that two points may be worth our noting regarding the violence perpetrated by revolutionaries and anarchists. The first is the toll of fatalities amongst the high profile heads of state targets. One Empress, one King, one Grand Duke, two Presidents, two Prime Ministers, and two Ministers of Interior are a grimly impressive total. And to this deadly toll of pre-1914 high profile targets must be added one more, an Archduke, Franz Ferdinand Archduke of Austria-Hungary, murdered in Sarajevo by a group of state-sponsored militant separatists wishing Bosnia to be part of Serbia, and directly supported by the Serbian Intelligence Service.[4] The second point is the international nature of the anarchist movement, especially with its various contacts and links formed by the various Italian individuals and several other anarchists who travelled and liaised with different cells.

In Imperial Russia, Italy, France and Spain political violence had occurred from the 1880s to the first decade of the twentieth century, such violence being usually countered by repressive measures by governments, which in turn were answered by further killings and violence by anarchists.

Notes

1 It is perhaps more appropriate to designate them "groups" rather than organisations given their essentially federalist nature and the constant splitting off and schismatic movements
2 Census of 1897–98, cited in R W Seton-Watson *The Russian Empire 1801–1917* (OPUS 1967) pp. 534–535
3 L Kochan *Russia in Revolution 1890–1918* (Paladin, Granada Publishing 1966) p. 114
4 C Clark *The Sleepwalker – how Europe went to war in 1914* (Penguin 2013) pp. 47–56 gives a full overview of the state-sponsored nature of the assassination

2 Ireland

Peaceful, patient and hopeful

Let us now turn to Ireland during the same period. By contrast with continental Europe, Ireland in the 1900s was reasonably tranquil. The bulk of the country was peaceful.[1] Ireland in the later years of the nineteenth century and early twentieth century had undergone dramatic change, with much progress in land ownership, social and economic conditions, and political self-determination

Land reform was started as early as the 1870s by British Prime Minister Gladstone who had determined, with a sense of religious zeal, to bring peace to Ireland. His first measure was religious, removing the primacy of the established Protestant church of Ireland. This measure related little to social and economic problems of the majority of the Irish populace, but it was not as irrelevant as it may appear to modern eyes. It was a radical move, a declaration of intent and the first change – even attack – on the 1801 Act of Union. Gladstone followed up this measure by his Land Act of 1870, designed to improve the lot of the small tenant farmer by ensuring adequate compensation if he were evicted for any reason except non-payment of rent. Landlords attempted to circumvent this by raising rents to unaffordable rates, then evicting. However, these activities by the landlords were countered by the formation of the Land League, formed and ably organised by Michael Davitt. Davitt had been imprisoned for arms smuggling for planned Irish insurgency and on release had travelled widely, met fellow Irish nationalists in the United States, and had reflected widely on Ireland's problems. Starting in Mayo, he organised the farmers who, by a combination of reasoning, dialogue and intimidation managed to wring a reduction of rents from landlords in times of adverse harvests, and prevented evictions. Due to Davitt's able organisation, the Land League grew and covered most of Ireland. Davitt's activities in making significant progress in Ireland's principle problem, should not be underestimated. A distinguished Irish historian in a work of long-term historical scope, wrote of Davitt

> Michael Davitt, an ex-Fenian, until the advent of Sean Lemass 80 years later, deserves to be regarded as the Irish leader who delivered the most tangible benefit to his people.[2]

The combination of Gladstone's Act and the subsequent 1881 Land Act, together with Davitt's organised tenancy, resulted in tenants being given a certain immunity against contrived rent increase and being able to purchase their rented land partly with down-payments and the rest by annual instalments. The 1881 Act in principle created almost dual ownership, that of peasant tenant farmer and landlord. Sole ownership by the peasant farmer was made possible by a further Land Purchase Act of 1903 under the guidance of the Chief Secretary for Ireland Wyndham. This gave landlords generous compensation in exchange for selling the land outright to the tenants. The small peasant farmer became, in time, a man of property and a freehold farmer.[3] The process was a continuous one, so that by 1921, of the 470,000 landholdings in Ireland, just over 400,000 were owned by their tenant-occupiers.[4] Progress in solving the Land question was accompanied by overall economic growth. This was facilitated by an increase in railway transport, this increase in turn was due to low labour costs and comparatively favourable terrain of Ireland, where railway expansion needed few tunnels or viaducts. In the 30 years between 1850 and 1880 an extra 60 miles of railway track was laid every year. After 1880 the railways expanded further with more rail companies and Irish investors acquiring and increasing shareholdings, resulting in the return in capital remaining in Ireland.

In 1891, legislation was passed setting up the congested districts board, to relieve poverty in the south and south-west of Ireland. Local industries were revived by subsidies, and also technical assistance and expertise was provided to small farms to improve yields. In addition to these measures, in 1899 a newly created Department of Agriculture was set up, under the direction of a forward looking, philanthropic-and-efficient landowner, Sir Horace Plunkett. There were further agrarian improvements, which were stimulated by the improvement of agricultural labourers' conditions and dwellings by Acts passed in 1882, 1883, 1885 and 1906. There were also other economic sectors which were placed under Plunkett's eager department. One example was the fishing industry which was given help in the form of direct grants and technical instruction and training, with the result that the value of fish landed on the coasts of the congested districts tripled over a period of 20 years.

By 1910 Ireland's economy and social conditions had been changed for by far the better. It was not booming, or perfect.[5] Two glaring examples of this were the Dublin working-class slums which grew, worsened and remained a scandal and a shame, and the numbers of unemployed unskilled labourers remained high. However, overall, the combined, massive effects of the easing of the Land question, the work of the congested districts board and the wide-sweeping improvements by the Department of Agriculture to conditions of agrarian workers and the expansion of rail transport, were changing Ireland to a more prosperous society.

These efforts, herculean as they were when compared to previous British intervention, were welcomed by Irish nationalists, but were also suspected of being part of the British intention to push away Irish self-determination and "kill Home Rule by kindness". Accordingly, the ultimate, unwavering objective remained self-determination but it was to be achieved by political means. This had been facilitated by local government reforms whereby certain powers of local government were devolved. Local councils responsible for urban and rural social amenities, including primary education, were elected under a progressive wide franchise (including women). These invariably produced nationalist majorities in local politics which afforded grassroots bases and support for the self-determination, by political means, at national level. The legislation of the past 20 years, up to 1914, in agriculture, land, local government and education, passed with the help and urging of the Irish Home Rule parliamentarians

> ... meant nothing less than the transfer of power from the Anglo-Irish ascendency to the Irish middle class and small farmers.[6]

As early as the 1870s, Isaac Butt, an Anglo-Irish lawyer, organised a campaign for the peaceful agenda of the rights of agricultural tenants and Irish autonomy in the form of Home Rule. Butt was to be ostracised by the Irish nationalist politicians led by the formidable Charles Stewart Parnell, but by the early 1880s Butt's work for the non-violent, parliamentary object of Home Rule was so influential that an Irish revolutionary of the 1840s, on returning from exile, wrote in frustration that he was,

> ... savage against the helpless driftless concern called home rule.[7]

Butt had given to Irish nationalism a practical direction.[8]

Leaders such as Butt's successor Charles Stuart Parnell and John Redmond led the Irish Parliamentary Party at Westminster in the late nineteenth and early twentieth centuries, and were regarded as the vanguard of the struggle for Irish self-determination. At crucial periods both Parnell and Redmond, leading their loyal Irish MPs, held the balance of parliamentary power at Westminster. In return for not obstructing government business and giving their support to the majority ruling party at Westminster, they exacted as their price, self-government, or Home Rule legislation. Bills had been introduced into the House in 1882 and 1886, but had failed to pass. Now at 1912, a third Home Rule Bill was introduced, finally giving Ireland self-government. It appeared that Irish patience, and their eschewing political violence by the majority of the population and instead placing of their trust in the non-violent, political way, was to be rewarded. In 1912 the ascendency itself, in the form of the three British governing officials of Ireland, Lord Lt Lord Wimborne, Chief Secretary Birrell and Under Secretary Nathan were sympathetic and fully in step with regard to the progress of Home Rule and

> ... this imposing triumvirate accepted the fact that they were on the way out, and that Irish nationalists under Redmond were to take over the country.[9]

Therefore, as at 1912, there was little combustible material in Ireland suitable for the fiery flames of political violence such as was occurring in Europe. A distinguished historian has described the situation, as late as 1916, as

> ... a strange limbo between disaffection and tranquility.[10]

The physical force movement in Ireland, the Irish Republican Brotherhood (which we shall meet in more detail later) was practically quiescent compared with the revolutionary forces and political violence occurring in Europe between 1890 and 1910. In Cork in 1910 it was a virtual home and reunion for Old Fenians.[11] Even the alternative Irish political movement formed for non-violence, Sinn Fein (which we shall also meet later in more detail) had reached a peak of active membership by 1908, and then was declining[12] and between 1910 and 1913 was "practically moribund".[13]

However, Irish peaceful patience and trust in the long-awaited Home Rule was to be yet again frustrated, not due to British intransigence, but due to the stubborn resistance in the north of Ireland. This resistance – and the British yielding to it – was to be the major factor and prime cause of Irish opinion turning away from peaceful political means to political violence. But this is to anticipate. Let us turn to one of those areas in Ireland experiencing a time of change, County Cork.

Notes

1 T P Coogan *The IRA – a history* (Roberts Rhinehard 1993) p. 13
2 T P Coogan *Ireland in the Twentieth Century* (Arrow Books, 2003) p. 13
3 N Mansergh *Ireland in the Age of Reform and Revolution 1840–1921* (George Allen & Unwin 1940) p. 195
4 R Kee *The Green Flag – a history of Irish nationalism* (Penguin Books 1972)
5 A full, comprehensive and balanced account of the economic changes in Ireland during the late nineteenth and early twentieth century is given by H D Gribbon chapter XII in X Martin, F J Byrne W E Vaughan *et al.* (eds) *A New History of Ireland – Volume VI Ireland under the Union* (OPUS 1996) pp. 260–356
6 F X Martin "1916 – Revolution or Evolution?" in F X Martin (ed.) *Leaders and Men of the 1916 Rising* (Methuen 1966) p. 242
7 Kee *The Green Flag* p. 362
8 D Thornley *Isaac Butt and Home Rule* (McGibbon & Kee 1964) p. 25
9 F X Martin "1916 – Revolution or Evolution?" in F X Martin (ed.) *Leaders and Men of the 1916 Rising* (Methuen 1966) p. 242
10 T P Coogan *Ireland since the Rising* (Praeger Press 1966) p. 2
11 P Hart *The IRA and Its Enemies – violence and community in Cork 1916–1923* (Clarendon Press 1998) p. 44
12 P Travers *Settlements and Divisions – Ireland 1870–1922* (Helicon 1998) p. 96
13 R M Henry *The Evolution of Sinn Fein* (Talbot Press 1920) p. 88

Part II

Michael Collins and the struggle for Irish independence

3   Cork, London, Dublin

The 1916 débacle

Michael Collins was born one of eight children to a father, Michael John Collins, who was one of a long line of tenant farmers in County Cork. Michael John Collins was a successful farmer, owning a 60-acre farm, and had time and leisure to devote to his young wife and family, and for intellectual pursuits including advanced Mathematics. Michel Collins' father died when he was six and he was brought up working on the farm by his mother and elder brother and sisters. He was schooled at the local school, whose headmaster, Denis Lyons, taught Irish history and influenced young Michael with past histories of rebellions and national feeling. After this school Michael went on to a school in Clonakilty and prepared for the British civil service entrance examination. A position in the civil service was then regarded as a reliable and secure future, and as such an opening for children from the lower social classes in an era when other career and academic opportunities still remained effectively closed.

Collins passed the examination, and was appointed to a clerical position in the second grade or division of the civil service. He opted for a post in the Post Office Savings Bank in London and moved to London in 1906.

His elder sister had moved to London for work some years before, and he moved in and shared her rented accommodation in West Kensington. Collins enjoyed London, mixing and socialising with other young men and women, especially those from Ireland, who had moved to London for work. Most of his spare time was preoccupied by Irish activities. He joined the London branches of the Gaelic Athletic Association and he played sports enthusiastically, playing for the Geraldines' hurling club. He later involved himself in the controversy as to whether players in GAA sports should participate in other non-Irish sports. He insisted that Geraldines jerseys and other equipment should be purchased from only Dublin-based firms. He started to attend Irish language classes, but these took second place to his other Irish activities. He was also efficient at his work, and took evening classes for the civil service promotion exams. However, he failed these, partly because he wished to change his employment (more of which in the second section of this book) and also because he spent most of his spare time on Irish activities. During Collins' childhood in Ireland,

and his time in London, three significant developments had occurred in the Irish nationalist movement. These were, the revival of the Irish Republican Brotherhood, the rise of Sinn Fein and the formation of the Irish Volunteers. Collins willingly became part of all three.

The Irish Republican Brotherhood (IRB) was formed in 1848 as a secret society dedicated to the establishment of an Irish Republic. After oaths and initiation ceremonies new recruits were made members. (The headmaster of Collins first school, Dennis Lyons was an ardent though discreet member of the IRB.) By the turn of the century, however, it had become a somewhat nostalgic society, looking back on and reflecting upon previous glories of Ireland's rebellious past. A small radical and reactionary group of the IRB were responsible for the murder in 1881 of the Chief Secretary for Ireland, and the Under Secretary, in Dublin's Phoenix Park. However, apart from that event, by the early twentieth century the IRB as a continuous insurgent organisation, was semi-moribund.

Then in the early 1900s several determined young members under the guise of forming literary and historical societies like the Dungannon Clubs, revitalised and refocussed the IRB into looking forward to obtain Irish independence through political violence. The revitalised IRB had a ready reservoir of recruits in the Gaelic Athletic Association and the Gaelic League. Active membership of either of these societies, besides ensuring that the potential recruit had a certain level of physical fitness and stamina, was also held to be an assurance of commitment to Irish self-determination and independence.[1]

The IRB were joined in the leadership by the veteran Irish revolutionary, Thomas Clarke. He was still recovering from a term of harsh imprisonment in British jails having returned to Ireland from the United States. Clarke was to be one of the leaders of the 1916 Rising. In 1909, Collins was recruited into the IRB whilst working in London. He was recruited through his activities in the London GAA, by Sam McGuire, a stalwart of Irish athletics (and to whom a much-coveted present day Irish sporting trophy is named). The suggestion that Collins should join the IRB was made when he met Harry Boland, an IRB member since the early 1900s, and at the time of encountering Collins he was on GAA business in London. Boland and Collins were to develop a genuine and long friendship, and were later to form an extremely efficient organising team back in in Ireland;and even later were, with extreme regret, to take opposite sides in a political conflict.

The second development was the emergence of Sinn Fein. Sinn Fein was the visionary concept and brainchild of Arthur Griffith, an Irish printer and journalist and staunch advocate of Irish independence. In the mid-1900s Griffith returned from South Africa (where he had been active as a journalist in pro-Boer and anti-British publications) and he formed Sinn Fein, literally translated to English to mean "Ourselves Alone". The bedrock of Sinn Fein was based upon his publication *Hungary – a parallel for Ireland.* It took as its model, Hungary, then a sovereign entity within the dual monarchy of the Hapsburg Austro-Hungarian Empire. Hungary was separate and autonomous in everything except a common imperial monarchy, defence and foreign policy.[2] (It may have been encouraging to Griffith that by the time he formed Sinn Fein, the principle of self-determination by dualism was held to be so beneficial in the Hapsburg Empire that the heir to the throne, Franz Ferdinand – to the despair of the aged reigning emperor – was planning, on his accession, to expand dualism and turn the Empire into a tri-monarchical structure which would give the Slav minorities similar autonomous powers.[3])

Sinn Fein argued that if, unlike the Hapsburg settlement of 1867 which established the dual monarchy, Britain proved unmovable towards some form of Irish autonomy and self-determination, then Ireland should go alone. By this Sinn Fein meant the Irish establish, by peaceful absenteeism, their own fully functioning institutions of state-courts and a legal system, banks and capital flow, agrarian development and land administration. When these were fully functioning, it argued, the British administration would be under-used and eventually wither away. The concept of passive absenteeism and the non-violent freezing out of British administration by no-use would grow in its appeal to Irish nationalism, and Sinn Fein would come to the fore later. However, in the mid-1900s it was regarded with suspicion by Irish nationalist like the IRB, looking to direct physical force and political violence as the way to achieve independence.

Collins joined Sinn Fein as part of his Irish activities in London, and at their political meetings composed and presented papers. There included papers on the Irish Famine of 1847 and the Finnish movement for self-determination during which he pointed to, as an example to follow, the Finnish revolutionaries who, allying themselves to the Russian revolutionaries, murdered the Russian Governor General in 1904, and sometime later gained a national parliament. He also pronounced on the Phoenix Park murders of Chief Secretary for Ireland and Under Secretary Burke in 1882, stating that he did not condone the murder as such, but justified it on expediency.[4] Collins fully embraced the physical force aspect as a solution to Irish self-determination, and whilst was content to be a member of Sinn Fein, at this stage tended to share the reservations of Irish nationalists for Sinn Fein's non-violent absenteeism.

The third significant development was that of the formation of the Irish Volunteers in Ireland. This was as a result of political events occurring between 1912 and 1914 which brought aspirations of Home Rule to a head, and to many, despair. Meanwhile, as at 1912, let us stay in London, but look also at events in northern Ireland. An Irish Home Rule bill, in accordance with Ireland's patient hopes, and the demands of the Irish Parliamentary Party at Westminster, passed the House of Commons; it was rejected in the House of Lords. However, the latter's powers had been restricted by recent legislation and were reduced to delaying a bill which, if passed three times by the Commons would automatically become law. The Home Rule bill finally passed the Commons again in May 1914. However, by this time the Ulster Protestants, totally opposed, had reacted speedily and violently under their leader Sir Edward Carson. Carson, a successful Anglo-Irish lawyer, was convinced of the benefits of the Anglo-Irish union. In the north, a petition against Home Rule, the Covenant, was raised with 40,000 signatures. A massive paramilitary force, the Ulster Volunteer Force (UVF), was formed whose members were openly drilling in formation and were armed by an illegal arms importation which the authorities had made little effort to prevent. In 1914, an ugly and highly controversial incident occurred where several senior British officers based at the military camp in the Curragh in central Ireland expressed extreme reluctance to take any action against the Ulster Volunteers. They were given an assurance by Sir Henry Wilson, as Director of Military Operations, that the Army would not be so deployed. The British government could no longer rely on its armed forces in any action to restrain or coerce Ulster.

These events of 1912 to 1914 in Westminster, London and in northern Ireland formed a crucial turning point in Irish nationalism in the south. As we have seen, up to 1912, Ireland was peaceful, hopeful and patient in anticipation of Home Rule. Those advocating physical force and conflict were marginalised. With the resistance of Ulster, the open drilling and arming of the Ulster Volunteers and the obvious capitulation of the British government to such resistance, Irish collective frustration gave the advocates of physical force their opportunity.

Ireland took Carson and his Unionists as a lesson and example. Thomas Clarke told fellow IRB leaders that this was the course that they too must follow.[5] Two of the IRB leaders and leaders of the 1916 Rising, MacDonagh and Plunkett, up to 1913 were adherents of Home Rule;[6] the events in the north changed their stance. Another leader of the 1916 Rebellion, Patrick Pearse, was as late as 1912 aspiring to be an MP at Westminster as an Irish Home Ruler, and in late 1913 had pointed out in the IRB publication *Irish Freedom* that

> there were *two* ways of righting wrongs, *reform* and revolution (italics mine).[7]

Now Pearse, after viewing the UVF formation, stated publicly that there was only one thing more ridiculous than an Orangeman with a rifle, and that was a Nationalist without one. Eion MacNeill, an eminent scholar of Irish history and literature, and Professor of Dublin University, formed the counter paramilitary force the Irish Volunteers in November 1913, and in doing so called for three cheers for Carson for showing Ireland the way forward. The British General Maxwell, deployed as commander of the forces that were to crush the 1916 Rising (and who was responsible for executing its leaders) was later to speak warmly of the Irish people and to condemn the poverty and squalor of parts of Dublin which could have easily been prevented. Maxwell firmly placed the blame for the Rising on the actions of the Ulster loyalists and the British government capitulating to this.[8] Pieras Beaslai, a member of the IRB and future IRA fighter in the Anglo-Irish War, who had viewed with concern the lack of support for the IRB in the 1900s, incisively wrote

> In an Ireland doped in an unlimited patience, and credulity, and an unlimited confidence in its Party leaders, and in the British Liberal government, and a confident expectation of Home Rule, came Sir Edward Carson to save the situation for the physical force party. He, more than any man, is responsible for the events which have created the Irish Free State.... Here was the opportunity of the IRB.[9]

The Irish Volunteers attracted a large number of recruits throughout Ireland. MacNeill conceived of the Volunteers defending Home Rule as a purely defensive force. But after 35,000 rifles and ammunition was illegally imported it was an armed defensive force. The IRB infiltrated the Volunteers at all levels and were determined that the Volunteers would be the forces used for the future Rising, which they saw as the only realistic means to gain Irish self-determination. A significant turning point towards political violence and armed conflict had occurred. It had been caused by Ulstermen in the north combined with a vacillating and nerveless British establishment.

In London, branches of the Irish Volunteers were formed and in 1913 Collins joined a unit. Therefore, by the time of the outbreak of the First World War Collins was both a Volunteer and a member of the IRB. With the outbreak of the First World War, the Volunteers split.

Redmond and his fellow Irish Westminster politicians had generously responded to the patriotic call in Britain, pledging full Irish support in terms of manpower and loyalty, an offer that was greeted with incredible short-sightedness and disdain by British authorities.[10] Redmond offered the Volunteers as the defence force for Ireland and called on the government to give support and facilities and implement this officially. His offer met with no response. In a summary of one historian (which encapsulates the British military view of the time)

> they were told, in so many words that one had to be careful about arming rebels.[11]

Then in September 1914, at review in a unit of the Volunteers at Woodenbridge in Wicklow, Redmond publicly committed the Volunteers to joining the war, urging them to continue drilling so that in due course they would join the firing line at the front.[12] This caused the split within the Volunteers. MacNeill issued a statement disowning Redmond and the direction he was taking the Volunteers, and his followers formed their own organisation, which became known as the Irish Volunteers. The remaining Redmondites became known as the National Volunteers. At the time, the Redmondite or National Volunteers were in a large majority. Up to an estimated 18,000 had remaining loyal to the National Volunteers, with only 1,200 forming behind MacNeill.[13] This was entirely in keeping with the general feeling in Ireland which was still in faith with the Home Rule Act, and the full realities of the Suspensory Act and the projected and looming Amending Bill were not yet fully apparent.[14]

Yet even then, dissident extreme nationalists' voices made themselves heard. Griffith's Sinn Fein publication stated in response to Redmond generous commitments at the outbreak of the First World War

> Ireland is not at war with Germany.... Our duty is not in doubt. We are Irish nationalists and the only duty we can have is to stand for Ireland's interests....[15]

Gradually MacNeill's Irish Volunteers gained more support and recruits throughout 1915.[16] Also, with the appalling casualties occurring on the western front throughout 1915, stark demographics came into play, reducing the difference in numbers between the National Volunteers and the Irish Volunteers.

Thus, the three significant developments in Irish nationalism in the twentieth century up to the First World War, the resurgence of the IRB, the emergence of Sinn Fein and the formation of the Irish Volunteers were all fully embraced by Collins. By the time he returned to Ireland from London he was an active member of all three.

Collins' time in London appears to have been a happy one for him in that he was constantly in work, worked hard, enjoyed much friendship and gave full vent to his Irish patriotism in his Irish activities. However, world events intervened. Britain was at war and, like other belligerents, deploying and using manpower in the army and navy on an unprecedented scale. The radical and unprecedented step was taken by the government to introduce conscription, which was due to come into force in Britain – but not in Ireland – in January 1916. Collins was most unwilling to serve in the British Army and resolved to return to Ireland. He gave notice to his employers, stating that he had no intention of waiting for conscription.

Collins returned to Ireland and joined the Plunkett household, located near Dublin. Count Plunkett was a Papal Count and Director of the National Museum. His son, Joseph, although terminally ill with tuberculosis, was a senior council member of the IRB and one of the "military strategists" planning the Rising. Joseph Plunkett and Roger Casement made secret visits to Berlin and attempted to negotiate German military assistance for the forthcoming Rising. Casement, born of an Anglo-Irish family, had worked for the British Colonial Office and in 1911 resigned after exposing human rights abuses against indigenous workers, by Belgian commercial interests in the Congo and by British firms in Peru. He had taken up the cause of Irish self-determination and placed his services at the disposal of the Volunteers. During Casement and Plunkett's visits to Berlin, Plunkett overestimated his own knowledge of military affairs and upset the German High Command;[17] the "delegates" received no promises of German military manpower in any forthcoming Rising. Count Plunkett had placed part of his estate at the disposal of the Irish Volunteers, and located there were young Irishmen who had fled England to avoid being conscripted. There they engaged in drilling and receiving elementary instruction in guerrilla fighting. In another part of the estate there was a makeshift arsenal where various home-made grenades and bombs were being made.

Collins' activities in the IRB also involved him working with another future leader of the Rising, Sean MacDiarmada. Although MacNeill was in overall command of the Irish Volunteers and had laid down their role as defensive, the IRB had infiltrated the Volunteers at all levels and were determined that they would take the offensive in the form of a national uprising. According to Plunkett and MacDiarmada's strategy, the Rising, aided and supplied by a clandestine shipment of arms from Germany, would begin in Dublin and then be supported and reinforced by Volunteer contingents from the rest of Ireland. These contingents would advance and hold a defensive line along the Shannon and link up with the Dublin Volunteers. Collins worked with MacDiarmada on the plan of taking and holding Dublin with a projected force of 5,000 Volunteers.

The story of the 1916 Rising has been told many times, and with repetition loses none of the tragedy of the mistakes and loses none of the futile, heroic bravery of the insurgents. It has been summarised as

> The Easter Rising as a whole, in which high drama and noble deeds were mingled with indecision, pure farce and division.[18]

The non-commitment by Germany of sending troops to assist, and the miscommunication and mistakes resulting in the arms shipment for Germany being lost, confusion and countermanding orders to all Volunteers by McNeill resulted in only 1,200 insurgents being deployed. These were supported by 152 members of a small workers' paramilitary group, the Irish Citizen Army.[19] The leaders of the Rising were relying upon a turnout of 5,000. The insurgents were centred in Dublin and largely unsupported by the rest of Ireland. The Rising was gallant and dramatic. Connolly ordered one of the Volunteers to hoist the traditional green flag of the Irish Republic from the top of the insurgents' headquarters at the Dublin General Post Office. (That same Volunteer was to play part in later years, thousands of miles away, in the attempts to gain recognition of the republic.) However, the Rising itself was a hopeless venture and there could be only one outcome. The result was foreseen by at least two of the leaders, the practical Connolly and the intense intellectual Pearse. Both realised the impact of making martyrs out of themselves and the other leaders. The fighting lasted a week and the insurgents showed resolve and bravery.

In our focussing upon Collins, there were five small but significant aspects of the Rising. One epitomised his commitment and attention to detail. At the start of the Rising, when the small number of insurgents were mustering in Dublin in various mixed garbs, and bits of uniforms and a strange assortment of weapons, Collins mustered in the full uniform of a staff captain of the Volunteers, immaculate and meticulous in every detail. (He was the subject of loud and ribald comment by his fellow insurgents which he did not take in good part.) The second aspect was when Collins was deployed as aide to the ailing leader Sean MacDiarmada in the GPO. During the course of his actions there, he came across two large tierces (barrels) of porter which had been brought along by some of the insurgents to fortify themselves during the forthcoming struggle. Collins immediately had the contents poured down the drains, stating

They said we were drunk in '98 – they won't be able to say that now.[20]

The third aspect was his bravery and initiative in the final days of the Rising, when the GPO became untenable. He led out a group of insurgents under heavy fire, and crossed the street, returning fire until they managed to gain temporary safety in other buildings. The fourth and fifth aspects had long-term consequences. Fourth, when the insurgents had capitulated they were taken into custody and processed, during which the six principal leaders and other leaders were identified and segregated from the rest. This was achieved with standardised procedures, but on other occasions it was by chance. So it was with Collins. He and a group of other insurgents were processed in a municipal hall and potential ringleaders, including Collins, were singled out and ordered to move to the other side of the hall for further interrogation. When the guards were preoccupied, Collins quietly stepped back to the where he had been and mingled with the others, to be "designated" a non-ringleader, and therefore safe from eventual execution.

The fifth aspect did not directly concern Collins, but its results were to aid him considerably in the future. The treatment of the captured insurgents by the British military was, overall, correct and at times sympathetic. There were two glaring exceptions to this, one where a British officer had prisoners shot out of hand[21] and another where a British officer[22] verbally abused prisoners and had them publicly stripped and humiliated, including the aged insurgent leader Thomas Clark.[23] Against these exceptions there were repeated acts of understanding, even kindness, by British forces, many of whose officers and men realised that the young insurgents deserved leniency, and some of the officers were conscious of the intense depth of Irish patriotism felt by the insurgents.[24] One such officer was Robert Barton. An Anglo-Irish landowner, commissioned and serving in the British Army during the First World War, his unit was deployed for duty during the Rising. Already sympathetic through his studies of Irish nationalism and Home Rule, he was profoundly impressed with the genuine patriotism of the insurgents, whom he treated with correctness, courtesy and consideration. By 1918 he was a convinced Irish nationalist and was to be an invaluable colleague of Collins in the economic sphere of the struggle in the Anglo-Irish War, and in the Treaty negotiations of 1921–1922.

Collins was taken into custody with the other insurgents. For him the fight of the 1916 Rising, in the words of an eminent historian had been

> seven mad suicidal, strange, incomparable days, a springtime of re-birth for Ireland.[25]

But for him the long-term struggle for Irish independence continued.

He was imprisoned along with other insurgents, first in Stafford Military Detention Barracks, and then taken to an internment camp in Fongoch in North Wales. There he kept himself physically fit, drilled with the other inmates, continued his Irish studies, and engaged in class discussions on Irish history, the mistakes of the Rising and the way forward, and organised group disruptions against various aspects of the prison régime. He also set up an IRB cell within the camp, planning for the future. In December 1916 the inmates were released, returning to Ireland in time for Christmas.

Notes

1 B O Connor *With Michael Collins in the Struggle for Irish Independence* (Peter Davies Ltd 1929) p. 20

2 How far there was a parallel with Hungary in the Austro-Hungarian Dual Monarchy, and the discussions it stimulated amongst Griffith's colleagues in Sinn Fein, is admirably and comprehensively discussed in R Davis *Arthur Griffith and Non-violent Sinn Fein*, chapter on "Republicanism and Dual Monarchy" (The Kerryman Publications 1974)

3 E Crankshaw *The Fall of the House of Hapsburg* (Papermac 1981) pp. 352–353; C Clark *The Sleepwalker – how Europe went to war in 1914* (Penguin 2013) pp. 108–109. What would have been less encouraging to Griffith – at that time advocate of pacific non-violent solutions – was that to Serbian nationalists working for a Greater Serbia incorporating the Serbian territories of the Austrian Empire, such a conciliatory, benevolent individual as Franz Ferdinand, whose solution would result in Serbian minorities gaining more autonomy and settling down content within the Empire, was far more dangerous than an out-and-out reactionary tyrant who would oppress the minorities. Hence the assassination of Franz Ferdinand in July 1914 by the revolutionary group *Uljedininje il Smrt* being planned and state-sponsored by Serbian military intelligence, C Clark *The Sleepwalker – how Europe went to war in 1914* (Penguin 2013) pp. 47–56.

4 T Ryle Dwyer *Big Fellow, Long Fellow* (St Martins Press 1998) p. 14

5 O Connor *With Michael Collins* p. 34

6 C Townshend *Easter 1916* (Allen Lane 2005) p. 95

7 F X Martin "1916 Revolution or Evolution?" and D Thornley "Pearse – Evolution of a Revolutionary" both chapters in F X Martin (ed.) *Leaders and Men of the 1916 Rising* (Methuen 1966) pp. 241 and 157

8 M Caulfield *The Easter Rebellion* (Roberts Rhinehart 1963) pp. 294–295

9 P Beaslai *Michael Collins and the making of the new Ireland*, (Phoenix Publishing 1926) vol I

10 Volunteers to the British Army from northern Ireland were allowed to form their own named division (the 16th Ulster, which fought with extreme gallantry and suffered terrible casualties at the Battle of the Somme) and to have the Red Hand divisional insignia. Volunteers from the south of Ireland were integrated into existing British Army formations with no effort made to acknowledge or recognise their identity. At one public meeting for recruitment the Secretary of State for War, Kitchener, accepted a Red Hand banner, destined for an Ulster unit, whilst at the same time ordering a Green Harp banner brought before him to be taken away (Coogan *Ireland in the Twentieth Century* p. 45).

11 F Packenham *Peace by Ordeal* (Pimlico Books 1992) p. 27

12 Kee *The Green Flag* p. 519

13 Coogan *Ireland in the Twentieth Century* p. 44; Kee *The Green Flag* pp. 517–519

14 Kee *The Green Flag* pp. 516–521

15 D Macardle *The Irish Republic* (Irish Press 1951) cited by Coogan *Ireland in the Twentieth Century* p. 44 footnote 53

16 O Connor *With Michael Collins* pp. 40–41

17 Caulfield *The Easter Rebellion* p. 22

18 Mackay *Michael Collins – a life* (Penguin Mainstream Publishing 1997) p. 49

19 National Library of Ireland MS 15,672 cited by Dangerfield *The Damnable Question* (Constable 1976)

20 Coogan *Ireland in the Twentieth Century* p. 54

21 Captain Bowen-Colthurst. A fellow officer, Major Vane, denounced him and persisted through official channels to bring Bowen-Colthurst to account. Bowen-Colthurst was found by a court martial to be guilty but insane. Major Vane was cashiered for such trouble making. In later years Vane was reinstated in his commission.

22 Captain Lee Wilson

23 T Ryle Dwyer *Big Fellow, Long Fellow* (St Martin's Press 1988) p. 31

24 Caulfield *The Easter Rising* pp. 250, 279; Dwyer *Big Fellow, Long Fellow* p. 34; Ryan *The Rising – the complete story of Easter Week* p. 258

25 Packenham *Peace by Ordeal* p. 28

4 Collins reorganises the Volunteers ...

After Collins was released, on alighting from the boat to Ireland he travelled straight through Dublin and on to his family home in County Cork. After a brief period at home he returned to Dublin where he obtained employment as secretary of the Irish National Aid and Volunteer Dependents Fund. These were two former Irish national organisations that combined to provide for Irish prisoners and their families. Collins performed his duties well. He had been given full lists of all the prisoners, and the names of Volunteers not taken prisoner and the nationalist sympathisers – these last two categories quite sensitive – by Kathleen Clarke who had full confidence and trust in him. His work with the Irish National Aid and Volunteer Dependents Fund involved him in travelling in Dublin and the surrounding areas. It afforded him cover to begin the work of reorganising the Volunteers in his travels in the area, whilst his colleague Michael Staines travelled further afield throughout Ireland with the Fund, and clandestinely revived both Volunteer and IRB cells.[1] In October 1917 Collins was elected to the Executive Council of Sinn Fein (though still somewhat sceptical of Griffith's gradualist, political approach to Irish freedom).

Reaction in Ireland to the 1916 Rising had been unfavourable, but it did change slowly. P S O Hegarty, a British civil servant in Ireland who joined the Irish Volunteers but later opposed physical force, accurately assessed the general Irish reaction as

> Ireland met it with misunderstanding at first, then puzzlement, then with a growing comprehension of its real meaning.[2]

The crushing of the 1916 Rising, the execution of the leaders, and the imprisonment and then phased release of the insurgents, and the overall lack of leaders at liberty, all meant that the physical force of Irish nationalism in 1917 had been nullified. Even after the 1916 Rising, and after the popular revulsion and reaction against the executions and against the treatment of the insurgents, the parliamentary non-political violent way of Irish Home Rule was still viable and desired by many of the Irish. The 1916 Rising and executions – these brought home and imposed upon the British the urgent need to pass Home Rule – but they did not, yet, render Home Rule irrelevant to the Irish.[3] For Collins and his IRB physical force nationalists, there was much to do in reorganising the forces and galvanising the struggle.

Also, the Irish nationalist movement was being effectively split into four parts, each with a leader. Count Plunkett had a small following with his Liberty League; Thomas Ashe, leader of the one successful Volunteer engagement outside Dublin during the Rising, was leading the IRB. Griffith led Sinn Fein. He was still opposed to physical force, though he was aghast and repelled by the executions and was becoming increasingly sympathetic to the Volunteers. The remnants of the Volunteers were still nominally under the command of Eion MacNeill. He had lost much ground and respect for his countermanding the 1916 Rising. However, his harsh sentence of life imprisonment in Dartmoor prison (and the stripping him of all academic awards and positions) did gain him some sympathy, and many of the Irish leaders accepted that he had acted with the highest motives. He was supported by de Valera, also in Dartmoor prison. There de Valera insisted and imposed upon his fellow prisoners that MacNeill was still their leader. De Valera was himself rapidly gaining a following as leader and spokesperson of all Irish prisoners in Dartmoor.

As part of his constant travels Collins also assisted in various by-elections taking place in Ireland for seats of Irish MPs at Westminster. He vigorously campaigned in the by-election of Kilkenny in August 1917 which was won by the Sinn Fein candidate William Cosgrave. It was the fourth by-election in that year to be won by Sinn Fein, Count Plunkett and de Valera winning seats in previous by-elections (Roscommon and East Clare), whilst an Irish insurgent still in a British prison had been nominated as a candidate and had won the seat (for Waterford). All four elected individuals refused to take their Westminster seats, looking to participate instead in an Irish assembly. Griffith's Sinn Fein policy of non-violent Irish freedom by sidelining British institutions was making significant progress, but in combination with the militant IRB and the reorganised Volunteers.

The nationalist strands of the IRB and Sinn Fein and the Volunteers finally unified under Sinn Fein at a meeting of the Sinn Fein National Convention in October 1917. At this Convention – the Ard Fheis – de Valera was elected President, Griffith magnanimously withdrawing his candidature to make way for de Valera. Also in October 1917, de Valera was elected head of the Irish Volunteers, and Collins was nominated Director of Organisation. This post meant that Collins would be in charge of recruitment, training supplies – and finances. Collins also maintained effective control of the IRB, which he reorganised.[4] IRB members were still present as Volunteers at all levels of the paramilitary force. In maintaining this control Collins, therefore, still wielded considerable overall influence within the Volunteers. Collins reorganised the Irish Volunteers, working with Harry Boland.

No biography of Collins would be complete without mentioning the background and work of his close friend Harry Boland. Boland's father was active in the Gaelic Athletic League and also in the post-Parnell Irish Party at Westminster. His son continued the athletic tradition and excelled at sports in the GAA. As we have seen, he met Collins in London through the London GAA activities when he, Boland, was visiting London and Collins was working there. It was Boland that suggested and facilitated Collins' joining the IRB. He, like Collins, took part in the Easter Rising, and was imprisoned in Britain. Being a particularly disruptive prisoner, he was transferred to the same jail as de Valera, and became a close associate, and shared de Valera's views on the type of Irish freedom, that is a republic as the ultimate goal. He was eventually released and the GAA and the Irish National Aid and Volunteers Dependants' Fund organised a hurley benefits match in his honour. He used the revenues taken to purchase ownership of a tailoring shop in Dublin. This would afford him a steady income, but also in the Anglo-Irish War the shop premises would be a meeting place and intelligence message drop. In 1917 he was made Honourable Secretary of Sinn Fein and in 1918, as part of the Sinn Fein drive in the 1918 election, he was elected as member for South Roscommon

Throughout late 1917, and through to late 1918, Collins reorganised the Volunteers in Dublin and in various parts of Ireland, organising and paying close attention to details, exhorting, providing a small amount of weapons and forming fresh Volunteer units.[5] He was in contact with officers of every Volunteer company throughout Ireland.[6] He worked with Boland who, on his side, reorganised Sinn Fein. They were an able combination, Collins on the militant side, Boland on the political side, and a close bond grew up between them[7] which facilitated even further the reorganisation work in Sinn Fein and the Volunteers. This close bond and this joint achievement made their political division and quarrel all the more painful to both, later. In the words of a distinguished Irish historian,

Sinn Fein was on the march. But so were the Volunteers.[8]

And this duality of progress was due to the closeness of Boland and Collins.

Notes

1 Hart *Mick – the real Michael Collins* p. 121
2 O Hegarty *History of Ireland under the Union 1801–1922* p. 703. O Hegarty was to become a long-serving, distinguished civil servant and historian for the post-1922 Irish State. See also footnote 366.
3 Kee *The Green Flag* pp. 591–592
4 Dwyer *Big Fellow, Long Fellow* p. 46
5 L Deasy *Towards Ireland Free – the West Cork Brigade in the War of Independence 1917–1921* (Mercier Press 1973) pp. 42, 53, 76, 81, 257
6 Bureau of Military History Archives (BMH) Witness Statement WM400/file S.76
7 Mackay *Michael Collins* p. 96
8 Coogan *Ireland in the Twentieth Century* p. 67

5 ... and de Valera enlists America

Whilst all this was occurring in Ireland, Eamon de Valera made a long, extended and historic visit to the United States. De Valera's objectives in going to the United States were, primarily, to publicise and influence United States opinion, up to and including President Wilson,[1] gain official recognition for Ireland and raise funds for the newly constituted Dail, or self-proclaimed Irish national assembly and government. President Wilson resolutely set his face against any form of recognition of Ireland as a nation–state. Wilson had little sympathy for Irish nationalism and the struggle against British rule, and insisted that Ireland was a British domestic issue.[2] De Valera's objective was ultimately to gain official recognition from the United States that Ireland was a nation–state. Another possible – and more practical – task was to facilitate an arms deal for the IRA, to supply them with the heavy calibre weapon, the submachine gun.[3] For Collins back in Ireland, raising funds was the priority. For de Valera in the United States, the priority was gaining US diplomatic recognition of the Irish nation, and of that nation as a Republic.

Harry Boland was smuggled out, disguised as a crew fireman on the White Star steamer "Celtic" departing Liverpool, and reached New York. There he made preparations for de Valera's visit,[4] establishing contacts, and discreetly gauging the political trends. De Valera was smuggled from Ireland by boat to the United States arriving on 11 June 1919. He was met by Harry Boland and Joe McGarrity, a self-made, Irish–American businessman, and staunch supporter of the Irish freedom cause. McGarrity provided de Valera with accommodation and extensive advice and guidance that Americans would expect him to act as President of a country.[5] At the time of de Valera's discreet arrival in the United States, opinions of those Irish Americans empathising, or active in the cause of Irish freedom, were divided as to the way forward. The association, named Friends of Irish Freedom (FOIF) advocated and campaigned for recognition of Ireland's right to self- determination. This way was opposed by those Irish Americans who held that the clearest and most effective way forward was to campaign for full and outright recognition of the Irish Republic as the legitimate government of Ireland.

The heads of the FOIF were Judge Cohalan and John Devoy. Cohalan was a judge of the New York Supreme Court, and a powerful influence in the US Democratic Party. Devoy was a prominent IRB leader in America who was visited by Pearse prior to the 1916 Rising. He worked with Sir Roger Casement during this period, making efforts to raise funds in the United States and, based in the United States – out of the reach of British Admiralty intelligence – coordinated messengers between the leaders of the Rising and the German Admiralty in their attempts to provide arms to the Volunteers.[6] Devoy was also the editor of the *Gaelic American*, a publication well known to and read in Irish–American circles. Together Devoy and Cohalan formed a powerful force. De Valera would have been better to have consulted and cooperated with them. Collins back in Ireland realised this, and wished for conciliation and as full cooperation as possible with both of them, hoping that,

the best and not the worst must be made of them.[7]

However, given de Valera's rigid and unbending vision of the Irish Republic, he was bound to side with Irish–American opinion which campaigned for full recognition of the Irish Republic as the legitimate government of Ireland and be directly at variance with Cohalan and Devoy and the FOIF. Before de Valera's visit to the United States, FOIF had already launched a fundraising campaign, the Victory Fund, and had raised a sum of which $250,000 was allocated for Ireland.[8] This however, was the subject of divided opinion. One opinion in the FOIF, led by Cohalan and Devoy held that this money should be used in the United States for the cause of Irish freedom, whilst another opinion, led by McGarrity, held that it should be given over without condition to the Dail in Ireland, to be used in Ireland to further Irish freedom.[9] De Valera felt that he could raise more by selling the Loan bonds, and, making his opinion very apparent and clear on his arrival, it did not augur well for good working relations with Devoy and Cohalan.

De Valera engaged upon a gruelling tour of America to plead and publicise the cause of Irish freedom. This strenuous tour was a coast to coast journey which started in New York then stopped in Boston, Baltimore, Washington DC (where he had interviews with sympathetic Senators), Chicago, Wisconsin (where as a pointed acknowledgement to indigenous people's rights he visited a Chippewa Indian reservation and participated in an initiation ceremony) and finally ending in San Francisco, California.[10] He planned to make the return journey to New York via the south of the country, but on learning of President Wilson's sudden illness (a debilitating stroke) he cut short the tour and went directly back to New York. Even so, it was an exhausting set of travels. In his public addresses, he often gave rousing and dramatic presentations, belying his normal reserved and quiet intellectual personality of the former professor of Mathematics. However, the latter did tend to become more apparent in his one-to-one, face-to-face meetings, where he tended to lecture the person to whom he was speaking and seemed disinclined to two-way discussions. In terms of generating publicity the tour was invaluable, he had made much effective propaganda,[11] and undoubtedly widened popular awareness in the United States of the Irish cause.[12]

However, within a short time of him being in the United States he had clashed with Devoy and Cohalan.

De Valera's title created problems. He was styled, or styled himself, from the press conference onwards and throughout his tour of the United States, as President of the Irish Republic. This was on the advice given to de Valera by Joe McGarrity, who knew the nuances of US politics and realised that some message of higher power had to be sent. However, his status and title bestowed by the Dail was that of Prime Minister (Priomh Aire) and this apparent self-styled promotion caused misgivings amongst his colleagues back in Ireland. Also, it was an ominous indicator to Devoy and Cohalan of this individual's personality, apart from the unwelcome public epithet of Irish Republic. It further paved the way for problems with Devoy and Cohalan.[13]

A disastrous interview with the press occurred when he advocated that Britain could adopt the US version of the Monroe Doctrine in its approach to an independent Ireland; Ireland would fully cooperate with this and British security would be guaranteed, as any power hostile to Britain would be unable to exploit Ireland as an invasion or infiltration base. However, he prefaced this solution by comparing Britain's relationship to Ireland with that of the United States to Cuba, so both the analogy and the logic of the solution was ill-received. Invoking and making comparisons with the Monroe Doctrine was risky at this particular time. Before the First World War, in 1908, the United States had been plunged into a minor war scare after a "plot" was revealed whereby Japan would ally itself with Mexico against the common enemy of the United States, and clandestinely station thousands of troops in Mexico. This "plot" had been a fabrication, entirely invented by German diplomacy in an attempt to obtain the United States as an ally against the Kaiser's phobia of the "yellow peril".[14] During the First World War in 1917 the United States had learned of proposed alliance – this time a genuine plot – conceived and planned by Germany, whereby Mexico would be offered, in a treaty of alliance, German military assistance if Mexico would engage in hostilities to recover her lost territories of New Mexico and Texas. According to the thinking and planning of both the German Foreign Office and High Command, this Mexican threat on her southern border would distract and fully engage the United States, and would prevent her from intervening in Germany's strategy of unrestricted submarine war blockade. (This strategy necessitated carrying out sinking of all neutral merchant vessels carrying supplies and provisions to Britain.) When the United States learned of this genuine German plot, it was the major factor in her entering the war on the side of the allies.[15]

Therefore, the sanctity and sensitivity of the Monroe Doctrine was absolute in the United States, and any attempt such as de Valera's to manipulate it for purposes of an aspiring claimant nation obtaining international recognition was regarded with extreme ill-favour. Also, within United States politics after 1917, any suspicion of being anti-Allies, and therefore pro-German was a potential vote loser. Therefore, being anti-British and pro-Irish had to be handled delicately; de Valera's blatant advocacy, vitriolic against British rule and strident for an Irish Republic, was indelicate.

De Valera caused further controversy during his stay in the United States by his pronouncements regarding the League of Nations. For him and his cause, recognition of, and admission of Ireland to, the newly formed League of Nations would be invaluable. Therefore, he wished the United States to embrace and join the League of Nations, thereby immeasurably strengthening the international body to which Ireland was seeking recognition and admission. However, he wished and advocated that the United States join the League of Nations (which the other great powers, and indeed US President Wilson so wished) but as a condition of her joining the League of Nations, Article Ten be eliminated. This article committed members of the League "to respect and preserve against external aggression the territorial integrity of members". If such an article stood, then Ireland as part of the United Kingdom was guaranteed by the League. (Modern Ireland has the same dilemma regarding its affiliation to the NATO military alliance. Article Four of the NATO Treaty pledges all alliance partners to ensure the territorial integrity of the members' existing frontiers, thereby accepting the UK/Eire border of northern Ireland.) However, much of American popular sentiment – including that of Devoy and Cohalan – was against United States participation in the League of Nations, and resented de Valera's intervention into US foreign policy, particularly as it was so obviously turning such a policy purely to Irish advantage.

In the first half of 1920 de Valera attended both the Republican and Democrat Presidential Conventions in Chicago and San Francisco. At the former he insisted on leading his "own" delegation and attested to have a resolution passed calling for the recognition of the Irish Republic, a proposal which was defeated. Instead a resolution was passed recognising the people of Ireland had a right to self-determination, and de Valera, with an ill grace, refused to accept or acknowledge the resolution asserting self-determination. The Convention then, tired of the conflict, decided against adopting the resolution. Ireland and any form of sovereignty remained unmentioned and unrecognised by the Republican Convention. Then, later in the year, de Valera's attempted at obtaining a similar resolution regarding the Irish Republic at the Democrat Convention was defeated outright.

Back in Ireland, Collins, whilst hoping that conciliation would prevail and a good working relationship would be established between de Valera on the one side and Devoy and Cohalan on the other, when it came to open dispute, he and his colleagues loyally backed de Valera. At one stage Boland was sent back to Ireland by de Valera to update the Irish cabinet about the situation in the United States, including de Valera's differences with Devoy and Cohalan; Boland was instructed by the Irish cabinet to take back with him a collective message of full support to de Valera from the cabinet. Collins himself stated in correspondence that he and the Irish cabinet stood right behind de Valera. However, later in early 1922, Collins privately apologised to Devoy (with whom he had a long established contact through the IRB) stating

> Our idea was to have some sort of worldwide Irish federation ... all joined by common ties of blood and race. Unfortunately some of those we sent to America did not understand the vital principle of that idea.[16]

By late 1920 de Valera was thoroughly frustrated with perceived United States politicians' refusal to afford official recognition to the Irish nation. More accurately, he was angry at their refusal to comply exactly with de Valera's specifications as to the type and form of such recognition and the way in which such recognition would come about, as laid down by him. Accordingly, after making tours in several states, he formed a separate Irish–American association on 16 November 1920, the American Association for the Recognition of the Irish Republic (AARIR).[17] Later the California branch of the FOIF also affiliated.

Irish–American opinions and associations were split more than before. Also, de Valera had failed in his primary objective in going to the United States, that of securing United States' official recognition of the Irish Republic, even Ireland's right to self-determination as a nation. However, he had succeeded in gaining in mass publicity and increasing popular awareness for the Irish cause. This publicity had translated into raising, by the end of his stay, over $570,000 for the Dail Loan. Even this undoubted achievement, as will be seen later, was accompanied by complications. Also, prior to his leaving for the United States, de Valera may have altered the narrative to give the impression that he was being ordered to go, and was being sent. When, just before his leaving, he stated this version to a fellow Sinn Fein member, the latter roundly rejected this version and directly replied to de Valera that the trip to the United States was de Valera's own idea, in order to be well away from the forthcoming trouble and struggle.[18] Whatever the version, what is certain is that de Valera had been absent from Ireland during a crucial period in the struggle for freedom, two-thirds of the period of the Anglo-Irish War which Collins organised and waged with great success.

It is to the period of conflict of the Anglo-Irish War back in Ireland, to which we must now turn and consider.

Notes

1 V MacDowell *Michael Collins and the Irish Republican Brotherhood* (Ashfield Press 1997) p. 58
2 M Macmillan *Peacemakers* (John Murray 2002), cited in Coogan *Ireland in the Twentieth Century* p. 77
3 MacDowell *Michael Collins and the Irish Republican Brotherhood*. Only Mac-Dowell, of all the authorities consulted, states this as one of de Valera's specific objectives or "missions". It is suggested that de Valera saw his role on a wider international political perspective. If contacts arose or could be facilitated as result of his visit, so much the better, but it may not have been one of the principal objectives he set himself or his fellow clandestine government envisaged from the outset.
4 Beaslai *Michael Collins* vol I pp. 307–308
5 D Hannigan *De Valera in America – the rebel President and the making of Irish independence* (St Martin's Press 2010) p. 6
6 Caulfield *The Easter Rebellion* pp. 29, 32
7 Cited in T P Coogan *The Man Who Made Ireland – the life and death of Michael Collins* (Roberts Rhinehard 1992) p. 190
8 T Ryle Dwyer *De Valera – the man and the myths* (Poolbeg Press 1991) p. 36
9 P Lavelle *James O Mara – a staunch Sinn Feiner* (Clonmore & Reynolds 1961) p. 143
10 The full itinerary was truly arduous; cities to be visited were, Philadelphia, Pittsburg, Youngtown, Akro, Cleveland, Cincinnati, Louisville, Indianapolis, Fort Wayne, Detroit, Chicago, Milwaukee, Indian reservation(s), Saint Paul-Minnesota, Des Moines, Springfield, St Louis, Omaha, Lincoln, Denver, Pueblo, Ogden, Salt Lake City, Seattle, San Francisco, Los Angeles and San Diego.
11 Kee *The Green Flag* p. 71
12 Dwyer *De Valera – the man and the myths* p. 120
13 T P Coogan *De Valera – long fellow, long shadow* (Hutchinson 1963) p. 207
14 B Tuchman *The Zimmerman Telegram* (First Ballantine Books) pp. 35–37
15 Ibid. p. 199
16 Cited by Coogan in *Michael Collins – the man who made Ireland* p. 193
17 D Hannigan *De Valera in America – the rebel President's 1919 campaign* (St Martins Press 2010) p. 57
18 Mackay *Michael Collins – a life* p. 116, citing T P Coogan *Michael Collins – a biography* (Hutchinson 1990) p. 102

6   The Anglo-Irish War 1919–1921

The so-called Anglo-Irish War, or the Tan War, had several confusing aspects. In such a conflict, summary analysis has always the inherent danger of over-simplification. However, two principal, vital points need to be made. First, the "war" or conflict by no means covered all of Ireland. Given the difference in numbers of combatants on both sides – the IRA when the combat was at its height had a maximum of 3,000 full-time fighters – this was inevitable. The IRA was always ill-equipped with fire-arms and short of ammunition. One of the most active IRA commanders, Liam Lynch, at the beginning of 1920 had for his entire brigade 15 rifles captured from an engagement, a few carbines captured from a police bar-racks and 12 vintage firearms of varying calibre; only 4 rifles were directly supplied by IRA general headquarters to his brigade. In an important attack in 1921 by men of Cork No 1 Brigade, the entire force was armed with shotguns, necessitating them engaging in close quarter firing exchanges. The ammunition shortages were such that actions had to be short and intensive, often having to be broken off and abandoned if opposition resistance continued.[1] One reason given by a former IRA com-mander for the defeat of encircling British troops at the engagement at Crossbarry in March 1921 was

> our luck in getting in the first half dozen blows (*i.e. rapid firing first*).[2]

The armed conflict had to be spasmodic and had to be irregular guerrilla fighting. In the words of an eminent Irish historian,

> There was never the remotest possibility of the IRA defeating the British Army.[3]

One of the most successful IRA brigade commanders wrote in his memoirs afterwards to advising against the

> visions of a smart brigade of regulars moving in strict order of rank through well-furnished quarters ... the reality was ... a group of

fellows mostly in peaked caps and not-too-expensive clothing wondering how to tackle the job in hand, and where they would stay that night or get their supper.[4]

It was ramshackle, and it was an ad hoc way of conducting armed conflict, but ultimately it achieved some success.

The Anglo-Irish War was bitter and intense, but it was spasmodic and regional[5] guerrilla warfare mainly in the south and west, and Dublin. Also, much of it was an intelligence war, of gathering intelligence, anticipating the opponents' move and assassinations, a type of war in which Collins excelled. Second, as can be seen in the above summary of the first phase, the Dail and its administrative and judicial action stepped in to the vacuum in the areas and localities left by the retreating British, thereby fulfilling the Sinn Fein ideal. On the one hand, it gained some real control. On the other hand, the Dail itself during the 1919–21 war was living an illusion[6] over the question of all-Ireland sovereignty. Large areas of the north and east – the traditional Ulster – refused to acknowledge, or accede to claims of an Irish nation. In June 1920, as a frustrated reaction to what was occurring in the south, the Ulster Volunteers carried out anti-Catholic rioting and pogroms, in which nine individuals died. The Dail tended to ignore this effective refusal of the north-east to acknowledge, and in its proceedings and day-to-day activities, by default and by silence accepted a nationalist Irish entry as confined to 26 counties.

Far from starting the conflict as a policy decision by the Dail, or the senior commanders of the Volunteers, it was forced upon them by a local action, when a local group of Tipperary Irish Volunteers ambushed and killed two RIC constables escorting gelignite to a local quarry. The police officers' arms and the gelignite was taken by the assailants. This occurred on 19 January 1919, two days before the Dail assembled and the Irish government in exile was formed. A few days later the Volunteers attacked an Army detachment in Macroom in Cork, injuring one soldier. These attacks were not sanctioned by either the Dail or central command of the Volunteers, and were pure local initiatives. However, Collins was not shocked by the action and did not condemn it. Far from it, it created precisely the situation Collins wanted, that whereby physical force could take over.[7] Speaking in the Dail in April 1919, Collins stated unequivocally that

> ... the sooner fighting was forced and a general state of disorder created throughout the country, the better it would be for the country. Ireland was likely to get more out of a state of general disorder than from a continuance of the situation as it stood.[8]

Up to this point it had been generally held by Sinn Fein and the Irish Volunteers that the Volunteers were to be purely a defensive force[9] and many individuals joined as a form of protection against the hated extension of

conscription. Even during the landslide 1918 election candidates and Sinn
Fein officials alike stated that another Rising, or similar action was no
longer necessary; the political could achieve results. However, Collins and
the IRB and others like Brugha had realised that further armed conflict was
essential, and Collins, in his work organising the Volunteers, ensured that
the offensive ethos was paramount.

Also, most important, the offensive strategy in the next conflict would be
that of guerrilla warfare, as opposed to the disastrous strategy of the Easter
Rising where insurgent forces had collected in a series of static defensive positions in Dublin and waited for opposing forces, superior in numbers, equipment and artillery, to eliminate them. Collins had taken the lessons learned
from the Easer Rising. These were not only the lessons from the static
defences of Dublin, but also from a small but significant action north of
Dublin. In 1916, outside Dublin attempts to mobilise the Volunteers into
action had petered out, either through the effect of MacNeill's countermanding the Rising, or through local miscommunication and uncertainty, or
through prompt action by the authorities. However, there was an exception
in Ashbourne, a small town in County Dublin. Here a group of Volunteers,
led by Thomas Ashe, a future hunger striker, and Richard Mulcahy, the
future IRA chief of staff, keeping their group mobile and flexible, attacked
larger force of RIC and after prolonged gun battle had forced them to surrender. Two Volunteers were killed, but also ten of the RIC were killed.[10] The
success of this mobile guerrilla attack was not lost on Collins. He realised and
acknowledged that the only way to fight was by organised guerrilla warfare.[11]

Accordingly, Brugha, as Dail Minister of Defence, issued the directive in
the Volunteer circular, *An t Ogleach,* which stated that Volunteers had the
authority of the (Irish) nation behind them in the form of the Dail, and
that every Volunteer was legally and morally entitled to slay, if necessary,
in order to overcome opposition and resistance.[12]

Collins organised a deliberate campaign of intimidation and killing of
Royal Irish Constabulary police officers. At the end of March 1919, an
ex-RIC officer and now a magistrate was shot in his home in Westport. In
April, an RIC officer was killed in Limerick and later on that month two
RIC officers were killed in an attack on a Tipperary police station. In June,
an RIC Inspector was killed in Thurles, whilst two RIC officers were killed
during an attack on a police barracks in Clare. The killings were then
extended to Dublin, and particularly targeted the Dublin Metropolitan
Police (DMP). In late July the Detective Inspector of the DMP was shot
dead in Dublin, followed in September and October by the shootings of
another DMP detective and an RIC officer. In late November, a DMP
detective was severely wounded (and disabled) and was followed in early
December by the killing of a DMP detective. A particularly able RIC detective, an Inspector from Belfast, was seconded to Dublin as part of an
attempt to arrest those responsible for the killings – principally Collins.
His diligent inquiries and activities soon posed a threat to Collins and his

intelligence officers.[13] By mid-January 1920 he too had been killed, shot down one evening as he returned to his hotel lodgings in Dublin. In the same month, an RIC police officer was killed in Country Meath, and in Tipperary a senior RIC officer, an Assistant Commissioner, was killed. In the second quarter of 1920 the pace of killing increased. In March RIC officers were shot and killed in Kilkenny and Limerick and an RIC Inspector was killed in Tipperary. In Cork, an RIC officer who had just returned from attending a colleague's funeral in Tipperary was shot and killed. In April two RIC officers were shot down on coming out of Sunday mass, a detective of the DMP was shot in Dublin, two RIC constables were shot in Cork and a police barracks in Tipperary was attacked, captured, looted and the contents of its armoury were seized.

The gradual result of this campaign of killing police was that the RIC withdrew from swathes of territory and re-grouped defensively into the larger police barracks, leaving the absented areas under the control of the IRA who were increasingly on the offensive. The original objective of raiding small police barracks was solely to seize arms and ammunition;[14] now there were territorial areas to be taken and controlled. In an early 1920 edition of *An t Ogleach*, there was an instruction to the effect that the era of trench warfare (i.e. defensive) was over and that from now on continuous guerrilla warfare was to be pursued, a trend which within two months had become all too apparent.[15] As if to emphasise this, in a two-day period in April 1920, the IRA, in a well- coordinated operation burnt over 100 smaller abandoned police barracks and police stations across Ireland.[16]

The mobility of British forces was also severely hampered by the refusal of the Irish dockers to handle military munitions and stores being brought into the port of Dublin at Kingstown, or the port of Cork at Queenstown. Also, the Irish railway unions refused to work or service trains being used by British forces, or to handle munitions and work on trains carrying munitions.[17] The Dail had issued an edict forbidding all train drivers, guards, firemen to engage in such work, and the majority of railway workers willingly complied. Those who hesitated or refused were subject to intimidation.[18] So effective was this action that the British administration considered closing down the Irish railway system.[19] The importance of neutralising the enemy's railway system was well-learned and underlined by a senior IRA commander, Liam Lynch (although when he stated it he was leading an anti-Treaty IRA division against the Irish government forces in the Civil War) when he exhorted his men

> ... a hundred bridges blown up was just as an effective blow as a hundred barracks blown up.[20]

The de facto retreat by the forces of order from areas of territory resulted in the Dail "governmental" institution taking over the functions of government and administration. Republican courts were established, and to uphold some form of law and order Sinn Fein police formed, on local ad hoc bases. The courts quickly became widespread.[21] This court system was organised by Austin Stack. Stack, a solicitor's clerk before the Rising, had joined the Volunteers and had been part of the disorganisation which resulted in the failure of the German arms shipment to Tralee Bay to reach the insurgents.[22] However, as an experienced solicitor's clerk his knowledge of legal system and procedure was put to good use in his report to the Dail of March 1919 and in overseeing the establishment of the Republican courts.[23]

The *Irish Times* was reporting that by mid-1919

The Kings governance had virtually ceased to exist south of the Boyne and west of the Shannon.[24]

Whilst Lord Dunraven informed *The Times* that

... an illegal government has become the de facto government. Its jurisdiction is recognized.[25]

By April 1920, 21 out of the 32 counties of Ireland had such courts operating.[26] Generally each court was presided over by a tribunal consisting of the local Sinn Fein Dail representative, the local IRA commander[27] and a third individual of good standing in the community. The Republican courts, both civil and criminal courts operated with popular support, the latter efficiently settling local and regional disputes. The result that the British courts were empty,[28] and practically ceased to function.[29] This was partially though fear in that no-one in an area controlled by the IRA would dare to bring a case to a British court, but also, as time progressed, because the Sinn Fein courts proved themselves efficient, quick and impartial at trying criminal cases and in settling civil litigation. The court staff and British appointed magistrates often resigned on "their" courts becoming so idle; some court staff even, discreetly, together with qualified solicitors took service as staff and counsel in the ad hoc Sinn Fein system that had come to prominence.[30]

This alternative criminal justice system functioned with perpetrators being arrested by the Sinn Fein police, often assisted by local units of the IRA. In some areas the Sinn Fein police were drawn from the ranks of the Volunteers and became de facto full-time police, but remained under the command of the local Volunteers commander.[31] Offenders were apprehended and brought before the Republican courts and sentenced. In one instance, one of the Cork IRA brigades was deployed in inquiries, and pursuing and apprehending individuals responsible for a £20,000 bank robbery.[32] (As well as a desire to maintain order, the motivation behind the IRA commander may also to have been to make clear to the local population that the robbery was indeed carried out by criminals, and not the IRA carrying on the custom of levying from, or being supported by the local population.) The Republican courts were particularly anxious to protect the rights of private property. This was shown in the civil proceedings of the courts, where matters of dispute were settled quickly and fairly, increasingly gaining the confidence of the populace. Courts of Arbitration settled land disputes. The impartiality in this court system was such that an Anglo-Irish peer, Lord Monteagle, in speech delivered in the House of Lords at Westminster, praised the high standards of justice and equity that prevailed in the courts.[33] Even Unionists living in the south of Ireland were reported to be acknowledging and using the Republican courts.[34] The political effects of the establishment of these Republican courts was substantial and cannot be underestimated as they were the most visible form of the new would-be Irish nation–state that was coming into being.[35] In addition Sinn Fein set up some form of local services and amenities. (Since the 1918 elections, Sinn Fein had majorities in 172 of the 226 local councils in Ireland.)

In the west of the country, as part of the clandestine Ministry of Agriculture policy, large-scale cattle herds were driven off the land and local Sinn Fein officials supervised the "reclaimed" land on behalf of the local inhabitants.[36] Also during this period of de facto Sinn Fein government, the Republican Land Bank was established under the directorship of Robert Barton (the same individual who as a British officer in the aftermath of the Rising treated the defeated Irish insurgents with a degree of kindness and understanding.) Barton himself perhaps epitomised the changes that were occurring in Ireland. He was an Anglo-Irish landowner, educated at Christchurch College Cambridge, and commissioned in the British Army during the First World War. His unit was deployed to Dublin during the 1916 Rising and he was profoundly struck by the conduct, commitment and sincerity of the insurgents. He resigned his commission due to the death sentences imposed upon the leaders of Rising and due to his being uncomfortable about the overall military repression.[37] He became convinced of the justice of the cause of Irish self-determination and by 1918 he was committed to Irish freedom. Appointed as Minister of Agriculture by de Valera in the Dail cabinet of January 1919, he started work on the Land Bank. Arrested and imprisoned for a seditious speech he was imprisoned, then escaped from Mountjoy jail. This was as a result of a jail breaking operation by the Volunteers, organised by Collins, who judged that Barton, as both as a Dail cabinet Minister and an expert in agricultural finance, was too valuable to be incarcerated.[38] Barton was both a hunted fugitive and an active Dail Minister of Agriculture until his recapture in 1920. At the same time as Republican courts and local government were operating, he organised and channelled funds and resources into the Republican Land Bank which advanced loans to farmers for land purchase, and implemented land commissions for land distribution to farmers and agricultural holdings in the west of Ireland. The activity was less dramatic than those of the Republican courts and the Sinn Fein police, but it is argued by one historian as "possibly more permanent"[39] in its impact on Ireland, and certainly was a significant factor in popular support in Ireland for the cause. Its fundamental objective was to break the financial bond between Britain and Ireland.[40] (Barton was also to play a significant role in the later stages of the Irish struggle for freedom.)

The situation by mid-1920 is ably summarised by one historian as

> Sinn Fein government operating simultaneously and in many ways more effectively than the king's writ.[41]

In 1920 the county Cork, parts of Tipperary, Galway and Clare were being described as really bad areas, and by 1921, the situation in Waterford, the west county Cork, and other counties in the south and west being described in briefings to British government as

> "desperate and damnable", "in a fearful condition" with one area which "had become a miniature republic."[42]

The RIC had retreated to the larger towns and into their enclaves in the larger police barracks. However, Collin's campaign of killing had another significant impact. Many of the RIC, being the subject of popular boycott in some areas[43] and the potential targets of murder in all areas, simply resigned. Gradual social ostracism and lack of government support since the end of 1916 had already reduced morale and numbers in some areas. As early as 1917 the county of Cork constabulary was 15 per cent below its established strength, and by 1918 the West Cork division was 20 per cent short of its strength, resulting in eight police stations being unmanned.[44]

Now outright intimidation and the all too apparent threat of being killed was causing even more resignations. Between May and July 1920, no less than 556 RIC officers had resigned. By August 1920 approximately 10 per cent of the force had resigned. This may seem a small proportion. However, in operational terms there is a general rule of measuring actual patrol strength "on the ground" at any one time, in that it is generally accepted that the potential numbers for such duties is reduced even in normal circumstances by up to a quarter of a police force, either due to being deployed on inside duties, court appearances, sick or on some form of secondment and/or training. Given this, a loss of 10 per cent through resignations with immediate effect in a comparatively short period, was a dramatic reduction in manpower. Recruitment in Ireland to the police force ceased.[45]

To compensate for the shortfall in police manpower in the RIC, and also to increase their numbers, the British government recruited in Britain and the UK. The shortage of dark green uniforms resulted in the new recruits being dressed in the shirts or blouses of the RIC but with khaki trousers, soon giving rise to a famous epithet, "Black and Tans", applied to police units that were soon to become infamous in Ireland. By mid-1920 there were 1,200 operating on active service in Ireland, and by the end of the Anglo-Irish War there were over 7,000 "Black and Tans" on active service in Ireland.

There has been much – and justified – controversy about the "Black and Tan" forces, and how they were recruited. Popular opinion castigated them as being former jailbirds, violent criminals recruited from the jails. In fact, the recruitment criteria stipulated that they be ex-British forces and of "good character", and had to produce Army discharge papers which showed honourable discharge. They were to be uniformly equipped, albeit adapting the traditional RIC uniform, and regularly paid, on a weekly basis of £3 10s week. Generally, they were battle hardened ex-British forces, inured to the horror of combat, with little understanding of the Irish situation or of the complexities of policing in times of civil disorder, but overall were well-disciplined. However, subsequent – and increasingly frequent – conduct of some units was to reveal a dramatic breakdown of discipline.

In addition to the new "Black and Tan" recruits to the RIC, another, autonomous, police unit was formed and recruited, the Auxiliary Division of the RIC, or "Auxies" as they became known. The recruitment criteria were that the individual must be an ex-officer of the British armed forces, and had to supply full details of their entire service record. They had different uniforms to the RIC, were paid £1 a day, plus expenses and they were divided into companies of 100 men. They were ruthless and resourceful[46] and, whilst attracting the same intense hatred and contempt of large parts of the Irish population as the "Black and Tans", were treated with wary respect by the IRA.[47]

At the height of the Anglo-Irish War the companies of Auxiliaries were deployed in Kerry, Clare, Tipperary, Meath, Roscommon, Sligo and Longford, with no less than three companies deployed in Cork and another three in Dublin.[48]

The British had declared Martial Law in the counties of Cork, Limerick, Tipperary and Kerry in December1920, and the following month this was extended to Waterford, Wexford, Kilkenny and Clare, affording soldiers and security forces increased powers of stop, search and detention.[49] By late 1920 the sheer numbers of increased troops, police recruits of Black and Tans and the undoubted – and ruthless – combat ability of the Auxiliary Division had resulted in the British regaining control of some areas. As a result of this re-taking of territory, the de facto Sinn Fein administration was forced either underground, or even ceased functioning. Kevin OHiggins later maintained that the Republican courts' useful work only lasted until late 1920, and Collins himself admitted that the Republican courts in south Cork were effectively suspended without a single session taking place for a period of eight months.[50]

The renewed offensive by the British was also accompanied by increased brutality by their forces, particularly the Black and Tans who regularly carried out reprisals. In July at Tuam, after two RIC men were shot down, Black and Tans retaliated by shooting through the windows of residential dwellings and setting fire to shops in the town. Templemore in County Limerick suffered similarly after an RIC officer was shot. In the same month in the village of Upperchurch following an IRA ambush of a police patrol, Black and Tans returned and drove a family out of their home, and burnt it to the ground. In September, in the east of Ireland in Balbriggan in County Dublin, an RIC Inspector was shot dead and the Black and Tans retaliated by entering the town, firing indiscriminately, burning shops and bayonetting to death two civilians. In the west of Ireland in Sligo, the killing of an RIC Inspector in Tobercurry was followed by the town being invaded by lorryloads of Black and Tans who fired shots into shops and burnt down the local creameries, instantly causing local unemployment. In the same month in Dineen in County Clare, after an IRA ambush killed four police officers, three neighbouring towns were burnt, and in one a local trade unionist was taken and shot, and his body thrown back into his burning family home. In their ruthless attacks and policy of reprisals, they may have terrorised the local population to sullen obedience, and have contributed to the British regaining control of several areas, but they also united the Irish population against them and increased support for the IRA. One local newspaper stated[51] that in throwing petrol on a Sinn Feiner's house

> ... they are merely pouring paraffin on the flames of Irish nationalism.

Even the most passive of the population, where the struggle intensified in Ireland, found themselves caught between the two conflicting authorities of the Sinn Fein and IRA on the one hand and the British forces on the other, and having to avoid being viewed as assisting either force. In the words of one Irishwoman, whose father was a prominent businessman and Sinn Fein figure

> to sit in the fence was just to be set up as a target for either side to fire at.[52]

One former Black and Tan was to write perceptively later

> ... no-one can serve two masters, yet the common folk of Ireland were forced to do so.[53]

Another scholarly individual, but an equally distinguished practitioner of guerrilla warfare, T E Lawrence, commented on the Irish situation

> You cannot make war on rising.[54]

When faced with this choice of two masters the majority of the Irish population were on the side of rising.

By mid-1921 there had been some efforts by the British to impose more discipline on the Back and Tans and the Auxiliaries, particularly by the commander of the latter, the eccentric Brigadier Crozier, in his short tenure as their commanding officer. He was a hard-line soldier but eventually became an advocate for justice and fair treatment for the Irish. He and government officials and policy makers in Dublin Castle attempted to impose more discipline on the Black and Tans and Auxiliaries and in doing so were at extreme loggerheads with other British generals. Amongst the latter was General Tudor whose

> belief in all that's good about the Back and Tans, his inability to believe a word against them is superhuman.[55]

By March 1921, 208 Black and Tan RIC and 59 of the Auxiliary Division had been removed as unsuitable; 39 more were removed by criminal prosecution. These efforts bore some results in that, when peace feelers between the British authorities and the IRA were bring made for some sort of truce in late 1921, Mulcahy and Collins both congratulated their British counterparts for the Dublin Castle efforts of doing most harm to Sinn Fein by restraining the "Tudor School" from going blindly on the rocks and wrecking their own boat.[56] However, these efforts achieved limited damage limitation. The Black and Tan and Auxiliary indiscipline and retaliations and reprisals had already alienated and engendered hatred in the population.

The conflict intensified, with the spasmodic struggle resulting in British regaining some territory and areas, but also with the IRA gaining victories in other parts. In October 1920, a party of the Essex Regiment was ambushed by 100 IRA, 15 miles outside Cork. Three soldiers were killed, and the rest were obliged to surrender, and their much-valued arms and equipment were seized.[57] IRA victories in this latest period were partly as result of a new tactic which the IRA had evolved. This was the flying column. In mid-1920 two senior IRA officers travelled a long distance, in parts of Ireland where the fighting was intense. By careful choice of timing and routes, they managed to travel without contact or being detected by the enemy. They realised that what two could travel so undetected, with suitable caution a small fighting unit could also successfully travel long distances and deploy. The flying column, of full-time fighting units of 30 men, was adopted. In November 1920 at Macroom in an ambush and a subsequent firefight, 18 of the Auxiliary Division were killed by the IRA. In December 1920, a flying column successfully ambushed British troops in County Limerick, killing four, and confiscating the arms of the others who surrendered.

In January 1921 at Ballinalee in County Longford and then at Dromkeen, the IRA successfully ambushed Black and Tans and Auxiliaries, and in County Clare six RIC were killed in a single ambush. In March 1921, at Crossbarry in County Cork, the IRA engaged British forces for 12 hours and inflicted heavy casualties, including 35 killed,[58] and then the entire IRA unit escaped, despite British reinforcements arriving and at one stage completely encircling them.

However, increased numbers of the security forces, and their gaining experience – albeit the hard way – were beginning to tell and the IRA also suffered combat defeats. In June 1920, a daring frontal attack on a government office in Dublin had succeeded, but in the same month three open order attacks on police barracks in Kings County and in County Tipperary had failed to capture them, and the numerous IRA involved retreated.[59] The following year in the space of a month in January to February 1921, IRA units were themselves taken by surprise at Peake, Mourne Abbey and Clonmult and suffered severe losses. By early 1921 some of the much-vaunted flying columns were making easier targets for the security forces and exposing the IRA to counter attacks. Some British units in the south-west were developing counter-initiatives at battalion level. They formed and trained small units of selected men, who made long-range raids or shoot-to-kill missions which impacted upon IRA units. One British officer stated that of the flying columns and the counterattacks

it was these that gave us back the initiative.[60]

On 20 January 1921, seven police barracks in County Tipperary and a police barracks in County Donegal were attacked by large groups of IRA. All the attacks were successfully repulsed.[61] An attempt to lure Auxiliaries into a carefully prepared ambush (over 150 IRA were mobilised and in position) around a Dublin railway station was met with a cautious advance by the Auxiliaries in large numbers; the IRA quietly retreated.

Then, in late May 1921, a full scale open assault by the IRA took place against the central Customs House in Dublin. One-hundred men were involved, and they successfully ensured that the building was completely destroyed and burnt. However, five IRA were killed by the British and a further 70 were captured. In terms of the loss of trained operatives, this was a considerable set-back for the IRA. An Army raid on one of Collins' safe houses resulted in seized correspondence; one of the documents was a letter despatch written to Collins the day after the Customs House raid, informing him that that it was a terrible business and that

we lost all those gallant fellows yesterday at the Custom House.[62]

The reason the attack – in broad daylight – took place was de Valera. Since his return from the USA in December 1920 he remained frustrated about his failure to obtain official recognition for the Irish nation–state. He was also concerned about the guerrilla war which had been so skilfully conducted by Collins and his associates. He was concerned that Collins was – justifiably – gaining eminence as a leader in the struggle. (His fury at Collins being referred to as "Big Fella" is well documented.[63])

De Valera unrealistically advocated a change of strategy, of cooling off the continuous war of attrition, sudden ambushes and shooting. This strategy was to be replaced by one of less frequent but almost set-piece battles of open engagements between large numbers of IRA pitted against British forces. Numbers of IRA combatants involved in such battles were suggested to be on or about 500.[64] In this way his authority over Collins and the shadow Ministry of Defence, and the cabinet, would be reasserted, the war would gain more favourable publicity and the IRA, by openly combating, would gain belligerent status, helping international recognition of the Irish nation–state. However plausible the reasons, the results of the Customs House raid – and any similar further open engagements were to be pursued – was and would be disastrous.

The IRA were also hindered at this period by a reorganisation which involved creating larger formations of divisions from the locally-based brigades and smaller units. This initiative, put forward by Brugha and backed by de Valera, was to enhance the image of the IRA as a combat army and the Irish nation–state as having belligerent status. Also, it was argued, it would improve the overall coordination and efficiency. The real reason was to ensure that the newly appointed divisional commanders (who would be full time and paid at £5 a week) swore allegiance to the Dail – and the Ministry of Defence under Brugha – and correspondingly weaken the hold of the IRB throughout the IRA. However, Mulcahy, as chief of staff, saw value and increased efficiency in the change, though foresaw and realised that it would take time due to the independent personalities of the IRA commanders who would be affected.[65] The process of divisionalisation took up to six months, and resulted in some of the newly promoted IRA commanders becoming more involved in staff work, meetings and strategy planning taking them away from "front-line" fighting. One distinguished former IRA commander despairingly termed it

> setting up a paper army division ... while the fate of Ireland was surely in the balance.[66]

Disputes occurred between newly appointed divisional commanders which Collins had to resolve.[67] All the while this process hindered the IRA fighting.[68]

By this time, both sides were looking to possibilities of some sort of truce. On the British side it was because they realised it was a conflict they could not win permanently and they realised the need to restore peace to Ireland; politically there was an imperative to reduce the unacceptable levels of violence. On the Irish side it was because, however brave and resourceful the IRA was, the sheer numbers of their opponents were taking effect. Providing ammunition to IRA units was always problematic.[69] At this stage of the war the shortage of ammunition was acute,[70] one IRA commander speaking of "our chronic shortage of ammunition."[71]

The British had frustrated most attempts to import fresh arms clandestinely. Within the Dail and the cabinet there was an increasing sentiment that the time was right for negotiations.

As an armed conflict, the Anglo-Irish war had been spasmodic and patchy. One historian maintains that it mostly was confined to Dublin and Munster.[72] There was comparatively little fighting in the west of Ireland; two IRA commanders active there conferred and agreed that it was only in mid-1921 that a policeman was killed in West Mayo.[73] Even in Munster, one IRA brigade commander of the Kerry IRA claimed that Kerry was only fully operational by the time the Truce came into force.[74] The definitive judgement on the war was encapsulated by the IRA itself. Collins stated simply, "We had not beaten the enemy but neither had he beaten us"[75] and was to write

We had not succeeded in beating the British out of Ireland militarily.[76]

Mulcahy, the IRA chief of staff, stated in the Dail Debate on the Anglo-Irish Treaty that the IRA had done nothing more than "drive the British out of a fair-sized police barracks."[77]

Even de Valera, with his virulent policy that the IRA should engage in open engagements with the British forces, when the Treaty negotiations leading to Irish self-determination were about start, stated of the Irish negotiating delegates, "You are asking them to secure by negotiations what *we were totally unable to secure by force of arms*" (Author's italics).[78]

The IRA achievement in the armed conflict of the Anglo-Irish War was as a result of differing regional levels of spasmodic engagement. The intelligence side of the war, however, was a different story.

Notes

1 F O Donohue *No Other Law* (Irish Press 1954) pp. 110, 129, 135
2 T Barry *The Reality of the Anglo-Irish War – refutations corrections and comments on Liam Deasy's "Towards Ireland Free"* (Anvil Books 1974) p. 38
3 Coogan *Ireland in the Twentieth Century* p. 85
4 Barry *The Reality of the Anglo-Irish War – refutations corrections and comments on Liam Deasey's "Towards Ireland Free"* p. 20. Tom Barry, commander of an IRA brigade, wrote this work in order to establish and maintain a balanced view of the limited nature of the IRA victory.
5 R English *Armed Struggle – the history of the IRA* (OPUS 2003) p. 17
6 Coogan *Ireland in the Twentieth Century* p. 680
7 B O Conner *With Michael Collins* (Peter Davies 1929) p. 16; Coogan *Ireland in the Twentieth Century* p. 74
8 D Figgis *Recollections of the Irish War* (London 1927) p. 243, cited in Kee *The Green Flag* p. 642. Kee also makes an assessment of how reliable an original

source Figgis is, although in this particular recollection he concludes that Figgis could be substantially correct.

9 D Fitzpatrick "Ireland since 1870" in R Foster (ed.) *Oxford History of Ireland* (OPUS 1998) p. 202

10 MacDowell *Michael Collins and the Irish Republican Brotherhood* p. 32

11 H Talbot *Michael Collins – his own story* (Hutchinson 1923) p. 93 cited by F Costello *Michael Collins – in his own words*, p. 21

12 Beaslai *Michael Collins* vol I pp. 274–275

13 Ibid. pp. 404–405

14 Ibid. pp. 310

15 *Irish Times* 31 March 1920

16 BMH 1694/file S.3017

17 *Annual Register 1920* pp. 6, 69–70, 133; National Archives Kew London Cabinet Papers 20 July 1920 CAB/24/109/60

18 *Irish Times* 10 August 1920 and *Annual Register 1920* p. 146

19 Cited in Mark Sturgis' diaries entry 19 August 1920, M Hopkinson *The Last Days of Dublin Castle – diaries of Mark Sturgis* (Irish Academic Press 1999) p. 24

20 M Hopkinson *Green against Green – a history of the Irish Civil War* (Gill & Macmillan 1988) p. 199

21 MacDowell *Michael Collins and the Irish Republican Brotherhood* p. 65

22 A full account of this is given in Caulfield *The Easter Rebellion* pp. 29–33 and Coogan *Ireland in the Twentieth Century* pp. 50–51

23 The term "Republican Courts" is used as a general term in this context to describe the de facto legal system established in areas from which the British had lost control. There were two types of courts, the first known as Arbitration Courts, were established as local, almost ad hoc, arbitration courts, deciding civil matters mainly concerning property. The Dail Courts which came later took over these functions – and on which Stack advised the Dail – were more formal in procedure, and also handled criminal cases. The main point in this narrative is that an Irish abstentionist legal system in large areas of Ireland replaced the British – and as such were fully accepted by the populace and functioned well – in large areas where the British lost control. (Although later in the Anglo-Irish War control of many areas were regained in the course of the British counter-offensive.)

24 *Irish Times* 1 May 1919

25 Cited by C Townsend *The Republic – the fight for Irish independence* (Penguin 2013) p. 130

26 Kee *The Green Flag* p. 678

27 BMH WS1443/file S.2779

28 Packenham *Peace by Ordeal* p. 40

29 Beaslai *Michael Collins* vol I p. 427

30 MacDowell *Michael Collins and the Irish Republican Brotherhood* p. 65

31 F ODonohue *No Other Law – the story of Liam Lynch and the Irish Republican Army* (Irish Press 1954) p. 63

32 Cited in Kee *The Green Flag* p. 678

33 Ibid. p. 679

34 Cabinet Papers 13 August 1920 CAB23/22

35 MacDowell *Michael Collins and the Irish Republican Brotherhood* p. 65

36 Coogan *Ireland in the Twentieth Century* p. 68

37 L Piper *Dangerous Waters – the life and death of Erskine Childers* (Hambledon & London 2003) p. 177

38 An account of Barton being sprung from Mountjoy jail is given in Mackay *Michael Collins – a life* pp. 121–122

39 F S L Lyons "War of Independence" in W E Vaughan (ed.) *A New History of Ireland Vol VI Ireland under the Union* (Oxford University Press 1991) p. 243

40 Townsend *The Republic – the fight for Irish independence* p. 94

41 Kee *The Green Flag* p. 680

42 Colonial Office Papers CO904/116, CO904/188/1 19 April, 19 May, 19 June 1921; Cabinet Papers 26 May 1921 CAB23/21

43 MacDowell *Michael Collins and the Irish Republican Brotherhood* p. 64

44 P Hart, *The IRA and Its Enemies – violence and community in Cork 1916–1923* (Clarendon Press 1998) pp. 58–59, citing *Return of Irish Constables and Sergeants* January 1917 National Archives Chief Secretaries Office, and *Chief Inspector West Cork Monthly Report* April 1918

45 O Connor *With Michael Collins* p. 149

46 Coogan *Ireland in the Twentieth Century* p. 82

47 Coogan *The Man Who Made Ireland* p. 14; MacDowell *Michael Collins and the Irish Republican Brotherhood* p. 66

48 *Irish Times* 28 September 1921

49 Cited in Mark Sturgis' diaries entry 10 December 1920, 4 January 1921 in Hopkinson *The Last Days of Dublin Castle* pp. 88, 105

50 Hopkinson *Green against Green* p. 7. In fairness to the assessment, it must be stated that Hopkinson in this work is somewhat scathing about the Dail, stating that its overall effectiveness in establishing its authority during the Anglo-Irish conflict has been exaggerated.

51 *Galway Express* 31 July 1920

52 Lavell *James O Mara – a staunch Sinn Feiner* p. 135

53 D Duff *The Rough with the Smooth* (London Books 1940) pp. 79–80, cited by Kee *The Green Flag* p. 708

54 *The Letters of T E Lawrence* ed. D Garnett (Jonathan Cape 1938) p. 308

55 Cited in Mark Sturgis' diaries entry 13 January 1921, Hopkinson *The Last Days of Dublin Castle* p. 110

56 Ibid. entry 17 August 1921 p. 213

57 *Annual Register a review of public events at home and abroad* (Longmans Green & Co) 1920 p. 120

58 *Daily Mail* 21 March 1921

59 *Annual Register* 1920 p. 66

60 Major Lowe "Some Reflections of a Junior Commander upon the Campaign in Ireland in 1920 and 1921" in *Army Quarterly* October 1922, cited in P Hart, *The IRA and Its Enemies – violence and community in Cork 1916–1923* (Clarendon Press 1998) p. 889

61 *Annual Register* 1921 p. 5

62 Report of Intelligence Branch of the Chief of Police CO904/156B, cited in Mark Sturgis' diaries entry 26 May 1920, Hopkinson *The Last Days of Dublin Castle* p. 182

63 Mackay *Michael Collins* p. 189; McDowell *Michael Collins and the Irish Republican Brotherhood* p. 84; Coogan *Ireland in the Twentieth Century* p. 91

64 MacDowell *Michael Collins and the Irish Republican Brotherhood* p. 86

65 Hopkinson *Green against Green* p. 13

66 Barry *The Reality of the Anglo-Irish War* pp. 42, 43, 52

67 Costello *Michael Collins – in his own words* (Gill & Macmillan 1997) p. 14

68 A detailed account and analysis of the process of divisionalisation is to be found in *MacDowell Michael Collins and the Irish Republican Brotherhood* pp. 86–87

69 Costello *Michael Collins – in his own words* p. 18

70 Hopkinson *Green against Green* p. 10

71 Barry *The Reality of the Anglo-Irish War* p. 42

72 Hopkinson *Green against Green* p. 10
73 Ibid.
74 Ibid., citing Bernie Scully of Kerry No. 1 Brigade; also, Costello, in his *Michael Collins – in his own words*, speaks of the chronic shortage of both arms and ammunition p. 18
75 Collins' speeches, cited by Taylor *Michael Collins* (Hutchinson 1958) p. 262
76 Michael Collins *The Path to Freedom* (Mercier Press 1968) p. 87
77 Cited in Kee *The Green Flag* p. 719
78 Beaslai *Michael Collins* vol II p. 281

7 Collins' Intelligence War

The Anglo-Irish War of 1919–1921 was primarily a war of intelligence, or a war between secret services.[1] Sean MacEoin leader of the Longford IRA shared his IRA colleagues' realistic assessment of the limited nature of the IRA's victory when he stated that whatever the IRA had achieved was by bluff and intelligence.[2] However, this combination was significant and an achievement. A leading counter-terrorist expert, and ex-senior British Army officer and former member of the United Nations Terrorist Sanctions Committee has defined terrorist conflict action as 90 per cent threat and 10 per cent action.[3] By this definition, the IRA actions combined with their intelligence success, were fully effective.

The intelligence capability of the IRA was such that by early 1920 the Irish consul in Dublin informed the US State Department that

> no event occurs in Ireland that the wonderful espionage system of Sinn Fein does not cover … no conversation can be conducted over their public telephone without it being known and reported to Sinn Fein....[4]

At this point it may be worth pausing to consider their opponents, British Intelligence in this period of the early twentieth century. British practice and use of intelligence operations was long established, arguably longer than any other major power.[5]

At the same time that the Volunteers were disputing amongst themselves whether to fight for England, and MacNeill formed the breakaway Irish Volunteers in 1914, British strategic intelligence had planned and executed action whereby all transatlantic cables off the cost of Europe were cut, rendering Germany reliant on radio communications. Then in the same year British intelligence, by a combination of liaison with the imperial Russian navy, manipulation of an agent in German-occupied Belgium and the timely seizure of the correspondence of a German agent in the Middle East, managed to break the entire German wireless code. Then British intelligence intercepted the details of an elaborate plot, conceived by the German Foreign Minister himself, whereby Germany would ally itself with Mexico, and send arms and supplies so that Mexico could make war on the United

States to recover the "lost territories" of Texas and New Mexico. Such a war would keep the United States fully occupied and prevent it from intervening against the German unrestricted U-boat warfare which required sinking of neutral merchant vessels heading for Britain. British intelligence then, with perfect timing at a later stage in the war, released and broke details of the plot on a stunned American President, forcing him to abandon his policy of neutrality and bring the United States into the war on the side of the Allies.[6]

At the same time as the arms landed at Howth in 1914 for the Volunteers and were being clandestinely distributed throughout Ireland in the first week of August 1914, British intelligence, in a superbly executed operation, rounded up 22 German agents in England. The impact on German intelligence was such that Germany was deprived of any intelligence operatives in Britain for the next ten months. The British Expeditionary Force crossed over to the continent entirely unreported or unmonitored by the enemy and arrived at the front in time for the battle of the Marne.[7]

At the same time as the 1916 prelude to, and the Easter Rising, British naval intelligence, based at room 40 in the Admiralty, was developing cryptology and analysis far superior to that of German intelligence, which ensured that, despite elaborate German preparations and complex strategic manoeuvres, they lacked any element of surprise over the British in the deployment of fleets before the crucial battle of Jutland.[8]

At the time of the Anglo-Irish War, British agents were in central Asia against Bolshevik agents' attempts to subvert Indian loyalty to the British Empire, monitoring their movements from border outposts in Kashgar in Chinese Turkestan and Meshed in north-eastern Persia and mounting counter intelligence operations.[9] At the time of the later stages of the Anglo-Irish war, British agents such as Lockhart, Dukes and Reilly, coordinated by Whitehall, were establishing cells within Bolshevik Russia, and even at one stage implemented a plot to overthrow Lenin and his Bolshevik regime.[10]

Through its three main agencies, Special Branch, Naval Intelligence and MI6, this constituted what was then a formidable intelligence service. In Ireland, the Director of Intelligence in Dublin Castle was an operative of this mettle and a worthy foe. Brigadier Ormonde Winter, known as "O", a former Lieutenant Colonel in the Royal Artillery then a temporary commander of a division in the First World War then an intelligence officer in India, was extremely able. He was somewhat foreboding and to the more open-minded, polished and effete administrators in Dublin Castle, "O – looking the most complete swine I ever saw ..." and, "a marvel – he looks like a wicked little white snake ... as clever as paint, probably entirely non-moral, a first-class horseman, a card genius, knows several languages and is a super sleuth...."[11]

Yet, despite such highly professional and far reaching intelligence services, British intelligence in Ireland can be summarised as the story of the Secret Services in Ireland in the post (*First World*) war was one of constant failure.[12]

Collins fully recognised the efficiency and might of British intelligence and that in neutralising this, the British would be helpless.[13] This intelligence success by the Irish was due to Collins. It was he who conceived and created the Volunteers, (and later IRA) intelligence department.[14] He formed this with care, and took time in assessing and selecting operatives.[15] He selected a small group of Volunteers to be his permanent intelligence staff, which grew to 12 full time employees. In charge of these were Liam Tobin, and eventually as second in command to him, Frank Thornton.[16] They worked in a discreet office at Bachelor's Walk, later transferred for greater security to Mespil Road which became the "war office".[17] Thornton became a highly efficient researcher, digging into many and varied sources to produce profiles and intelligence sheets of British individuals considered dangerous (and in many cases marked down for assassination). Tobin, though the strain took considerable toll upon his physical appearance and health, became a superb intelligence officer (and also an efficient killer) and next to Collins was the most dangerous Irish enemy to British intelligence at Dublin Castle.[18]

In addition to creating a clandestine intelligence department, Collins a short time later, in July 1919, created a full-time autonomous fighting operational arm of this intelligence department, for special or dangerous tasks. In stark terms, this became the assassination or killing section. The number of such operatives eventually reached 12, and they became known as the "twelve apostles" or, "The Squad". Like the intelligence department they were full-time, paid a fixed salary, each individual being paid the amount that he was formerly earning in the job he had given up to become a "Squad" member.[19]

Collins realised – and British complacency largely ignored – that by 1919 the majority of the Irish were potential sources of pieces of information, no matter how small, and that they would notice and that many would make efforts and go out of their way to ensure that the Volunteers (later IRA) were informed of what they had found or noticed. (The British would make the same complacent mistake in Malaya and Singapore in the late 1930s, where large numbers of Japanese residents, and visiting traders were all potential sources of valuable information.[20]) There was also the converse, in that there were always some informers against the IRA, for various motives, either out of conviction, or ex-Irish soldiers who had served in the British Army and still had a strong residue of loyalty to the Crown or those motivated by money or revenge. As the struggle intensified, units of IRA sought out suspected spies and shot them, leaving their bodies on display with a large warning note labelling them as spies and that this was the result of informing.[21] In March 1921, bodies of two individuals were found shot dead in Kerry and Cork, with notes pinned to the bodies reading "SPIES BEWARE".[22] Mistakes were made by some units, other units were remarkably efficient, even when an informer fled Ireland and went to the United States, pursuing him later and he was found shot dead in Manhattan New York.[23] The overall result was an effective climate of intimidation against informing by Irish people on the IRA.

In terms of incoming intelligence, Collins and his intelligence department had a myriad of sources and informers in place. He had his contacts and agents in the Post Office and branches[24] throughout Ireland. (In a non-digital age, mail was an essential form of communication). This afforded him access to official correspondence.[25] In mid-July 1920 a group of IRA men made a well-coordinated raid on a temporary postal sorting office in Dublin. The raiders were well informed about the layout and numbers of personnel in the office, and knew exactly where to go and seize the official correspondence which they did, and escaped quickly.[26] Similar advance information from the inside was fully available to those IRA individuals who, in in mid-1920s, raided the Rotunda Post Office in Dublin, and were equally successful in the selection of and carrying off all the transit official Dublin Castle correspondence.[27] At a comparatively early stage in the conflict the internal RIC communications were compromised. Collins and the IRA had access to the police codes for messaging.[28] The mid-Clare IRA Brigade officer requested in early November 1919 that Collins send him a monthly update on the latest police code; Collins sent it to him within four days.[29]

Collins and the IRA were given significant logistical support by the Irish trade union movement. In mid-1921 Collins was informed – significantly by a source within the administrative offices in Dublin Castle itself – that the British military were to train operatives, who would then be furnished with false documentation purporting that they were part of the executive of various Irish trade unions, allowing them to infiltrate meetings and union headquarters, gaining details of members. He forewarned the President of the Irish Congress of Trade Unions and formulated arrangements whereby certain branch secretaries would be alerted so as to be on their guard.[30] He anticipated that the target of such activities would be the transport unions, with the eventual objective of breaking the railwaymen's boycotting of servicing and driving British troop trains.[31] Railwaymen and stewards assisted in secretly transporting equipment by rail, stealing stores and supplies, and in the intelligence function they were used to carry messages and letters from Collins to and from IRA commanders in the provinces[32] and constantly to report movements of individual army officers and individuals whom they thought might be agents. Collins' Deputy Head of Intelligence, Frank Thornton, recalled that the

men working on the railways were our most valuable assets.[33]

Within Dublin the city was a veritable warren of premises secured for IRA intelligence purposes. There were no less than 12 addresses, including a draper's shop, a shop selling dairy produce, a tobacconist, a fishmongers and chemist, as well as private addresses where which the sympathetic owners, proprietors or counter staff acted as live letter boxes for receiving letters, documents and snippets of intelligence. Messages were also taken, and meetings and rendezvous could be held in premises secure for the IRA at Barry's Hotel, in Great Denmark Street, Flemings Hotel in Gardners Place, The Grafton Bar in Stephen Green and two private addresses in Upper Abbey Street and Parnell Street.[34] In addition, there were two premises that were known to be very secure and could be used for dropping and circulating particularly sensitive, or extremely urgent snippets of intelligence. These two premises were a tailor's shop owned by Harry Boland, and O Hegarty's bookshop. Working in the latter was a former girlfriend of Collins', whom he had met and enjoyed a relationship with, whilst they were both working in London before the outbreak of the First World War. Finally, solely for meeting ultra-sensitive informants such as those serving in the RIC or the DMP, a carefully chosen safe house in Clontarf was used.[35]

Whilst Dublin was Collins' intelligence section, it was essential that local intelligence officers and their sections were also established as extensively throughout Ireland as possible. These varied in efficiency, depending upon the commitment and combat activity of the particular IRA unit. Generally, each IRA brigade had an intelligence officer, who was in communication with local units at battalion and at company level and with Collins and his intelligence section in Dublin. One local intelligence section that was extremely active, and played a vital intelligence role in the Anglo-Irish War was that of Cork No. 1 Brigade, under Florrie O Donoghue.

O Donaghue had been a member of the IRB since 1917, and in the same year was made a communications officer in the Cork Brigades of the IRA (then the Volunteers). In December 1919, Collins, as part of his reinforcing the Volunteers and building an intelligence organisation, visited the Cork Volunteers.[36] O Donaghue was appointed shortly afterwards as Brigade intelligence officer, and by March 1920 was active full-time in the IRA. He gradually built up a network of contacts and agents which provided invaluable information to all three Cork IRA brigades. Contacts included workers at the British military barracks at Fermoy, and Post Office workers in Buttevant, Ballyvonaire and Mallow.[37]

Collins valued IRA intelligence officers of the IRA brigades and was vigilant that they would be fully and properly used. Good intelligence prior to an operation was essential to its success, as was proven in several important engagements such as the ambush in Newmarket, County Cork attack of October 1920.[38] As much as possible he guided and exhorted IRA unit commanders to put their intelligence officers to proper use, and protect them, forbidding their use on operations raiding mail from post offices and stressing their role to be proactive intelligence providers.[39] He encouraged and praised initiative in the intelligence officers, and gave guidance and advice as to the how to have extrapolated more intelligence from the information and any documents they had already acquired.[40]

Some of Collins' most valuable intelligence assets were within the RIC, the British military and Dublin Castle. During the course of the Anglo-Irish War he had four such agents, fully committed to helping him and the IRA.

One was a detective in the DMP, the "G", or Political Division, Joe Kavanagh. Affected by the sight of the defeated rebels in 1916, he became increasingly uneasy about the role the police force was being forced to play in what seemed to be repressing his fellow Irishmen. Kavanagh by 1918 was committed to assisting Collins. He forewarned Irish Sinn Fein leaders, including Collins, de Valera, and Griffith about the forthcoming raids of 18 May 1918, which only Collins heeded, and resulted in the arrest of important figures like de Valera, Cosgrave and Griffith. (It was part of an elaborate – and totally transparent – ploy by the British government who claimed that Sinn Fein was being directly supported by Germany.) Kavanagh working at Dublin Castle, hastily made a list of those to be scooped up in the forthcoming raid, gave it to a known IRB individual, who immediately took it to the tailor shop owned by Harry Boland in Middle Abbey Street, from where it was urgently taken to Collins in one of his Dublin clandestine offices. Kavanagh continued to supply Collins with a stream of snippets of information, but unfortunately was terminally ill with cancer. Before his condition became too severe for him to continue his clandestine activities, and indeed his police duties, he had already identified and persuaded another officer to take up this role.

This individual as James MacNamara. MacNamara, despite hailing from a staunch Unionist family and being regarded by the RIC as both loyal and highly valued, was to supply Collins with the same flow of snippets of intelligence that Kavanagh formerly provided until late 1920. Then, after a police raid on premises recovered some of Collins' files, these led to several officers being under suspicion of passing classified information. No tangible evidence was found incriminating MacNamara, but he was dismissed from the service. Sympathetic RIC colleagues, sadly, viewed this as yet another crass mistake the authorities had made. MacNamara, as pointed out by Collins, was grateful to leave with his life.

Another Collins informant within the security forces was Dave Neligan, a former RIC officer who, after resigning from the RIC because of unease at what was occurring to his fellow Irishmen, re-enlisted on Collins' urging and became a member of the Dublin G Division. In the late stages of the Anglo-Irish war he was eventually seconded to the British Secret Service. The information he was able to pass to Collins and the IRA was invaluable. Ironically, during the truce period, when the Treaty negotiations were taking place in London between Lloyd George and his three government colleagues on the one side and the Irish delegation on the other, Neligan was deployed by the British Secret Service to go to London and keep Collins, as part of the Irish delegation, under close surveillance.

A fourth informant within the security forces was a young Detective in the Dublin G Division, Ned Broy. Broy had been a conscientious and loyal police officer, but the Easter Rising of 1916 and the execution of its leaders had stirred and finally confirmed his inner convictions towards Irish freedom. He approached Collins through a close friend and agreed to be one of Collins' agents. His duties included that of confidential clerk in the G Division admin section, affording him access to information that would be invaluable to Collins and the IRA. At an early stage of the Anglo-Irish war, Broy managed, in April 1919, to smuggle Collins into the head-quarters of G Division, into the confidential files section. Collins spend almost a night there, locked in by Broy, and was able to gather intelligence and assess what level of intelligence the police and security forces had on him and the IRA. This gave him an invaluable advantage in the forth-coming intelligence struggle during the Anglo-Irish war.

A senior member of the IRA central headquarters, reflecting upon the Anglo-Irish War, stated that the IRA had not beaten the English despite their (the English) being disciplined, but because they were not.[41] In this he was not only speaking of the physical acts of retaliation committed by the Black and Tans and Auxiliary Division, but also certain lapses by the British in intelligence. These were fully exploited by Collins in the most important part of the Anglo-Irish War, the intelligence war. One of the most invaluable sources that was available to Collins was as a result of lax vetting by the British. A Dublin Post Office worker was selected to be the confidential clerk of the Under Secretary for Ireland, Sir James MacMahon. The individual, Nancy O Brien, was Collins' cousin. Collins was incredu-lous,[42] particularly as O Brien's duties within Dublin Castle included hand-ling top secret de-coded messages.

Besides Collins and his intelligence headquarters having contacts within the British security authorities, the Cork IRA also recruited such an inside agent, through its intelligence officer Florrie O Donaghue. Collins was quietly proud of the way the Cork IRA brigades' intelligence officers developed and became highly efficient under "his" encouragement and tutelage, as was O Donaghue proud of the role – arguably indispensable to the whole war effort – the Cork IRA intelligence carried out. The chief clerk at the military headquarters in Cork, was Josephine Marchmont. Her credentials as a loyal British civil servant were apparently sound, her late father being a long-serving RIC officer and her being the widow of a Welsh soldier killed in France. However, O Donaghue learned from indirect sources that she was unhappy due to her mother-in-law in Wales refusing to give up custody of the two children, after their father was killed. O Don-aghue contacted Marchmont who agreed to willingly work for the Cork IRA if her children could be somehow restored to her in Ireland. O Don-aghue arranged that IRA members abduct the children (who proved them-selves willing victims) and brought them back to Ireland where they were given accommodation with local families, with Josephine having almost unlimited access to them. From then on Marchmont provided a large and steady amount of intelligence regarding British troop movements, dates and times of raids, and copies of secret documents to the Cork IRA.

All told, throughout the Anglo-Irish war, Collins' intelligence was constantly receiving a flow of important and invaluable intelligence.

Inevitably, as with all intelligence services, as amounts of intelligence received increased, and as it was circulated more, mistakes occurred. On one occasion Collins handed over some papers detailing the reorganisation of another department to a Volunteer who either mislaid or lost them. They were found by a workman, unconnected to either the IRB or Volunteer who, taken aback by the contents, confided in a friend for advice as to what to so. One of the friends was connected to the IRB, and Collins soon became aware of what had occurred. He speedily despatched men to recover the papers. The workman and friends were firmly persuaded to forget all about the incident.[43] The significant aspects of this incident were the speed of Collins' damage limitation action, and the climate of the times that the workman did not immediately report the papers to the authorities, but – fortunately for him – acted more cautiously.

The British made several attempts to penetrate Collins' intelligence organisation in order to gather information and eventually capture or eliminate Collins. There was a scheme for paid informers in place. One such individual who attempted to take advantage of this was Timothy Quinlisk. Quinlisk's father was an ex-RIC officer, retired, and Quinlisk himself served as a sergeant in the British Army during the opening years of the First World War, until he was taken prisoner and placed in a prisoner of war camp. He volunteered and became one of the few POWs suborned by Sir Roger Casement in the latter's attempt to form a pro-German Irish Brigade. The progress of this small group of turned POWs was chequered, and Quinlisk himself was discharged for misconduct after falling foul of the German civil authorities. Returning to Ireland – discreetly – he tried during the Anglo-Irish War to join the IRA, claiming he would be an able training officer. He was refused, so he turned to the British in Dublin Castle, claiming he had information and could act as informant. He then approached the Cork IRA, mixed with them and on one occasion claiming he could procure at least one automatic weapon for them.

In November 1919 Quinlisk wrote an update to his British handler, stating he had information about Collins and his whereabouts and that further information would follow.

Quinlisk finally gave himself away when he was told by Collins that he, Collins, would be in Cork and staying at a certain hotel on a certain date. Quinlisk immediately informed Dublin Castle of this and they sent instructions to the RIC in Cork to arrest Collins when he would arrive at the hotel, a message that Collins and the IRA were made aware by their sources inside Dublin Castle. Quinlisk travelled to Cork on that date, presumably to be on hand to claim the reward. On that same day, 18 February 1920, he was abducted by members of the Cork IRA and killed on the outskirts of Cork. Collins' source in Dublin Castle had already, three months previously, informed Collins that Quinlisk had applied to be an informer, and he had been accepted. (Quinlisk had even had the effrontery, when he wrote offering his services to Dublin Castle, to sign himself as "late Corporal Royal Irish Regiment".)[44]

A hotel porter in Dublin's Wicklow Hotel was another paid informer who passed on to his British handler various pieces of information about comings and goings, meetings and rendezvous of Sinn Fein Dail members. As a result of his information some Republican sympathisers were arrested and questioned, which led to further information being gained. One early morning in March 1920, on Collins' orders, he was shot dead in the reception area of the Wicklow Hotel. Another individual, an NCO in the Royal Army Pay Corps, Fergus Molloy approached a close IRA associate of Collins'. Molloy claimed the British were recruiting him into their Secret Service to infiltrate the IRA and he offered Collins to be double agent. After a series of meetings with Liam Tobin and another of Collins' intelligence department, Molloy promised to obtain various information and even facilitating Tobin to be clandestinely smuggled into Dublin Castle. He was assessed by Collins and his team to be false, and was shot shortly afterwards.

One of the most dangerous British agents sent against Collins was an individual, Burns, operating under the cover-name, Jameson. Having worked for the British Secret Service in India, Jameson posed as a left-wing agitator, by profession a seller of musical instruments. He first came to the attention of and made contacts with the IRA through an Irish front organisation propounding left-wing propaganda at London Hyde Park Speaker's Corner, casually placing himself in a speaking place adjacent to those proclaiming the cause of Irish freedom. He eventually made contact with the Dublin IRA and Collins himself. Despite other agents and informers being killed in Dublin, Jameson persisted in his mission and did gain some information from – and about – Collins and twice travelled to and reported back to MI5 in London. Collins and Tobin however, became suspicious of him, and set him up with a deal whereby Jameson would procure a small consignment of small arms. This Jameson did and the revolvers were duly handed over and, with Jameson accompanying, were transported to and hidden at a Dublin address. This same address was raided shortly afterwards (the revolvers had been relocated at a safe address). The next time Jameson requested a meeting with Collins he was taken to a quiet location and shot.

There are two significant aspects of Jameson's false attempts and death. The first is that, despite being brave, clever and thoroughly professional, it could be argued that he was lost from almost the start due to a crass intelligence failure. Detective Inspector Redmond, the Belfast CID officer who was seconded to Dublin to lead the investigation into the killings – and himself soon to be shot – arrived at the Dublin police headquarters. In one of his preliminary meetings with the Dublin detectives Redmond scornfully berated them on their failure to gain any intelligence about Collins, and sarcastically contrasted this by informing them that an agent which London had sent over very recently had already gained information. Present at the briefing was MacNamara, who quickly passed this snippet onto Collins and the intelligence section, who made the possible connection to the newly arrived Jameson. Whilst it could scarcely be anticipated that Collins would have an agent at the heart of the Dublin police and present at that briefing, nonetheless Jameson's deployment and presence in Dublin should have been on a strict need-to-know basis, and not made common knowledge amongst the Dublin police. The second even more remarkable aspect was that Collins received a copy of one of Jameson's debriefings sessions in London, which Jameson had given direct to Sir Basil Thompson, Director of MI5.[45] Collins apparently had a source close to the Director General of MI5 himself.

Collins himself was a consummate operative. He was extremely cautious not to be in any photographs, and there are only two available images of him on photo. In one photo he was part of a group at the historic meeting of the Dail, and in which he deliberately distorted his face and made an exaggerated snarl. In another he was in a short but highly effective promotion film for selling subscriptions to the National Loan; the film and the limited amount of copies were kept firmly in the possession of the IRB.[46] This reticence served him well, as in mid-1920 the intelligence chief at Dublin Castle, General Winter, implemented a policy reinforced by the powers under Martial Law whereby large-scale arrests would be made of suspects, who would be detained, resulting eventually in only a few convictions, but during the period of detention would be photographed and identity details taken. Within a matter of weeks it was apparently yielding good results for intelligence purposes.[47]

In Dublin, Collins took great personal risks,[48] cycling about in the open on the basis that being in plain sight was the most efficient cover. On one occasion in January 1921 he was stopped by an army patrol and asked his name, responded as a joke, tongue in cheek that it might be Michael Collins, to which the patrol, sharing the apparent joke, sent him on his way with a friendly warning. On another occasion Collins and a colleague were stopped late at night by an Auxiliary patrol; Collins indicated discreetly that his colleague was deaf and dumb and that they were both provincials new to Dublin and had lost their way. Again, he and his colleague were sent on their way, with this time a stern warning about being found on the streets at a late hour. On another occasion, he escaped detailed scrutiny by pretending to be drunk and acting the harmless nuisance; the army patrol passed him off onto the police who, tiring of his pestering and whining, unceremoniously threw him out of the station onto the street.[49]

By late 1920 the guerrilla war and the intelligence war were both being fiercely fought. The IRA in its guerrilla warfare was enjoying mixed fortunes against police forces and British troops. Prime Minister Lloyd George, whilst discreetly making overtures to the IRA for peace through an Irish business-man, was also vaunting British military successes in the war. On the 9 November 1920, he stated in the House of Commons that

we are hitting back. we have murder by the throat.[50]

However, in the intelligence war, Collins had effectively broken any British intelligence within Ireland. So complete was this that Britain resorted to an elaborate operation to inject, in stages into Dublin, a group of highly trained military intelligence officers. Their task was to gather intelligence, make arrests, kill where necessary and eliminate Collins and his intelligence department. They became known as the "Cairo Gang" because some had been recruited and trained whilst on missions in Cairo, or because they frequented one of the popular bars and cafes in Dublin named the Cairo Café. They gained some initial success in gathering intelligence. However, on two occasions they apprehended Frank Thornton, and on another occasion Liam Tobin and another of Collins' intelligence department. Little realising whom they had in custody, the security forces released all three. Collins judged that the Cairo Gang was getting too close. Using all his con-tacts, and tasking his intelligence operatives to focus on the Cairo Gang, Collin's operatives gathered enough intelligence to enable Thornton to compile identity profiles of the Cairo Gang and pinpoint their locations. On 23 November 1921, two weeks after Lloyd George's claim of having murder by the throat, the British received a terrible response.

In the early morning, groups of selected IRA simultaneously visited numerous addresses in Dublin and murdered 19 British intelligence officers of the Cairo Gang. One officer managed to fight back, wounding two of the IRA men coming to kill him, and making the others retreat, and the officer escaped unscathed.[51] In total, almost half of the group of Secret Service operatives forming part of the Cairo Gang escaped assassination, either because they were not present at the anticipated locations or had not been pinpointed by Thornton and his intelligence colleagues' profiling. Also, two members of the Dublin IRA, one the commander of the Dublin IRA, had been captured the previous evening and were subsequently killed by British troops (allegedly shot whilst trying to escape). However, the effect of assassinating 19 British intelligence officers was cataclysmic. Black and Tan detachments that same afternoon arrived at Croke Park in Dublin, where a Gaelic football match was being played, and fired on players and crowd, killing 14. Later a group of civilians was rounded up in Lincoln Place Dublin and told to run, and were fired on, killing seven. The ferocity – and blatancy – of the reprisals indicated what an impact Collins' killing operation had made. The surviving intelligence officers were rushed to safe locations[52] and it was the end of any further British intelligence efforts in Ireland. Collins, in his own words, had paid the British back in their own coin. It also stimulated the peace process; Lloyd George cynically noted that the killings were one set of intelligence operatives successfully, pre-emptively striking another, and continued the unofficial peace negotiations. By this time Lloyd George was recognising Collins and the IRA as a worthy, formidable foe. He was reported to have exclaimed, at one stage of the conflict

> the tenacity of the IRA is extraordinary. Where was Michael Collins during the Great War – he would have been worth a dozen brass-hats.[53]

The Anglo-Irish war had several months more to run, and more bloodshed was to ensue, but with the British, despite pouring more troops into Ireland, realising that it was a conflict they could not win. By early 1921 Lloyd George's government was under pressure about its repressive Irish policy, and industrial strife with the main unions in Britain was adding to its troubles. Within the IRA, units were becoming overstretched and with de Valera's return from the United States the peace process gained momentum. De Valera had allies in Cathal Brugha the clandestine Minister of Defence, Austin Stack the Home Affairs Minister, and Liam Mellowes Director of Purchases, all of whom were opposed to Collins either through jealousy or resentment against the influence of the IRB. These three individuals would be fully supportive of de Valera in his advocating some form of truce. Since the Government of Ireland Act of 1920, six counties in northern Ireland were firmly set on the course of separation from the rest of Ireland, and Sinn Fein and the Dail were attempting to organise a boycott of Belfast goods. Unofficial peace feelers on both sides were ongoing over a period of months, but one of the main barriers was British insistence that IRA be disarmed, a prospect even the pragmatic Collins described as

> everything broke down because of an impossible condition. Of course no-one could dream of entertaining such a proposition.[54]

On 11 May 1921, Lloyd George publicly stated that he would meet de Valera and/or Irish leaders for talks without precondition. Between May and July, kick-started by an initiative by the South African Premier Jan Smuts, there were a series of meetings, some open, some discreet between Irish leaders, go-betweens and British civil servants. Finally, a face-to-face meeting took place between General Macready on the British side and Sinn Fein cabinet members Duggan and Robert Barton on the other at which an official truce was agreed – with the IRA being permitted to retain their arms. De Valera travelled to London with a small group of his cabinet, but pointedly excluded Collins. Having arrived in London de Valera excluded the rest of his delegation, even his close ally Austin Stack and had several meetings with Lloyd George. At these meetings it was made clear to him that the British could offer the 26-county state dominion status, the state having its own army, but certain naval bases in the new state to be retained by Britain. He could be in no doubt that this was the most Britain would offer.

The Irish delegation returned and an official delegation was formed, that would be the Irish delegation that would negotiate and obtain terms from Britain as to the final settlement. De Valera this time included Collins in the delegation along with Arthur Griffith, Robert Barton, Gavin Duffy and Barton's cousin, Erskine Childers. Childers was an English establishment figure, educated at Haileybury and Cambridge, parliamentary legislation drafter at Westminster, ex-British Army in the Boer War, decorated for services in the British Navy in the First World War and since the early twentieth century had passionately espoused the cause of the Irish freedom. Distrusted by some because of his background, including Griffith, he became a Republican judge in the Sinn Fein courts during the Anglo-Irish War and an unpaid director of Barton's Land Bank.[55] He was a prolific propagandist for the Republic and had attracted much publicity in both Britain and Ireland.

De Valera excluded himself from being part of the delegation, loftily asserting that he, as Irish President, must remain unsullied by negotiations. He ordered Collins to be part of the negotiating team. Significantly he had excluded Collins from the initial London-bound delegation on the grounds that Collins must remain low profile for intelligence purposes in the event that hostilities were renewed, but now he had no qualms about contradicting himself. One interpretation may be that de Valera was retreating and absenting himself and any responsibility from a settlement which would inevitably not gain Republican status for Ireland.

Notes

1 Coogan *Ireland in the Twentieth Century* p. 85
2 Hopkinson *Green against Green* p. 9
3 Brigadier Michal Chandler, in M Chandler and R Gunaratna *Countering Terrorism* (Reaktion Books 2007)
4 United States' consul in Dublin, reports to Washington 2 January 1920 and 14 January 1920, cited in Mackay *Michael Collins* p. 134
5 A Cave Brown *Bodyguard of Lies* (Bantam Books 1975) p. 2
6 Tuchmann *The Zimmerman Telegram* pp. 6, 7, 11, 14–21
7 R Deacon *A History of the British Secret Service* (Grafton Books 1963) pp. 214–215, 282–305
8 J Keagan *The First World War* (Hutchinson 1998) pp. 285, 291–294
9 P Hopkirk *Setting the East Ablaze* (John Murray 2006) Prologue
10 Deacon *A History of the British Secret Service* pp. 282–305
11 Cited in Mark Sturgis' diaries entries 1 September 1920 and 22 October 1920 Hopkinson *The Last Days of Dublin Castle* pp. 32, 60; Kee *The Green Flag* pp. 674–675
12 Deacon *A History of the British Secret Service* pp. 282. Arguably British intelligence had failed in Ireland during the war, especially concerning the Easter

Rising. British intelligence at Dublin Castle had constructed a rebel nationalist hierarchy with Casement and MacNeill at the top. By this logic it followed therefore that MacNeill's last minute public countermanding of the Rising was because Casement's mission had failed when he landed in Ireland and was captured shortly afterwards. The Rising, therefore, would not occur. At the Royal Commission of Inquiry into the Rising afterwards, the Chief Secretary Austin Birrell frankly admitted "The rebels had kept their secrets to themselves" L O Broin, "Birrell, Nathan and the Men of Dublin Castle" in *Leaders and Men of the Easter Rising Dublin 1916*, F X Martin (ed) (Methuen 1967) pp. 7, 11.

13 Costello *Michael Collins – in his own words* p. 21
14 O Connor *With Michael Collins* p. 115; O Donaghue *No Other Law – the story of Liam Lynch and the Irish Republican Army* (Irish Press 1954) p. 116
15 Beaslai *Michael Collins* vol I p. 333
16 Ibid. p. 330
17 O Connor *With Michael Collins* p. 132
18 Neligan *The Spy in the Castle* (Abe Books 1968) pp. 72–74
19 Beaslai *Michael Collins* vol I p. 331; BMH WS423/file S.1469
20 P Thompson *The Battle for Singapore* (Portrait Books 2005) pp. 38–40
21 Kee *The Green Flag* p. 702
22 *Annual Register* 1921 pp. 21–22
23 *New York Times* 14, 15, 17 April 1922
24 L Deasy *Towards a Free Ireland – the West Cork Brigade in the War of Independence 1917–21* (Mercier Press 1973) p. 210; O Donaghue *No Other Law* p. 117; BMH WS1263/file S.2569; BMH WS1003/file S.310
25 Kee *The Green Flag* p. 675
26 *Annual Register* 1920 p. 83
27 Beaslai *Michael Collins* vol 1 p. 36
28 Ibid p. 333; BMH WS615/file S.89
29 Mackay *Michael Collins* p. 134
30 Collins to W O Brien 6 July 1921 O Brien Collection NLI, cited in Costello *Michael Collins – in his own words* p. 24
31 Ibid.
32 Beaslai *Michael Collins* vol I p. 38; BMH WS1676/filS.2989
33 BMH WS 615/file S.89
34 Beaslai *Michael Collins* vol I p. 426
35 Ibid. p. 333
36 M Hopkinson *The Irish War of Independence* (McGill-Queen's University Press 2002)
37 O Donaghue *No Other Law* p. 177
38 Ibid. p. 102
39 Collins' orders cited in R Taylor *Michael Collins* (Hutchinson 1958) pp. 105–106
40 Collins despatch to Mid-Limerick Brigade 6 October 1919 Collins Papers National Library of Ireland; Collins' despatch to Cork No. 1 Brigade 8 January 1920 Military History Bureau; and despatches to Longford Brigade Collins Papers National Library of Ireland, cited by Costello *Michael Collins – in his own words* pp. 18, 26 and Taylor *Michael Collins* p. 106
41 Hopkinson *Green against Green* p. 9
42 Collins reaction cited in Mackay *Michael Collins* p. 25
43 Beaslai *Michael Collins* vol I p. 404
44 Ibid. p. 360
45 Coogan *The Man Who Made Ireland* p. 196
46 Apart from a copy sent to the Irish representative accompanying de Valera in the United States, for showing at US cinemas, where appropriate

47 Cited in Mark Sturgis' diaries entries 12 August 1920, 24 August 1920, 30 August 1920 Hopkinson *The Last Days of Dublin Castle* pp. 19, 28, 30
48 Kee *The Green Flag* pp. 674–675
49 Taylor *Michael Collins* pp. 125–126
50 Speech in London's Guildhall November 1920 cited in Kee *The Green Flag* p. 693
51 Cited in Mark Sturgis' diaries entry 21 November 1920 Hopkinson *The Last Days of Dublin Castle* pp. 76–77
52 Ibid.
53 T Jones *Whitehall Diary* ed. K Middlemass (Oxford University Press 1971) Volume III p. 60
54 Hopkinson *The Last Days of Dublin Castle* vol III Note 33 p. 253
55 Piper *Dangerous Waters – the life and death of Erskine Childers* p. 200

8 Treaty and Civil War

The negotiations in London lasted from late July to December 1921. Facing the Irish delegation was a truly formidable British negotiating team; Prime Minister Lloyd George, Austin Chamberlain, Lord Birkenhead and Winston Churchill. Much of the negotiations were carried out through sub-committees which dealt with more specific issues, and valuable work was effected. In the main body of the negotiations the British, initially aloof and finding having to sit down with individuals they considered terrorists, at first awkward, but as time passed both sides developed mutual respect, Birkenhead and Collins developing both empathy even admiration for each other. Collins was conscious of hostility of de Valera and his allies back in Dublin who would inevitably have a jaundiced view of any compromise short of a united and Republican Ireland. During the negotiations, there may have been an attempt by Cathal Brugha to discredit Collins with the British when a failed IRA arms raid on a London barracks, with the alleged collusion of an Irish guardsman, occurred in late November 1921.[1] Collins convinced the British team that he had no knowledge, and unequivocally condemned any such breaking of the truce. During the negotiations Collins returned to Dublin every weekend, ostensibly to report back to de Valera, but also to keep an eye on the political situation. The talks kept foundering on the issues of the north and the status of the new nation-state, dominion within the Empire or republic. Dominion status was gradually accepted by the delegation (though not without the secretary to the delegation, Erskine Childers, constantly upbraiding them, and quietly sending reports back to de Valera). The delegation realised that the British were implacable on this point. The exclusion of northern Ireland was wrung out of the Irish delegation by Lloyd George's keeping in reserve commitment made by Arthur Griffith to accepting this in a written memo he had made in preliminary talks with a senior British civil servant, Tom Jones. At a very late stage in the negotiations, Lloyd George produced this and sprung it on Griffith in front of the other Irish delegate, to which Griffith, fully honour bound, vehemently asserted that he would stand by this; the others except Barton followed. Barton's resistance, already worn down by the fact his fellow delegates were against him on this point, was finally broken by brinkmanship and theatre from Lloyd George, who on the 5 December 1921 cited the necessity of a quick resolution. He combined this with the threat that if no such agreement was reached as threatened, then war would resume within 72 hours (in the small hours of the following morning Auxiliaries were already re-deployed on the streets of Dublin[2]) and that the responsibility of a renewed war would lie squarely with the Irish delegation. Barton relented, and, on 6 December 1921, the Treaty was signed.[3]

None of the Irish signatories of the Treaty had liked the compromise, but Collins, Griffith and Barton held that the advantages – peace under a settlement of an Irish state that few would have thought possible five years ago – far outweighed the disadvantages of a renewal of the conflict with the British who would be on a full war-footing. However, Collins was under no illusions and was already describing Dublin as "the main difficulty".[4] The next task for Collins, Griffith and the Irish delegation was to obtain ratification for the Treaty by the Dail. De Valera was instantly hostile, his disfavour turning to rage at the alleged manner in which he, the President first had knowledge by the Treaty by popular newspaper.[5]

Eventually, after acrimonious cabinet meetings where Austin Stack and Cathal Brugha ranged themselves against Collins and Griffith on the side for de Valera, the Treaty was debated in the Dail. Between 14 December 1921 and 7 January 1922, the historic debate on the Treaty took place in the Dail. The sessions were at times, long-winded with some speakers digressing but for the most part the debates were furious and passionate, with Collins being targeted by the group opposed to the Treaty. This targeting was not just because they were opposed to the limited gains the negotiations had yielded, or because they held out for the ideal of a Republic, but also some of them were personally jealous of Collins and his reputation. The final days of the debates included a vitriolic personal attack on Collins by Cathal Brugha in which he called into question Collins' whole conduct and value during the Anglo-Irish War, an attack which, transparent in its personal jealousy, was listened to with embarrassment and gained Collins more sympathy and support.[6] The Dail voted and ratified the Treaty by 67 to 54 votes. De Valera and the anti-Treaty delegates walked out, and a new government was formed under Arthur Griffith as President, Mulcahy as Defence Minister, and Collins as Minister of Finance. Four of the five signatories of the London negotiations were in the new cabinet; the fifth, Robert Barton had sided with de Valera and the anti-Treaty delegates. More painful to Collins was the opposition of his long- time friend Harry Boland who also sided with de Valera.

The next stage was the Second Dail and the Provisional Government received powers and functions transferred from Westminster, to draft a Constitution and call a general election for the people of Ireland to vote on the Treaty. The majority of the business and commercial interests were for the Treaty. One IRA intelligence officer from North Cork summed up the pro-Free Staters as

> the Farmers Union, and the businessmen, middlemen, landlords and capitalist class.[7]

This was a powerful, and numerous, section of the Irish population. Also, in addition to Irish business and commercial circles, the vast majority of the Labour movement and the trade unions, were for the Treaty. In fact, the majority of the Irish population, even the Southern Unionists, were solid with Griffith, Collins and the government in wishing to have done with conflict and were grateful to be part of an Irish nation and benefit from the gains of the Treaty.

Ranged against the Treaty were a hard core of the old guard IRA, principally the Cork, Kerry and Tipperary Brigades of the IRA; a militant political grouping led by de Valera and including Erskine Childers, Robert Barton, Austin Stack and several female members of the Dail such as Mary MacSwinney, widow of the IRA hunger striker Terence MacSwinney, Kathleen Clarke, widow of the executed leader of the 1916 Rising and Constance Markiewics, leader of the Cumann na mBann and imprisoned for her part in the 1916 Rising; and the extreme left of the labour movement led by Liam Mellowes, an IRA commander, Director of Supplies, and an avid follower of James Connolly. The Republican ideal was impractical at this stage but its adherents were intransigent. This was especially true of Erskine Childers. He had such an intense empathy with Mary MacSwinney, Kathleen Clarke and Constance Markiewics that the anti-Treaty group became scathingly known as "the women and Childers' party".

One historian trenchantly summed up the Republican position by stating that it was clinging

> to fantasy. It was a struggle between those who were willing to come down to earth from the loftiest heights of Irish nationalism and those who were not.[8]

However impractical their ideal and however much a fantasy, the anti-Treaty-ites had significant military strength. In a Convention held in Dublin in March 1921 the anti-Treaty faction of the IRA led by Rory O Connor, IRA Director of Engineering, broke away from the main IRA, repudiated both the Dail and de Valera and his Dail colleagues and formally adopted the title "Irish Republican Army" and stated their sole allegiance was to the Republic. Meanwhile, on the Provisional Government side Mulcahy as Minister of Defence and Lieutenant General O Connell, the new chief of staff, began recruiting for the new Irish Army, the Irish Free State Army, integrating many of the massive numbers of new recruits who joined the IRA just after the Truce. However, many of these enthusiastic young men, anxious to fight on further, eschewed such recruitment and declared allegiance to the anti-Treaty units. Collins, as Minister of Finance, assisted Mulcahy in finding and allocating – with difficulty – funds for the new army.

More ominously, the anti-Treaty forces started to build their war chest by spasmodically robbing banks and "requisitioning" or seizing vehicles. Then, in the second week in April 1922, Rory O Connor, Collins' former Director of Purchases in the Anglo-Irish War, led a group of anti-Treaty-IRA and seized the Four Courts. This was the central law court buildings complex in the heart of Dublin, which they fortified, designated their "headquarters" and issued a series of written demands to the Dail that elections should be postponed and that the Republic be upheld. Griffith's Provisional Government of the new Irish state was, in its very infancy, faced with a de facto militant rival government. Both Collins and Griffith realised that it was essential during any forthcoming stand-off between the Provisional Government and the anti-Treaty IRA and Republicans, that they, the Provisional Government, did not go onto the offensive, strike the first blow and become the aggressor. The British government was fully understanding of this.[9]

Harry Boland intervened in mid-May 1922 and he brokered and brought the political faction of de Valera and his associates together with Collins, Griffith and the Provisional Government. Between these two, the Provisional Government or Treaty-ites and the anti-Treaty faction, an electoral pact was formed whereby both would canvass and run in the election under a united Sinn Fein, with candidates being apportioned to the de Valera and Griffith factions (66 pro-Treaty Sinn Fein candidates and 57 anti-Treaty Sinn Fein candidates). By Ireland's electoral system of proportional representation a Sinn Fein voter, depending upon his stance on the treaty, would be able to vote for one Sinn Fein candidate, then his second choice another Sinn Fein candidate. Ireland welcomed this pact, as it apparently clarified what had been an extremely confused and acrimonious political scene that appeared to have dominated Irish government since the Treaty. However, it was regarded with grave suspicion by the British, particularly the powerful right wing of the Conservative Party. O Connor and the anti-Treaty IRA had already caused concern with their seizure of the Four Courts; now the concern was increased with Collins and Griffith and the government allying with extremist anti-Treaty elements. Their suspicions were not allayed by the bitterness of the electoral campaign and the accompanying violence, where candidates were attacked, voters were intimidated and even prevented from attending meetings. Also, some elements of the IRA were still settling old scores,[10] and O Connor and the anti-Treaty IRA, soon to be known as the Republican forces, were still holding parts of Dublin, arming and still vehemently denouncing any political party and declaring no allegiance save that of a Republic.

The election was held on 16 June 1922 and the results were resoundingly pro-Treaty. A total of 58 pro-Treaty Sin Fein representatives were elected, 17 Labour members, 7 Farmers Party, 6 Independents and 4 Southern Unionists from Dublin University. All these small parties, together with the pro-Treaty Sinn Fein were solid for the Treaty. There were in total 92 elected members for the Treaty opposed by 38 anti-Treaty Sinn Fein members. The anti-Treaty vote had been 133,864, against the pro-Treaty vote of 486,419. A Provisional Government was formed. Griffith remained resident of the Dail, whilst Collins was appointed head of the Provisional Government. Mulcahy remained Minister of Defence in the Dail, but not part of the Provisional Government.

Immediately after the election there emerged a somewhat paradoxical situation in Ireland. Having freed itself of what was deemed repressive foreign government – British troops and civil servant were evacuating barracks, Dublin Castle and other government premises – the country in a sense had a proliferation of governments. There was the Dail, sanctified by the tradition of the revolutionary clandestine government during the years of struggle and claiming allegiance of all Irish; there was the new Provisional Government, governing with the mandate of an election majority; there was de Valera and his anti-Treaty-ites who refused to recognise either, and claiming they were the true government of the Republic of Ireland; and finally there was O Connor, and Liam Mellowes, Collins former Director of Purchases in the Anglo-Irish War, and the anti-Treaty IRA or Republican IRA, holding fast in the Four Courts. They had the single-minded objective of the Republic like the political faction of de Valera and adherents, but recognised no authority save that of the anti-Treaty army.

A week later any satisfaction with such a resounding popular mandate for the Treaty was eclipsed by an event in London. General Sir Henry Wilson, returning from a wreath laying ceremony to the fallen dead of World War I, was shot by the IRA and died on the doorstep of his Belgravia apartment. During the peace negotiations and the elections Wilson had been active in openly supporting Sir James Craig and the northern Unionists in their ongoing sectarian violence against the Catholic minority. His public demands to the Stormont government included the virulent question "who governs Ulster – you or Collins".

A born intriguer, in the late 1900s, as a Brigadier in charge of Britain's military Staff College he had committed a British Expeditionary Force to aid France in any forthcoming conflict with Germany long before the British Cabinet had made the slightest move away from the foreign policy of strict neutrality.[11] He had been involved in 1914 in the "Curragh Mutiny" when British Army officers stationed in Ireland had threatened to resign their commissions rather than be deployed against the militant Ulster Volunteers.[12] Now, in the confusing turmoil in Ireland during the post Treaty period he was intriguing with the extreme right wing of the British Conservative Party to bring down Lloyd George's coalition government and even possibly revise the Treaty settlement.

He had been marked down as an IRA target since mid-1921, and the killing was carried out on Collins orders,[13] but the British right wing Conservatives and others jumped to the conclusion that it was the work of O Connor and the anti-Treaty IRA.[14] So convinced were the British that the anti-Treaty-ites were responsible for Wilson's murder, and so intense was their ire that an astonished General Macready was summoned to Downing Street where it was put to him that he should be in charge of an operation whereby British troops should retake the Four Courts in Dublin. Macready sensibly repudiated the idea, and stated firmly that perhaps it would be better that the Irish government take such action against its own insurgents.[15]

The House of Commons debated the killing four days later and the anti-Irish fury-and also fury against the coalition-was intense. Political pressure against Lloyd George's coalition government for punitive action was immense, and Lloyd George and Churchill in their turn harried Collins into taking action against the anti-Treaty IRA. Collins initially refused to bow before such pressure to take action and strike the first blow against the anti-Treaty IRA. Shortly afterwards however, he was faced with no alternative following action by the anti-Treaty IRA itself. A group of anti-Treaty IRA sallied from the Four Courts and raided garages, and "requisitioned" vehicles and fuel. They were seized and apprehended by troops from the new Free State Army. The anti-Treaty IRA then sent another group out and they captured and kidnapped no less a personage than the chief of staff of the Free State Army, General O Connell.

Collins sent an ultimatum to O Connor and his forces in the Four Courts to evacuate. The anti-Treaty IRA occupied other buildings in Dublin. On 28 June 1922, with artillery borrowed from the British Army, the Four Courts were bombarded and the hostilities of the Civil War started. It was to be ten months of bitter conflict.

De Valera hastily joined the Dublin Republican forces as a serving fighter. For three days fighting occurred in Dublin, with the anti-Treaty, or Republican forces being defeated. O Connor and Liam Mellowes were amongst the Republicans taken prisoner. The Republicans then fell back and the struggle evolved into Republican forces attempting to hold Munster or the south-west. Liam Lynch, IRA commander of the south-western brigades of the IRA (grouped in the newly formed 1 Southern Division in the later stages of the Anglo-Irish War) and staunch Republican, had been detained with fellow IRA commanders in Dublin. However, they were allowed to go free on the assumption that they would not involve themselves in the struggle. These individuals immediately took command of the Republican forces in the south-west and pursued conflict. They were joined in that area by de Valera, escaped from Dublin. They were also joined by Erskine Childers who was either ignored or isolated by many Republicans through either distrust, or that he was so notorious that he was too dangerous to be with. He was given tasks on the Republican general staff, and took charge of Republican propaganda through editing the virulent *War News* which he published often on the run and under difficult conditions.

Collins was appointed commander in chief, his place being taken as head of the Provisional Government by William Cosgrave. Cosgrave, quiet and unassuming, had been Dail Minister of Local Government and had been effective in organising the parallel administration of Sinn Fein institutions in the newly liberated areas of Ireland during the Anglo-Irish War. Collins and Mulcahy deployed and expanded the Free State Army. Although the latter was initially outnumbered by the former, in terms of 13,000 to 9,000,[16] the eventual defeat of the Republicans in the Civil War was inevitable. The majority of Ireland was for peace and Republican status, however ideologically desirable, meant less than a final end to conflict. The Free State Army had the support of the financial resources of the new state and was replenished with arms and vehicles from Britain. In terms of intelligence the Free State had the advantage of an overall supportive population and many of its troops had local knowledge from the previous conflict of the Anglo-Irish War. The Republicans lacked cohesive strategy, beyond that of static defences which when breached, retreated to further attempted stop lines. Their troops, although tough and experienced, were less formally disciplined and instances were reported of lax sentry duty and defensive lines being left to go for drinks.[17]

Also, there was unease on both sides about fighting former comrades. Even the intransigent Rory O Connor had mistakenly calculated that his Republican forces occupying the Four Courts would not be forced out by the Free State troops; he mistakenly calculated that the lengthy occupation of the Four Courts would eventually provoke Britain into halting the evacuation of her troops and engage in storming the Four Courts, a significant gain for Republican propaganda.[18] Up to 20,000 of the IRA in late 1922 formed themselves into a loose association named the Neutral IRA, working for an end to conflict. Most were Republican in sympathy,[19] but held that internecine conflict was a price too high.

The overall direction of the Civil War saw the fall of Dublin, the Republicans falling back on a defence line from Wexford to Limerick, the fall of Limerick, the Republicans falling back on Cork, the fall of Cork, the Republicans falling back on parts of Kerry and other isolated pockets of resistance in Tipperary. It was near constant retreat by the Republicans. One historian has pinpointed the fall of Limerick as the point after which the anti-Treaty forces never ceased to be in retreat.[20] Some of those anti-Treaty forces felt the struggle was over as early as when the fighting in Dublin finished.[21] In June and August 1922 Free State troops were deployed by sea and landed at points in the south and south-west, taking the Republicans by surprise.[22] With the advance of Free State troops the Republicans resorted to increasing guerrilla warfare, and the civil population became more alienated.[23] One former Republican fighter recalled in the Civil War we were in the same position that the Brits had been in the first period. They fought the people and we fought the people.[24]

Significantly, at this stage of the war the Republicans became known as Irregulars. The Free State troops, overall, avoided the mistake the British made of taking reprisals on any of the population suspected of sympathising with the Republicans. However, the Provisional Government showed it could be ruthless. The Republicans in the later stages of the war were reduced to engaging in desultory sabotage causing much economic damage, especially to the rail and road networks. They also resorted to spasmodic attacks and shootings. One such attack occurred in Dublin and was in accordance with a Republican general order of November 1922, known as "orders of frightfulness" which stipulated all members of the Dail who had voted for the Emergency Powers were to be shot on sight. Two members of the Dail were shot in early December, one fatal. Immediately Mulcahy called an emergency cabinet meeting which agreed unprecedented retaliatory and deterrent action. The following morning Rory O Connor, Liam Mellowes and two other Republican IRA captives were taken from Mountjoy jail and were shot by firing squad. These executions hit the Republicans hard. In fact, in the ten months of Civil War, the Free State executed three times the number of captured Republican prisoners than the British executed IRA in the Anglo-Irish War of three years. The executions were a key event in the breaking of the Republicans.[25] In January 1923 Liam Deasy, an officer in IRA Cork No. 3 Brigade during the Anglo-Irish War and deputy chief of staff in the Republican anti-Treaty IRA, was captured by Free State troops. He issued a manifesto to all Republican IRA troops to cease fighting in what was an unwinnable struggle. Some Republican commanders closed ranks against this, but amongst others it was the final blow.[26] In May 1923 the acting chief of staff of the Republican troops, on de Valera's orders, issued a final order to dump arms and cease fighting, whilst de Valera issued a valedictory communiqué to "Soldiers of the Republic, Legion of the Rearguard", assuring them that their sacrifice had not been in vain. Nonetheless, the Civil War was over and the Republicans had been decisively defeated.

The Civil War had lasted less than a year, but it cost Ireland dear. The material damage has been estimated at £30 million, and cost the lives of 540 Free States troops, with lives lost on the Republican side running into thousands.[27] Prominent and dedicated individuals who had made invaluable contributions in the recent struggle against Britain died in a war against their own former comrades. Such individuals may have held differing views of the final goal of Irish freedom, but were of a tenacity and patriotism beyond reproach and had they lived time may have reconciled them to once again give good service to their country. (Within less than five years de Valera himself had modified his own opposition and had entered the political parliamentary system of the Irish Free State.)

Cathal Brugha who was tenacious and unbending in patriotic endeavour died in a single, last-man defence of a Republican position in Dublin at the start of the Civil War. At differing stages of the Civil War, and certainly in the Dublin fighting at the start, there was a reluctance on both sides to fire on former comrades. However, by June1922, feeling amongst sections of the Free State Army towards Brugha were unequivocal; he was regarded as a total extremist and dangerous fanatic, and his death in the fighting was welcomed.[28] However, he had fought in the 1916 Rising and had served selflessly in the Anglo-Irish War – Collins was later to say that he could forgive Brugha anything due to his fervent patriotism – and a future Ireland was deprived of a sincere, unceasingly striving patriot by his death on 5 July 1922.

Harry Boland, close friend of Collins and fellow comrade in the IRB, superlative organiser of Sinn Fein during the vial period 1917–1919 and helper of de Valera during the latter's visit to the United States, was captured by Free State troops in a Dublin hotel and fatally wounded in a confused scuffle in the hotel bedroom on 31 July 1922.

Arthur Griffith, founder of Sinn Fein, head of the negotiating team which ensured the peace Treaty with Britain was signed, resident of the Dail, under constant strain and working all hours, collapsed and died of a brain haemorrhage at the early age of 51, on 12 August 1922.

Erskine Childers, intense and unbending, gun runner for the Volunteers at Howth in 1914 and since then never deviating in his passion for his adopted country, and determinedly pursuing the propaganda war for the Republicans, was captured in possession of a loaded firearm by Free State troops. Taken to Dublin he was tried, sentenced and executed. Characteristically he forgave all the Irish Ministers in the Free State government, and made his son promise that he would also so forgive, and also made him promise that if he ever in future went into Irish politics he would never mention nor use his father's name.[29] Equally characteristically he sympathetically urged the firing squad to advance a few paces forward, if it made their task easier on that morning of 24 November 1922.

Sean Hales, one of five brothers from the Cork area, three of whom fought since the beginning of the Anglo-Irish War in the Cork IRA unit, had been elected to the Second Dail for a Cork constituency. A fourth brother (Donal) loyally served throughout the Anglo-Irish War as de facto Irish consul in Genoa, and attempted to facilitate a much-needed arms deal for Collins. One of the Cork IRA brothers, Tom Hales, had undergone intense torments in a British interrogation, refusing to give information about Collins. Tom had now chosen the Republican side and was commanding an anti-Treaty IRA unit. Sean, intensely loyal and steadfast, was a pro-Treaty-ite and government member of the Dail and was shot down outside the Dail by Republican gunmen carrying out Liam Lynch's "order of frightfulness" on 7 December 1922.

O Connor and Mellowes, as we have seen, were amongst those executed in reprisal for this slaying. Mellowes was a link to both the 1916 Rising and the socialism of Connolly, and amongst the IRA was a voice of concern for the deprived social classes of Ireland, a future voice cut short by the executions of 8 December 1922.

Liam Lynch was veteran of the Volunteers and the IRA, officer commanding No. 1 Cork Brigade and tireless organiser and coordinator of the Cork Brigades during the Anglo-Irish War. Commander of the 1 Southern Division IRA, gentle, yet inflexible for the Republic, and the commander in chief of all Republican forces, was killed in a skirmish with pursuing Free State troops in the Knockmealdown Mountains of Tipperary, on 10 April 1923.

As well as theses lives, the Civil War claimed the life of the individual who has been named, by an eminent Irish historian, as "the man who made Ireland", Michael Collins.

At the start of the Civil War hostilities, Collins had been made Commander in Chief of the Free State Army. Together with Mulcahy he expanded the new army, organised training – often extremely brief – for new recruits and pursued the war. By 5 August 1922 he had been confident enough to send a memorandum to Cosgrave assessing the military situation as steadily progressing favourably with the only military formation left to contend with being the Republican 1 Southern Division. However, he was wracked by ill-health due to the strains of the past five years and overwork. A stomach condition, combined with a vulnerability to colds severely hindered him. One biographer described his last week

> He lived it suffering mentally and physical. Full of ideas, he found it hard to work. The shadow had begun to fall.[30]

He made a tour of inspection of the south-west, partly for public relations to show himself and the government in the area of Cork where he had grown up, and also to maintain the morale of the National Army, still engaged in operations against the Cork and Kerry anti-Treaty Irregulars. He was also going for exploratory talks with some anti-Treaty IRA elements as a prelude to possible peace. As part of a series of brief stops and visits in County Cork, he and his party had reached Macroom on 22 August 1922, and then set out for the small town of Bandon. One group of hard-line Irregulars had set up an ambush on the road. A short time before, de Valera, also active in the area, had attempted to persuade them not to carry out this action, but he was brusquely dismissed, being informed that he was a mere staff officer and had no operational command in this area. After waiting all day, the ambush group had decided that the convoy containing Collins was not coming and had begun to disperse. At that point, Collins' convoy consisting of a motorcycle outrider with an open saloon car, a Crossley tender and an armoured car appeared and the remaining ambush group opened fire. The commander of the convoy ordered all vehicles rapidly accelerate according to standard procedure, but

Collins characteristically countermanded the order and ordered to return fire and fight. After a half-hour firefight, in almost the final shots before the ambush party retreated, Collins was hit in the head and died shortly afterwards.[31]

His body was transported from the scene to Cork, then by sea to Dublin where it lay in state then a funeral, at which tens of thousands lined the street and the cortege was over two miles long. Collins as buried in Glasnevin cemetery, in the area reserved for the fallen of the Irish armed forces.

All deeply regretted Collins's death in Ireland and Britain.[32] De Valera, on receiving the news, was visibly upset. Frank Aiken, one of the Republican IRA commanders wrote personally to Mulcahy, the Free State chief of staff, offering deepest sympathy and acknowledging that Collins most of all was responsible for building the nation.[33] Even Erskine Childers, bitter opponent of the Free State régime, acknowledged him as an Irishman who worked untiringly for the good of Ireland. Hundreds of Republican IRA, taken prisoner and held in Kilmainham jail, at the news of Collins death spontaneously knelt in prayer and recited aloud the Rosary for Collins's repose.[34]

Lord Birkenhead, with whom he and Collins had worked tirelessly together during the Treaty negotiations, paid a tribute that

> he was ... daring and resourceful ... I never doubted that both Collins and Griffith, having once given their word, would sacrifice life itself in order to carry out their promise.

Lloyd George sent a message to Cosgrave, as acting head of the Provisional Government in which he stated,

> His engaging personality won friendships even amongst those who met him as foes, and to all who met him news of his death comes as a personal sorrow.

General Macready sent a personal letter to Cosgrave in which he stated,

> I deeply regret that he should not have been spared to see in a prosperous and peaceful Ireland the accomplishment of his work.[35]

However, perhaps the most moving, and appropriate tribute came from General Mulcahy, in his funeral oration at the graveside which encapsulated the situation in Ireland and Collins's role,

> Men and women of Ireland we are all mariners on the deep, bound for a port still only seen through storm and spray, sailing on a sea still full of dangers and hardships and bitter toil. But the Great Sleeper lies smiling in the stern of the boat, and we shall be filled with that spirit which will walk bravely on the waters.[36]

Notes

1 Mackay *Michael Collins* pp. 219–200
2 Coogan *Ireland in the Twentieth Century* p. 105
3 A comprehensive and outstanding account of the Treaty negotiations – arguably one which to date remains unsurpassed – together with Lloyd George's final negotiating coup, is to be found in Packenham *Peace by Ordeal* Part 3 pp. 102–229, 237–242
4 Taylor *Michael Collins* p. 165
5 De Valera's being informed in such a manner is disputed and all but disproved by Coogan *Ireland in the Twentieth Century* p. 107
6 *Treaty Debates Public Session* 6 January 1922 Irish Stationary Office pp. 324–325
7 Hart, *The IRA and Its Enemies* p. 145
8 Kee *The Green Flag* p. 731
9 Cabinet Papers, meeting 5 April 1922 CAB/23/20
10 Hart, *The IRA and Its Enemies* p. 111
11 B Tuchmann *The Guns of August* (Macmillan Press 1980) pp. 57–61, 63–64
12 G Dangerfield *The Strange Death of Liberal England 1910–1914* (Capricorn Books 1961) p. 136; C Clark *The Sleepwalker* pp. 213, 488–489
13 Kee *The Green Flag* pp. 738–739; Hart, in his comprehensive and frank work on Collins in *Mick – the real Michael Collins* pp. 396–397 states there is no convincing evidence of Collins' orders or involvement. However, Coogan, after extensive researches, ascribes responsibility to Collins, and states that he, Collins, ordered it as a specific operation, with Liam Tobin sent over to London to co-ordinate, *Ireland in the Twentieth Century* p. 120, *The Man Who Made Ireland* pp. 375–376.
14 M G Valiulis *Portrait of a Revolutionary General – Richard Mulcahy and the founding of the Irish Free State* (University of Kentucky Press 1992) p. 153.
15 C Kostick *Revolution in Ireland – popular militancy 1917–1923* (Pluto Press 1966) p. 180; Kee *The Green Flag* p. 739
16 Mackay *Michael Collins* p. 270; Kostick in a later work, although partisan towards left-wing Republicanism, puts the difference as high as Provisional Government Free State troops 14,000 to Republican IRA troops 50,000 *Revolution in Ireland* p. 181.
17 L Deasy *Brother against Brother* (Mercier Press 1998) p. 70
18 Mackay *Michael Collins* p. 266
19 O Donaghue *No Other Law* p. 288
20 C Townsend *The Republic – the fight for Irish independence* (Penguin 2013) p. 416
21 Deasy *Brother against Brother* p. 85
22 Ibid. p. 72
23 Ibid. p. 73; BMH WS 1665/file S.2981
24 Cited in Hart *The IRA and Its Enemies*
25 O Donaghue *No Other Law* p. 289
26 Hopkinson *Green against Green* citing Tom Barry, arguably one of the ablest IRA commanders both in the Anglo-Irish War and the Civil War as an anti-Treaty IRA commander.
27 J M Curran *The Birth of the Irish Free State* (Alabama University Press 1988) puts it at over 3,000.
28 Coogan, in *De Valera – long fellow, long shadow*, p. 327 in his characteristically extensive and comprehensive researches, cites accounts by Neligan that Free State troops at the scene of the fighting, the Hammam Hotel in Dublin, were determined that Brugha should not be taken alive.

29 His son, also named Erskine, faithfully kept the promises made to his father. He eventually became President of Ireland.

30 F O Connor *The Big Fellow* (Picador 1998) p. 291

31 Given the extremely divisive nature of the Civil War there has been speculation about whether there was collusion between member(s) of the convoy and the Irregulars in bringing about what would be an assassination. MacDowell, in his *Michael Collins and the Irish Republican Brotherhood* points to Free State general Emmet Dalton, who was with Collins in the open top saloon and also the driver of the armoured car. This speculation and the individuals allegedly involved are dealt with in detail – and rejected – by Mackay in his *Michael Collins – a life* pp. 297–298, and in Dwyer *Big Fellow, Long Fellow* pp. 330–331

32 P Bew in his comprehensive history of Ireland *Ireland – the politics of enmity 1789–2006* (Opus 2007) cites the *Galway Observer* of 2 September 1922 reporting that in the poorer areas of Dublin women were dancing on the day of Collins' funeral. However, this can be countered by an account of Mackay in his *Michael Collins* p. 294 of a woman from a similar deprived area who was publicly weeping and lamenting Ireland being bereft without Collins.

33 Dwyer *Big Fellow, Long Shadow* p. 33

34 T Barry *Guerrilla Days in Ireland* (Anvil Press 1962) p. 180

35 Mackay *Michael Collins – a life* Epilogue

36 Collins 22 Society Graveside Oration found on www.generalmichaelcollins. com/life-times/graveside-oration/ and U O Connor "Tribute to Collins with the impetus of poetry" *Life* 21 August 2016 found on www.independent.ie/life/ ulick-oconnor-tribute-to-collins-with-the-impetus-of-poetry-34977479.html

Part III
The sinews of war

9 Preparing in London, active in Dublin

Collins arrived in London and moved in and shared rented accommodation with his sister in West Kensington. He started working in the Post Office Savings Bank. This was a period long before the digital era, in which online financial management for much of the population is almost the norm. It was in a period long before the era of television, let alone 24/7 news coverage, with constant updating of financial and market trends available to mass audiences in easily understood summaries and soundbites. In this era, the Post Office telephones system, telegraph, telegrams and mail were the main means of communication and the Post Office services and its Savings Bank essential for the day-to-day management and small safe investments for most the population. The work was routine and dull, involving the scrutinising and issuing of dividend warrants and auditing of savers passbooks every time a withdrawal was above a certain threshold. However, it afforded Collins training in very basic procedures and forms, and an introduction to basic elements of record keeping and auditing. Even at this stage, he was found to have agile mathematical ability.[1]

Collins spent four years with the Post Office Savings Bank, and enrolled in evening classes at King's College London, taking accountancy, commercial law, taxation and economics. Passing the full range of these examinations would give him a position in the Customs and Excise, both of these governmental functions having recently been unified in this department. Apart from the potential career prospects in the civil service, these subjects would give him substantial technical knowledge of finances and a broad understanding of economics. In fact, he failed the exams, due to his spending an inordinate amount of his spare time in his various Irish activities, which left little time for study and revision. However, he had gained from his classes a good working knowledge of finance from these courses. In 1910, no longer being interested in a civil service career, he resigned and gained a better salary by joining a stockbroking company, Horne & Company, in the City of London. This was a position of more responsibility, being overall supervisor of the messengers. Whilst not directly involved in finance or transactions, it gave him an overall awareness of the private financial sector, and the various functions and departments making up a stockbroking firm. Then in August 1914 he left this job, returning to the public sector and gaining a larger salary as a clerk at the Board of Trade. His progress in acquiring financial knowledge can be witnessed by his reply to the job specification, that he had good knowledge of financial trade and that he had also studied the construction trade and, within that, trends in unskilled labour. Also by this time he was fully proficient in type-writing – the then equivalent of IT skills – and in both bookkeeping and formulating trial balances. After less than a year at the Board of Trade he resigned and took a position with the Guaranty Trust Company, New York, in their London office in the City of London.

There is some interpretation amongst historians regarding this move. One interpretation suggests that he took a position with a New York based finan-cial firm to be available for transfer to the United States if events turned for the worse, i.e. conscription or possible arrest for his Irish nationalist activ-ities. Another interpretation is that this may have been long-term planning either by himself, or by the IRB. One historian has raised the question of whether the IRB intended, even instructed, Collins in London to gain as much practical knowledge as he could of the financial system, to be put to good use for the Irish cause later.[2] This possibility appears supported by an event in late 1915 when Collins returned back to Ireland on his own initi-ative and contacted Clarke in Dublin to see what was afoot. Clarke received his inquiry coldly, looked sharply at Collins and brusquely told him to return to London and await *further* orders (italics mine).[3] Whether Collins pursuing a financial occupation in London was planned or not, his experi-ence in various jobs in the public and private financial sector were certainly to be of benefit to him and to the Irish struggle. Guaranty Trust was a posi-tion in a major international financial and investment corporation, adding further to Collins' already varied experience in trade and finance.

Indeed, the work experience of young Michael in London, lasting just under a decade gave him both basic and advanced knowledge of finance, revenue raising and economics, in the words of biographers, "… dealing in finance stood him in good stead for later in life …"[4] and "… fit him admir-ably for the cabinet post of Minister of Finance."[5]

He also put it to good use in his Irish activities in London. By 1914 he was IRB Treasurer for London and south-east England, recording and hus-banding funds and discreetly acting as both collector and courier. As we have seen, on conscription coming onto force, Collins was anxious to avoid being drafted, and returned to Ireland to be part of whatever forth-coming struggle. He informed his employers in London that he was leaving, and would not be waiting around for conscription. His employers, on hearing this, assumed that he was eager, and was going to volunteer for the British Army, and gave the departing Collins an extra week's wages as a bonus. Typical of Collins, he donated this bonus to the IRB on his return to Ireland. Equally typically, he meticulously recorded the "donation".

On his return to Ireland he combined his Irish activities with his professional métier, becoming financial adviser to Count Plunkett and his family. Then came the Rising with Collins participating and, as we have seen, imprisoned.

After Collins had been released from prison and returned to Ireland he obtained a post with the National Aid and Volunteer Dependents Fund, an amalgam of two previous organisations The two organisations which had been combined were the Irish National Aid, which was sponsored by Dublin Corporation, and the Volunteer Dependents Fund which was founded and run by Kathleen Clarke, widow of the executed 1916 Rising leader Tom Clarke.[6] The latter's main remit was to disperse the remainder of funds which had been collected in the United States to finance the 1916 Rising. Both organisations combined after the 1916 Rising to provide for Irish prisoners and their families. Collins was granted a small salary and was placed in overall charge of the finances. In this he was tireless in efficiency and effort. By mid-1917 large numbers of Irish prisoners taken in the 1916 Rising were being released. From the moment the prisoners stepped off the boat train, Collins organised short ad hoc welcoming ceremonies, worked out the necessary travel arrangements and costs of the prisoners to travel from Dublin to their home towns and provided them with the exact sums of monies needed. In many cases he provided extra monies for possible additional expenses with which they might be faced. He was constantly moving to and fro around Dublin and the surrounding area to different addresses, ensuring the dependents of those prisoners still in custody or those prisoners badly injured and unable to find work, had appropriate sums of money for their support. They were given cash payments, of which Collins kept meticulous records. Within 18 months of managing the Fund, Collins had written over 3,000 letters, dealt with over 2,000 cases and handled over £100,000 accumulated because of appeals to the Fund.[7] Indeed, he was held to have made a brilliant success of the working of the Fund.[8]

Notes

1 Taylor *Michael Collins* p. 46
2 Coogan *Michael Collins – a biography* p. 17
3 Mackay *Michael Collins* p. 43
4 Taylor *Michael Collins* p. 48
5 Mackay *Michael Collins* p. 42
6 M Forrester *Michael Collins – the lost leader* (Sphere Books 1971) pp. 50–60
7 Hart *Mick – the real Michael Collins* p. 118
8 O Connor *With Michael Collins in the Fight for Irish Independence* p. 99

10 Filling the war chest
The National Loan

In 1919 the news of the formation and meeting of an Irish Dail was met with extreme scepticism by the British press.[1] One normally open-minded and liberal British publication bitingly commented

> One fancies that the Ministers of Finance and Home Secretary and all the other dignitaries will be hard put to it to find an outlet for any executive capacity they may possess.[2]

The formation of the parliament, the Dail and the government was impressive. The ringing pronouncements of national self -determination and resonating Declaration of Independence was rousing and inspiring. But defiance alone does not make for a strong economy and nation states have outgoings. The aspiring Irish state needed to work out costs and pull in revenues to meet these. Certain basic costs of its legislature and executive were immediately identified. The President's (or Prom Aire's) annual salary was fixed at £500, with Ministers' salaries at £350. Dail representatives were given an entitlement to travel and accommodation expenses whilst on and conducting Dail business. The Dail needed fixed premises to convene, printing costs for the records of its proceedings, and further printing costs for the vital propaganda front. Further costs were to be incurred for its fledgling diplomatic service, essential to the nascent state in its quest for international recognition.

The Dail considered raising taxes but decided against this. The Volunteers (or by then the IRA) were to bomb out and burn down the taxation offices of the British administration in Ireland (much to the delight of farmers and businessmen, whose tax records were thereby destroyed). However the Dail never ordered or encouraged Irishmen to withhold taxes to the British administration (although Collins did propose and argue for such a tax boycott during Irish cabinet discussions[3]) and they certainly realised that imposing their own taxation system upon the Irish would be unfeasible, be detrimental to the Irish economy and would impact upon Irish support. Yet revenues were needed.

It was announced in the Dail in early April 1919 that the Minister of Finance was to raise a projected £1 million pounds, through the purchase of bonds. It was anticipated that about half would be raised at home, and about half would be raised abroad. In terms of raising monies abroad, de Valera would travel to the United States two months later, partly to avoid arrest (he was a convicted felon on the run) partly to raise the funds but with an overriding priority of obtaining diplomatic recognition for Ireland from the United States.[4] Harry Boland would precede him as Dail ambassador to the United States.

The importance of obtaining funds was emphasised by de Valera announcing the Loan to the Dail

> It is obvious that the work of our Government cannot be carried out without funds.

He continued,

> ... The Minister of Finance is ... preparing a prospectus which will shortly be published for the issue of a loan of one million pounds Sterling, 500,000 to be offered to the public at home and 325,000 abroad, in bonds and such amounts as to meet the needs of the small subscriber.[5]

In this de Valera was emphasising the current lack of funds available to the clandestine government, and also the lesser amount anticipated from foreign sources and subscribers making Ireland-based fundraising all the more important. (In fact, the potential foreign sources, particularly from America, then an unknown potential in April 1919, would eventually prove lucrative.) De Valera's announcement also emphasised the importance of the "small subscriber", that is, the appeal to all classes in Ireland. Collins prepared the prospectus in which he was irritated by de Valera's quibbling over almost every word.[6] However, Collins did more than prepare the prospectus. He, as Minister of Finance, took charge of the whole enterprise.

Before starting work on the Loan, Collins added to his financial training and knowledge by asking an accountant named Henry Mangan for some instruction in elements of municipal finance. Mangan was an experienced local government accountant and had worked as Accountant to Dublin Corporation for some years and was of course a Sinn Fein sympathiser. Mangan gave Collins some lessons, and found Collins the most brilliant brain he had ever met. He was reported to have stated,

> In fact after three lectures Collins knew much more about it than I did.[7]

In organising the National Loan and concealing the transfer and storage of the collected funds, Collins was to prove his knowledge and brilliance.

Three trustees of the Dail Loan were appointed; de Valera, Dr Michael Fogarty and James O Mara, together with a Secretary to the Trustees, Daithi Donnchadha. Dr Michael Fogarty, Bishop of Killaloe was known to be sympathetic to Sinn Fein, and throughout 1918 had been vociferous in his condemnation of the British extending conscription to Ireland. James O Mara was an Irish businessman, with extensive commercial experience, and supported the cause of Irish freedom. He had been made Assistant Financial Director of Sinn Fein in 1917. He and Collins recognised each other's abilities in finance. O Mara was to play a crucial role in support of de Valera's fundraising in the United States. Daithi Donnchadha was a former civil servant and a staunch Sinn Fein supporter from Limerick. These four individuals were invaluable in their differing ways in support of the Loan. However, the organiser and the ceaseless dynamo of the Dail Loan was Collins.

To start the Loan, the prospectus would offer the sale of £500,000 in bonds. It was anticipated that half of this would be raised in Ireland, the other from abroad. The target at this stage, therefore, in Ireland was £250,000, and a selling campaign started. Collins appointed four trusted individuals as Loan organisers, each one responsible for each of the four provinces of Ireland, and they were empowered to appoint sub-organisers where necessary within "their" respective areas.[8] The four organisers for the provinces were paid £30 per week, as were the 47 sub-organisers.[9] Collins, through the Dail cabinet, allocated £500 to pay two reliable printers. He and the Loan organisers, with great discretion, arranged with the printers to print Loan material and literature. The two printers were Dollards printing house located in the same area as Dublin Castle itself, and Mahon Printing of Tarnahll Street in north Dublin.[10] Newspapers and local printers in other parts of Ireland were also contacted to advertise the Loan. In at least one location local Volunteer units took the initiative, and discreetly commandeered the local newspaper offices and printed masses of Loan posters.[11]

The British, after a delay born of complacency, reacted. By mid-September 1919 editions of newspapers were being suppressed. Pre-emptive raids on newspapers in the hours before the release of the first editions were carried out. On 17 September, the Cork Examiner was suppressed after such a raid.[12] In a space of 20 days the *Cork Examiner* and 21 local newspapers had been closed down for illegal advertising.[13] Printers who were found to be producing any Loan material, or what could widely be construed as any Loan-related material, had their premises summarily closed and their printing material and equipment dismantled and confiscated.

Individual Loan sellers, or those publicly speaking on behalf of the Loan were arrested. On the 23 September three newspapers in Limerick were suppressed. In order to prevent fundraising meetings, in September a proclamation was issued by the authorities prohibiting public meetings in County Tipperary.[14] These suppressions of newspapers and some printers and arrests of Loan sellers were carried out efficiently and had some preventative effect, but often the arrests of individuals produced more good publicity and empathy for the Loan. This was certainly the case when members of the Dail were arrested in their own constituencies for encouraging and exhorting subscriptions of the Loan. Alexander McCabe the Dail representative for South Sligo was arrested whilst addressing a public meeting and imprisoned for unlawful assembly and soliciting subscriptions to the Loan in September 1919[15] and his sentence of hard labour evoked much anger and sympathy. The following month James Dolan the Dail member for Leitrim was arrested at a public meeting for unlawful assembly and soliciting subscriptions to the Loan; he was sentenced to two months imprisonment. On his way to the courthouse he was cheered by crowds and, significantly, whilst his trial was ongoing the crowds remained outside singing *"The Soldiers Song"*.[16] A local Catholic curate in County Kilkenny was arrested for possessing correspondence relating to the Dail Loan. In December 1920, he was tried at Waterford and sentenced to two years imprisonment, to be served in a British prison.[17] The effect of arresting and imprisoning a member of the local Catholic clergy caused outrage. All told, the British attempts to suppress the raising of subscriptions resulted in the reverse effect, favourable promotion of the Loan.

Collins found another method of promoting the Loan. Together with Diarmuid O Hegarty, they featured in a short promotion film. O Hegarty was a former civil servant in Ireland, recruited into the IRB, fought in the 1916 Rising, was imprisoned and then released by the British and he worked with Collins in the Irish National Aid Association. The short film was made costing £600, and was money well spent.[18] The film showed Collins and O Hegarty sitting working on documents and signing Loan certificates for a queue of subscribers. In this film symbolism was exploited to the full. Prominently shown amongst the subscribers waiting to receive their documents were relatives of the leaders of the 1916 Rising (Pearse's mother, Connelly's daughter and Clarke's widow) and Arthur Griffith. Collins and O Hegarty were sitting signing against the background of St Enda's School,[19] a pioneering educational project of the 1916 insurgent leader Padraig Pearse (one of the Loan advertising slogans was "Pearse gave everything – can you give a little?"). Also, Collins and O Hegarty were working diligently at a table formed by the execution block of Robert Emmet. The completed film was then taken into packed cinemas, where projectionists were either asked or persuaded by various degrees to run it inbetween the main films. The film was then quickly and discreetly taken out of the cinema before the authorities were alerted, to be shown again later, or on the following days, in other cinemas. Eventually cinemas all over Ireland had "hosted" the film, and copies were sent to the United States to be shown in cinemas with sympathetic managers and proprietors.

Marketing and promoting the Loan was intensified on Sundays,[20] the day when the majority of the population would attend church and afterwards ad hoc Loan meetings could be arranged after the services. On this day the part-time Loan workers would be free from their day jobs, and have more time to devote the Loan. Also, local Catholic clergy, the majority of whom who were sympathetic to the cause, would be available and on hand.

During the years of armed struggle from 1919 to 1921, in the conflict for independence, the Catholic Church in Ireland would frequently and consistently condemn the killings carried out by Irish Volunteers and insurgents, as well as British atrocities. The bishops, as a whole, were deadlocked, anxious to avoid giving moral sanction to either side.[21] Generally, they dismissed the Irish Volunteer (or IRA as it became) claims that they were retaliating and resisting British atrocities, tersely holding that two wrongs did not make a right.

However, the Loan as a peaceful activity per se was a different issue. Archbishop Harty of Cashel actively supported the Loan. Archbishop Walsh of Dublin contributed to the Loan. In this he made extensive efforts to have this publicly known, even requesting his fellow clergyman Cardinal O Connell in New York to ensure that the donation was publicised in the US press.[22] (Any Irish newspaper which made mention of donations to the Loan, or any matter relating to the Loan, or naming the subscriber(s), were suppressed under British counter-measures.) One of the Dail trustees, Dr Fogarty, Bishop of Killaloe, donated £100 directly to Collins in the early days of the Loan flotation. Such support and contributions from the higher clergy were significant as statements. Many of the lower clergy took their lead accordingly. Parish priests facilitated the Loan promotion on Sundays, ensuring Loan workers had access to congregations after church service, at ad hoc meetings in the vicinity of the church. They would also discreetly announce the dates and places of subscription meetings. In one area in Donegal handbills and Loan literature was distributed to the congregation as they were leaving the service.

The vast majority of the contributions were voluntary. However, almost inevitably there was a certain amount of intimidation,[23] either peer pressure or more blatant. In some localities in the west of Ireland at meetings, names of those who refused to contribute were taken, as well as those who had done so, raising the possibility of such individuals being "revisited".

The Loan started with much publicity but made slow progress in incoming subscriptions. By mid-December 1919 Collins was to write to de Valera, updating him on the Loan. In this he stated that the net revenues received from the Loan amounted £30,000, with further potential £35,000 pending in subscriber applications,[24] well short of the target of £250,000. There were varying levels of efficiency in the local committees and not all Sinn Fein clubs and areas were fully active. Some districts appeared at best grudging in response. Collins wrote in frustration

> If you saw the bloody pack down there, and their casual, indefinite, meaningless purpose way of carrying on.[25]

Also, the methods of Loan promotion and fundraising in the early stages were trial and error, although Collins was always aware of good ideas and methods which appeared to be working and did his best to make sure different local committees were made aware of these. In September 1919, the Dail itself was proscribed by the British administration as an illegal organisation. Between the formation, coming together and "opening" of the Dail, the British regarded it as a symbolic formation, part of Irish nationalists working through their Sinn Fein elected representatives towards a political non-violent means of increasing self-determination. In terms of impact, it was a talking shop, albeit a hallowed one, and harmless. Now it was raising funds it could pose a tangible threat, as those monies could (as correctly forecasted) be used for illicit and more violent purposes. The proscription of the Dail made promoting the Loan more difficult, as no reference could be made to it in any advertising or publication. Indeed, by early October Collins assessed that the principle British efforts against the Irish national movement were concentrated and focussed at suppressing the Loan. By December he was writing to de Valera over in the United States

> My Dear Dev,
>   The situation has been getting more and more difficult here ... the hindrances have been enormous ... the main enemy objective is directed to secure the failure of the enterprise.... Advertising is impossible practically.[26]

However understandable though the difficulties were, such slow progress would be fatal, as it was essential that the Loan raising was a success in Ireland. Funds, raised by the Loan in Ireland, were needed as soon as possible, given that the funds to be raised in America by de Valera would be delayed in materialising due to the problems of distance couriering and there was a delay in starting the flotation and promotion due to legal difficulties. It would not be until late 1920 that the funds raised in America could start arriving – those that were actually sent (see Appendix I) – and be at the disposal of Collins and the Irish shadow government.

Collins was undaunted. In the words of one biographer

> from the beginning he does not seem to have though at all of the impossibilities latent in the scheme.... He was a born improvisator and from the moment he was appointed Finance Minister the department of finance began to function.[27]

His efforts were unstinting. He exhorted the local committees maintain their efforts, and sent them materials and ideas. By mid-1920 he had organised the distribution of half a million copies of the Loan prospectus to local Loan committees around the country, and two million promotional leaflets to the committees. Painting slogans on walls and buildings, although very ad hoc, had been found to be extremely effective by Sinn Fein in the general election which had produced their landslide victory. Collins urged all local fund committee to obtain and deploy the "painting squads", and this tactic was repeated again, on a more organised basis, especially in the west of Ireland, to promote the Loan. Even stencils carrying the slogans were prepared enabling multi-slogans to rapidly appear on paths, walls, letterboxes of houses and post boxes.[28] He was diligent in issuing receipts to donors. Remarkably, given the circumstances of the clandestine nationwide Loan, every contributor obtained a receipt.[29]

To stop police from surrounding, cordoning off areas and preventing public meetings where subscription would be sold, from going ahead, advance distraction groups were organised in local areas. These groups would create minor incidents, or suddenly gather together and force crowded entry to public buildings such as the local court house, diverting police resources to contain this potential disorder, whilst businessmen and interested investors and contributors would be able to come together in another location and subscribe unhindered.[30]

Another strategy adopted by Collins was donor targeting. He ordered each Dail representative to forward to him, urgently a list of ten "likely subscribers" within their respective constituencies. To these individuals he would send a personal letter and a Loan prospectus. "Likely subscribers" generally meant those who were comparatively wealthy, and it was felt that they would be more likely to subscribe – or subscribe more – if they were approached by Collins himself.

This constant contact and liaison and flow of information and instructions between Collins, as central government in exile Minister of Finance, and the localities, was crucial.

Also, the Dail itself made political promises and commitments. Voters – and potential subscribers – in the East Limerick constituency were categorically promised that the Limerick Technical Schools, which had been recently closed under the British administration, would re-open with full student intake.[31]

In certain areas in the west of Ireland promotion and collection continued with a steady increase. The mid-Cork area, under the energetic Dail representative Terence MacSwiney, collected at a frenetic pace, which Collins monitored and constantly encouraged. In many areas Volunteers took an active part in collecting funds.[32] Unlikely subscribers appeared. One individual in the north of Ireland, a non-Catholic, contributed over £600 by a series of payments to the Dail Loan collector. Dail "representatives" in Argentina raised £1,600.[33] British Army officers stationed in Germany in the immediate post-Armistice years, apparently sympathetic to the cause of Irish self-determination, were found to have subscribed to the Loan.[34]

With the New Year the slow rate of Loan progress had been reversed. By mid-January 1920 the demand for Loan subscriptions began to increase perceptibly, the amounts raised by the Loan growing steadily with no indications of falling demand. Therefore, in the third week in January 1920 it was announced that Loan period would be extended. Collins made a further exhortation to Loan workers to maintain and increase the efforts, whilst encouraging those areas and constituencies where substantial amounts had already been collected. At these later stages of the Loan, IRA commanders engaged in collecting even when engaged in conflict. One prominent Loan collector was commander of the North Cork IRA Brigade, combining his guerrilla leader function with that of clandestine fund raiser.[35] Sean Moylan, future commanding officer of a Cork IRA Brigade, whilst leading an IRA company in fighting in early and mid-1920, also engaged in collecting for the National Loan.[36]

The monies, illicitly raised, were discreetly transferred by three main methods, namely through banks, and by use of cash couriers and by conversion into gold specie.

Funds were transferred through bank transfers. In the era of cheques and in the large cities the banks would send runners with messages, specie and coins to be transferred and cheques from different banks to be exchanged and cleared. In some areas local bank managers were sympathetic to the Loan, and the cheques to Dail Eireann could be deposited, and the monies in bank drafts were then forwarded by the bank to their Dublin branch.[37] It was then collected by Loan workers and physically delivered to the Dail Ministry of Finance Offices at 72 Harcourt Street. Where local bank managers were more cautious, or simply hostile, then there was refusal by the bank to accept any cheques made out to the Dail Eireann. In such cases the money was first placed into the account of a sympathetic respected individual of the locality.[38] Cheques sent direct to the Ministry of Finance in 72 Harcourt Street were counted then deposited in the Sinn Fein Bank. Parish priests and curates, besides making personal contributions and facilitating local subscription meetings were also responsible for sending direct to Collins a large number of small amounts from various parishioners, which they, the priests and curates, held in trust.[39] Therefore, as well as facilitating Loan promoting, they were also very active as collectors and fund movers, and potentially less likely to come under suspicion than non-clerical Loan workers.

Funds, on reaching Dublin, were counted at Harcourt Street and then placed in the Sinn Fein Bank at 6 Harcourt Street. By 1919 Sinn Fein's significance in the Irish nationalist movements for freedom was unchallenged but, as has been seen, in the early years of the twentieth century it was a struggling force. However, one of its achievements during these difficult early years was the establishment of the Sinn Fein Co-operative People's Bank in 1908. It was set up to carry out all the functions of retail banking with the additional purpose of assisting in the development of Irish industries. The founders included Arthur Griffith and the bank was consciously set up without registering, complying or in any way acknowledging the requirements of British law and banking regulation. It was an early symbolic and tangible achievement of the Sinn Fein policy of peaceful abstention from any British institutional framework. Part of its success was that it attracted a significant number of household deposits. Based at 6 Harcourt Street, this was where the incoming Loan subscriptions were deposited. The main accounts in which the monies were deposited were either those of the sympathetic Bishop Fogarty of Killaloe, or the equally sympathetic Lord Mounteagle.[40] The banks documentation and records were kept deliberately chaotic.[41]

From the Sinn Fein Bank in Dublin, the monies were then transferred to the Dame Street branch of the Munster and Leinster Bank, and the Camden Street, College Green and Sackville Street branches of the Hibernian Bank. The monies were placed in the names of sympathisers. These were individuals who were comparatively unknown to the British authorities. Also, accounts were opened in fictitious names. From these account holders in these banks, monies could be drawn out and given to or made payable to those actively engaged in the struggle. From the Munster and Leinster Bank in Dublin, monies were also further transferred or made payable to the National and Provincial Bank in London, to the account of Art O Brien.

Art O Brien was from a prosperous and cultured Anglo-Irish family, having been educated in Europe and lived and worked in London. He joined the Gaelic League in London in the 1880s, and espoused it because of Irish freedom, and by the 1916 Rising had become a close confident of Collins within the IRB. He founded the Irish National Relief Fund in London to provide assistance to the families of Irish rebels imprisoned in England and became the leader of the small Sinn Fein organisation in Britain. In early 1919, on Collins' instigation O Brien was appointed the envoy of Dail Eireann in Britain, setting up and running its "London Office" over the next few years, to which monies from the Dail Loan were sent. Besides using the monies for the upkeep of the Sinn Fein London Office, the account could also be used to further transfer monies and obscure the flows.

Like those of the Sinn Fein Bank, the official records of transactions through the Munster and Leinster and Hibernian Banks, where the Dail Loan monies were placed, were extremely lax. Papers and statements concerning transactions relating to Mulcahy, seized in a raid by British troops (from which Mulcahy only just escaped[42]) were correctly judged by British intelligence as

> the banks transactions as disclosed in the commandeered stuff ... are casual to the point of conspiracy.[43]

Cash couriers were used skilfully. The use of the postal service to transfer donations, either notes or cheques, was discouraged. Warnings were issued to Loan organisers for caution in postal donations. This was somewhat ironic, given the later period of the Anglo-Irish War, when the postal service was severely compromised by the IRA raiders and Collin's intelligence officers, to the extent that one British periodical commented with tongue in cheek that

> it would really save time if official correspondence were forwarded direct to Sinn Fein.[44]

Collins issued specific instructions to Loan organisers and workers that if donations had to be set by post, then not to the address of Dail Eireann and/or Harcourt Street, but donors should address the envelope to a trusted friend or associate in Dublin, who on receipt of the letter could then physically bring the donation round to Harcourt Street (and a receipt could be issued either to the bearer or sent to the original donor). Cash couriers were the preferred method of transfer and such individuals were available. Couriers carried monies from other parts of Ireland to Dublin.[45] Also, some provincial banks sent donations by cash to Dublin by special messengers, often carrying sums of £20,000.[46] Couriers travelled by rail to Dublin at some risk to themselves, as passengers at railway stations were frequently searched.[47] Sometimes local parish clergy acted as couriers, when their duties caused them to visit Dublin.[48] On arrival at Dublin some couriers took the monies direct to Harcourt Street, whilst others were met by two Dublin-based couriers, who took possession of the monies and brought it to Harcourt Street. These Dublin-based couriers also fetched and carried monies around Dublin between banks and Harcourt Street. The two Dublin couriers were Daithi Donnchadha, Secretary to the Dail Loan Trustees, and Sean McGrath. Both these individuals were staunch Sinn Fein supporters originally from Limerick. Both became adept at cash couriering, changing routes, planning the next stage of their "run", stopping at retail premises and throughout acting naturally. On one occasion Donnchadha left Dublin, travelled to Limerick and took possession of a large donation from the Mayor of Limerick. Then he couriered through Limerick, successfully avoiding the heavy military presence, and took it back to Dublin by train. The train itself was subject to a passenger search but Donnchadha, outwardly relaxed, well dressed, smoking his customary cigar and travelling first class, was not approached.[49] In their journeys around Dublin both couriers often had thousands of pounds on their person, yet never came under suspicion and were never stopped by the authorities whilst couriering.

Some of the funds collected were converted into gold. Shopkeepers and small business owners in and around Dublin were requested to hoard gold sovereigns and half sovereigns. Loan collectors would visit them and pay them an appropriate amount of notes in exchange for gold. The entire amount of Loan funds collected and converted into gold was worth

£24,957. To this could be added some gold bars and foreign coins, the total amount being valued (when the entire amount was surrendered to the Free State Bank of Ireland in 1922) at £25,071. Most of the gold was packed into four boxes in an empty infant's coffin, and hidden at the house of Batt O Connor in Brandon Road, Dublin. O Connor, a builder by trade, spent several hours of hard labour constructing a hiding place for the five containers in a narrow space under the concrete floor. A smaller amount of gold was also stored, in a constructed hiding place, at 3 St Andrews Street in Dublin.[50] O Connor's skill as builder was to be put to good use several times by Collins.

Collins had wished to have as much as possible of the Loan in gold.[51] Whilst cash, and to a lesser extent, bank drafts could be used quickly for expenditure – especially clandestine purchase of arms – gold would always hold its value. This was the era when the financial security of states and countries depended upon gold. A decade was to elapse before the economic crisis of 1929–31 forced Britain to abandon the gold standard for its reserves.

By June, the target of the £250,000 Loan for Ireland had been passed. In July 1920 the Dail passed a motion that the domestic (Ireland) Loan fundraising be closed by the end of the month. The total amount raised was £371,849, a magnificent achievement, almost a 50 per cent increase over the original target sum. In modern twenty-first century values, this was over £29,300,000. The population of Ireland had contributed this amount and had given generously,[52] with an estimated 15 per cent of the million households in Ireland contributing.[53] The largest amounts, in proportion to the populations, came from the south and west, the poorer parts of the country. Cork had given over £44,000, County Limerick over £53,000.[54] The provincial totals were

Connaught £59,977
Leinster £87,499
Munster £172,533
Ulster £41,319

In the words of a historian, writing in a several-volume monumental work of Irish history

Collins' exuberant energy turned an unlikely gamble into a resounding achievement.[55]

The timing of the success of the National Loan was vital, as its successful conclusion – and accumulation of funds – coincided with the increase in British military activity and the deployment of the Black and Tans and Auxiliaries into the conflict.[56]

It is most appropriate, however, to allow the last word on Collins and the Dail Loan to Collins' fellow countryman and a fellow (later) Minister of Finance. Speaking at the annual Michael Collins commemoration at Beal na mBath, August 2010, the then Irish Minister of Finance, Brian Lenihan, stated

> … it was the task of raising the loan to finance the work of the revolutionary government that preoccupied him as Minister of Finance. History has recorded the extraordinary success of that venture in the most adverse of circumstances of suppression and constant hindrance by the British authorities. It was a truly remarkable feat and it added greatly to the authority and capacity of the First Dail at home and abroad.[57]

The British authorities were determined that this feat would not go unanswered. The British press had been sceptical about the self-appointed Dail's ability to govern, but the authorities in Ireland were alarmed at the Dail's apparent success in gaining funds.[58] As part of an intelligence reorganisation within Dublin Castle, an elderly magistrate was summoned from the north[59] and arrived in Dublin in December 1919 to carry out government work. The individual, Alan Bell, was an ex-RIC officer, who had joined the RIC in 1879 and had worked his up. In the 1880s he investigated the activities of the Land League, identifying sources and tracing its funding. In Dublin, he was assigned to various intelligence duties and a major part of his work was to investigate and find the National Loan funds. In January and February 1920 a series of raids were carried out, targeting premises which the British assessed as being the clandestine offices of Collins' Ministry of Finance. Documents were recovered from the raid on the Sinn Fein Bank at 6 Harcourt Street; these included cheques and receipts. From these Bell surmised that Loan funds had been placed or transferred into banks in Dublin.

Bell was established in rooms in the old police courts in Dublin,[60] and he started his inquiry. Bank managers of different Dublin branches of the Munster & Leinster Bank and the Hibernian Bank were summoned to appear for interview before Bell on certain dates. The letter summoning them also stipulated that they were expected to bring and produce any evidence regarding any transactions that had taken place at or between their respective banks and Sinn Fein. Ten bank managers in total received such summonses, and the inquiry started on 8 March 1920. The banks protested at what they considered intrusiveness but representatives were sent to the inquiry; however, the bankers attending were instructed by their bank to adopt a "stiff attitude" towards the inquiry.[61]

The press had gripped the story. The *Irish Times* briefly mentioned the opening of the inquiry and its objectives, whilst *The Times* of London gave fuller details, stating that bank managers were appearing before Alan Bell and that they were expected to produce documents. The *Irish Independent* reported that there was general public hostility to the inquiry, whilst the official publication of the Dail, the *Irish Bulletin* denounced Bell, recounting his previous inquiries into Land League funds, and claiming that the inquiry was the opening stage of an attempt to destroy the Irish economy.[62] Within 24 hours the inquiry, its objectives and the full identity of the individual leading was fully publicised.

In the forthcoming days Bell interviewed[63] four witnesses, three from the Hibernian Bank and one from the Munster & Leinster Bank. Overall, they were uncooperative, showing this in two ways. None of them had brought bank documents; the somewhat truculent justification by them included replies to the effect that the bank ledger was a heavy document to bring along, or that the individual was not asked to bring any documents (despite the specific requirement contained in the summons) or that the individual judged it contained no relevant information. Also, none of them gave positive or confirmative answers to any of the questions or names or accounts mentioned, the only times they so confirmed was when Bell accompanied his question with evidence that this was indeed so. Their attitudes presumably were in accordance with their bank management instructions of a "stiff attitude" and also that they were aware that Bell had no legal powers to sanction uncooperativeness, a point heavily publicised by the press.[64]

Given the exposure of the whole inquiry before its start and the plodding nature of its progress, arguably Collins and colleagues at the Ministry of Finance would have had time hastily to move any monies they deemed at risk. However, despite his difficulties, Bell had uncovered significant indicators. Confirmation was obtained of joint accounts in the names of Kelly and Gleason and of Clerkin, and there was tentative confirmation of an account of Robert Barton. Also accounts in Michael Collins' name were acknowledged as possible, and of a transfer of £1000 from one of these possible Collins accounts, to a UK account in London in the name of Art O Brien. There was also tentative confirmation of an account in the name of Richard Mulcahy. When the names of Mulcahy and Collins as possible accounts at the respective banks were raised, the witnesses were indeed anxious to remain vague and declared themselves uncertain. One of the witnesses, when asked whether he knew of an account in his branch in the name of Michael Collins answered,

> I would not like to say that from memory.... It would be too dangerous for me to speak from memory.[65]

His answer may have used an extravagant phrase in emphasising that he could not be certain, or it may have had the underlying statement of fear or repercussions. Either way it was to prove dangerous, not for the witness but for Bell himself.

However vague and unconfirmed the links that Bell had managed to establish, Collins judged that he was getting too close and had to be stopped. The authorities were aware of the sensitivity of Bell's work and had detailed officers of the DMP to act as bodyguard to escort to Bell on foot to and from his residence in Dublin to the inquiry; however, neither escort detail escorted Bell whilst he was on the tram, only seeing him safe on to it, and meeting him when he alighted. Accordingly, on the morning of 26 March 1920 two of Collins' men from "The Squad" observed Bell get onto his morning tram and they then followed on bicycles. They signalled to other members of The Squad, waiting at a further tram stop that their target was on the tram. The three waiting Squad members got on, identified Bell, bundled him off the tram and shot him.[66] He had been killed in broad daylight, on a weekday in the morning rush hour.[67]

There was widespread condemnation of Bell's murder. General Macready and Sir Edward Carson both accused the *Freeman's Journal* of being partly responsible for Bell's murder due to its high level of publicisation of what should have been a confidential inquiry. In fact, judging from the *Irish Bulletin*, the Dail official publication, Collins and Sinn Fein were already fully aware of Bell's former law enforcement activities and that he formed part of Dublin Castle's intelligence gathering. (A British Secret Service officer based at Vaughan's Hotel in Dublin for a considerable period and who showed no concern or fear about any of the shootings and assassinations which were occurring was said to be profoundly shaken by Bell's murder.[68])

The *Times* asserted the murder as a cold-blooded atrocity, whilst the *Irish Times* stated the murder outdid in extreme crime the Phoenix Park murders of 1881.[69] The killing was generally regarded as a murder of an elderly and gentle retired magistrate who had continued to do his duty. Bell was a retired magistrate, was indeed elderly, and possibly of a gentle personality, but he was also an indefatigable and tenacious law enforcement investigator who was becoming dangerously close to finding the Dail Loan funds. When it came to protecting the Dail funds, Collins had given a clear, unequivocal and terrible answer.

The British authorities were not quite finished with Collins' funds. Whilst British intelligence overall was inadequate in Ireland, the Head of Intelligence at Dublin Castle, Ormonde Winter, was a formidable opponent. One innovation Winter had implemented was the "Raid Bureau". This was an intelligence unit dedicated to analysing the vast amounts of paperwork seized in raids. His Raid Bureau had steadily garnered some intelligence, and one or two documents led him to possible bank account details. Where Bell had attempted to reply upon robust inquiry, Winter adopted more ruthless methods. In October 1920, he and officials – without any due process or authorisation – attended banks and, by intimidation of staff, had certain suspected accounts opened and the amounts in them sequestered. A sum of £4,000 was seized from one account and another later resulted in just over a further £13,000 seized. It was carried out illegally[70] and after the Anglo-Irish War, as part of the settlement, the British restored £18,000 to the Free State. Winter himself, in his autobiography, gave a detailed account of his duties in Ireland (where he respectfully acknowledged Collins as a worthy foe) but he carefully omitted any mention of these seizures.[71] Collins was furious at how the seizures were effected and vowed

> we shall see the return of the monies just as some day Ireland will exact the full reparation of all the stealing and seizures of the British in the past.[72]

Notes

1 O Connor *With Michael Collins* p. 114
2 *Manchester Guardian* 24 January 1919
3 Dwyer *De Valera – the man and the myths* p. 29
4 Dwyer *Big Fellow, Long Fellow* p. 83
5 Dail Proceedings April 1919, cited in Coogan, *The Man Who Made Ireland* p. 106
6 Dwyer *De Valera – the man and the myths* p. 29
7 BMH WS511/file S.990
8 Beaslai *Michael Collins* vol I p. 349
9 A McCarthy "Michael Collins – Minister for Finance 1919–1922" in G Doherty and D Keogh (eds) *Michael Collins and the Making of the Irish State* (Mercier Press 1998) p. 57
10 Beaslai *Michael Collins* vol I p. 349
11 BMH Witness Statement WS 1610/file S.2917
12 *Annual Register* 1919 p. 111
13 Dwyer *Big Fellow, Long Fellow* p. 92
14 *Annual Register* 1919 p. 111
15 *Leitrim Observer* 25 October 1919
16 *Leitrim Observer* 22 November 1919
17 *Nenagh Guardian* 8 January 1921
18 Townsend *The Republic* p. 93
19 Dwyer *Big Fellow, Long Fellow* p. 92
20 BMH WS 1610/file S.2917
21 Kee *The Green Flag* pp. 646, 652, 659
22 P Lavelle *James O Mara – a staunch Sinn Feiner* (Clonmore and Reynolds 1961) p. 146
23 Dangerfield *The Damnable Question* p. 313; BMH WS 1694/file 3017
24 Collins to de Valera 19 December 1919, cited in Beaslai, *Michael Collins* p. 413
25 Cited in Mackay *Michael Collins – a life* p. 119
26 Collins to de Valera 15 December 1919, Beaslai *Michael Collins* vol I p. 413
27 O Connor *The Big Fellow* 1937 p. 86
28 *Irish Times* 8 November 1919
29 Coogan *Michael Collins* 1991 chapter 12; also BMH WS 1610/file 2917; BMH WS 1552/file S.2873
30 Beslai *Michael Collins and the making of New Ireland* vol I p. 349
31 *Nenagh Guardian* 23 August 1919
32 BMH WS 954/file S.2272; BMH WS 1552/file S.2873; BMH WS 1062/file S.2357; BMH WS 1075/file S.2368; BMH WS 1539/file S.2860; BMH WS 1221; BMH WS 1046/file S.2371; BMH WS 1399/file S.2722; BMH WS 1512/

file S.2848; BMH WS 1694/file S.3017; BMH WS 1178/file S.2460; BMH WS 1336/file S.2673BMH WS 1337/file S.2663; BMH WS 1402; BMH WS 1331; BMH WS 2656; BMH WS 1121/file 2421; BMH WS 1592/file S.2906; BMH WS 983/file S.2297

33 BMH WS 1769/file S.96
34 Beaslai *Michael Collins* vol I p. 350
35 Hart *The IRA and Its Enemies* p. 250
36 Ibid. p. 249
37 Beaslai *Michael Collins* vol I p. 353
38 BMH WS1610/file S.2917
39 BMH WS 954/file S.2272
40 O Connor *With Michael Collins* p. 177
41 "The Sinn Fein Bank – the winding up matter" *Irish Times* 23 December 1923
42 Dwyer *Big Fellow, Long Shadow* p. 140
43 Cited in Mark Sturgis' diaries entry 17 November 1920, Hopkinson *The Last Days of Dublin Castle* vol II p. 74
44 *Pall Mall Gazette* July 1920, quoted by Mackay in *Michael Collins* p. 163
45 BMH WS 1439/file S.2737; WS 1770/file S.909; WS 1121/file S.2421
46 Beaslai *Michael Collins* vol I p. 352
47 Ibid.
48 BMH WS 1771/file S.909 Part VI
49 M Comerford *The First Dail*, Joe Clark 1969 cited in a www blog "Daithi O Donnchada-photopol", found on http://photopol.com/martello/daithi.html
50 Beaslai *Michael Collins* vol I p. 351
51 O Connor *With Michael Collins* p. 116; Beaslai *Michael Collins* vol I p. 352
52 Apart from just over £11,000 from subscribers in Britain and France and £800 direct from the Irish–American society Cumann n Gael
53 Mitchel *Dail Eireann* (Gill & Macmillan 1993) p. 64
54 Taylor *Michael Collins* Appendix C p. 296. Also an extremely comprehensive detailed breakdown and analysis is to be found in the detailed scholarship of G Evans' thesis, *The raising of the first internal Dail Eireann Loan and the British response to it* Masters thesis University of Maynooth 2012 see Note 65.
55 F S L Lyons "War of Independence" in W E Vaughan (ed.) *A New History of Ireland Vol VI – Ireland under the Union* p. 243
56 Costello *Michael Collins – in his own words* p. 49
57 Irish Department of Finance, *Minister for Finance speech at Beal na m Blath 22 August 2010*, found on www.finance.gov.ie/viewdoc.asp?DocID=6422
58 BMH WS 707/file no S.602
59 *Irish Times* 8 November 1919
60 BMH, WM 707/file S.602
61 *Irish Independent* 12 March 1920
62 *Irish Bulletin* 9 March 1920, *Irish Times* 9 March 1920, *The Times* 9 March 1920, *Irish Independent* 9 March 1920
63 In dealing with Bell's inquiries the author acknowledges his indebtedness to, and draws upon, the published research of the Master's thesis of Gary Evans, student at the Maynooth University of Ireland. It is postgraduate research of which its author must be extremely proud, and is a credit to the distinguished university.
64 *Freeman's Journal* 9 March 1920
65 Evans *The raising of the first internal Dail Eireann Loan and the British response to it* citing deposition TNA Dublin papers CO 904/177/1
66 BMH WS 423/file S.1469
67 *Annual Register* 1920 p. 34
68 P Beslai *Irish Independent* 28 May 1957

69 *The Times* 7 April 1920; *Irish Times* 27 March 1920
70 Cited in Mark Sturgis' diaries entry 26 October 1920, Hopkinson *The Last Days of Dublin Castle* vol II p. 60
71 O Winter *Winter's Tale* (Richards Press 1955) pp. 288–348
72 Dwyer *Big Fellow, Long Fellow* p. 108

11 Funds from America, funds in America

As we have seen, de Valera had several objectives in his visit to the United States. One of them – although not viewed by de Valera as the main objective – was to raise funds for the Dail Loan. As such it was planned to be the US side of the dual approach to raising funds, namely fundraising for the Loan in Ireland and Britain, and fundraising for the Loan in the United States. Even before de Valera set out, his deviousness and fact-twisting came to the fore – and was recognised – in an incident. This occurred after one of the meetings where his visit to the United States was planned. Emerging from a meeting he stated to one IRA member that "they" were sending him to America. He received the stinging and dismissive reply

> Nonsense, it's your own bloody idea to get over there out of the trouble.[1]

De Valera arrived in the United States in June 1919. In November 1919, James O Mara, one of the Dail Loan Trustees, joined him to assist in the Loan.

James O Mara was brought up in Ireland and worked in one of the factories in the family business, of a bacon manufacturer and curer. He studied part-time at the Royal University of Ireland. Despite his studies being interrupted several times, he showed tenacity and gained first class honours in 1898. Making his way up the family business, he worked in London as an agent, and travelled to Romania in 1902 and returned to London having gained a trade deal importing Romanian bacon. Like many Irish ex-patriots in London he was warmly sympathetic to the cause of Irish freedom. He returned to Ireland in 1914, and put his business acumen to use for the cause of Ireland, becoming Assistant Financial Director of Sinn Fein in 1917. He and Collins had already recognised each other's financial and commercial abilities and shared common views on ways forward in the struggle for Irish freedom, although O Mara was less enthusiastic on the physical force aspects. In 1919 the Dail appointed O Mara as one of the three trustees of the National Loan. Whilst de Valera was travelling, lobbying and making speeches, O Mara was hard at work in his commercial element, raising the United States Loan. De Valera, in his anxiety and drive to obtain United States' recognition of the Irish Republic, initially underestimated the true potential in the United States for financial support. Collins realised its potential from the outset and it was he who ensured that O Mara would be part of de Valera's United States visit, and ensured that Arthur Griffith, as Acting President of the Dail,[2] made an official request to O Mara to go to the United States.[3]

O Mara too fully realised the fundraising potential from the outset, perceiving that in America

was the vein of potential gold waiting to be tapped.[4]

O Mara took personal responsibility for raising funds in the United States for the Dail.[5]

De Valera, on his arrival and during his meetings with Cohalan and Devoy, proposed to float the sale of bonds for the Irish Republic. However, Cohalan, drawing upon his considerable legal knowledge, strongly counselled against this. He advised that the sale of such bonds within the United States would be illegal (and tantamount to fraud) as the Irish Republic did not exist as a legal entity, had no recognition in international law, and was not recognised as such within the United States. This was wise counsel and was accepted by de Valera, albeit grudgingly. It also delayed the start of his Loan raising activities within the United Sates until a way round could be found.

O Mara consulted, pondered and, with Cohalan's help,[6] finally resolved the issue, enabling a Loan campaign to go ahead without falling foul of the United States anti-fraud laws. Redeemable – and re saleable – bonds were not to be offered. Instead certificates of indebtedness of the Irish Republic,[7] or "bond-certificates" were offered. Sellers were sternly instructed that the term "bonds" was never to be used, and never to refer to themselves as "bond sellers" and to avoid claiming that they were offering or "selling bonds". The "bond-certificate" or certificate of indebtedness would be exchangeable at cost price for gold bonds issued by the Treasury of the Irish Republic one month after the Irish Republic received international recognition and the British forces of occupation had been withdrawn from the territory of the Irish Republic. From the time of the "bond-certificate" or certificate of indebtedness being purchased to actually being able to be exchanged for a gold bond, no interest was paid on the bond-certificate of indebtedness. Thereafter, when it was exchanged for a gold bond it was interest bearing to the holder at 5 per cent.

Popular US perception often failed to distinguish differences between what they were accustomed to, i.e. government backed and guaranteed bonds, as against this new "bond-certificate". The *Wall Street Journal*, a month after the fundraising campaign started, virulently criticised the "so-called bonds of the so-called Irish Republic" warning that these were "... sold as bond, the de Valera issue is nothing more than a swindle".[8]

To counter this de Valera exercised further caution against the possibility of running the risk of investment fraud by his outlining the terms of the Loan. As part of these terms he publicly emphasised that the Loan was "a sentimental appeal" and not an offer to investors and that each subscriber needed to distinctly understand that they were "making a free gift" of the money, and that repayment would be entirely conditional on "the recognition of the republic as an independent nation".[9] An identical qualification was inserted into the promotional material issued, as the front page stated, *"A Bond-Certificate Campaign"*. The careful caveat was used stating that subscriptions or tenders for the bond-certificates

> are, in all cases, voluntarily made with the express stipulation that there is no obligation to repay the principal or to pay interest until the Republic of Ireland has been internationally recognised and after the Republic has been freed from British military control.[10]

O Mara methodically organised the collecting campaign, using both his business and commercial skills to the full. All workers involved in the Loan raising were inspired and had confidence in O Mara and his judgement.[11] He based his headquarters in New York on 411 Fifth Avenue, with a branch or sub-headquarters established in Chicago.[12] Both offices had fully paid staff. He appointed organisers who followed de Valera in his journeys throughout the United States and as they arrived at each location or area, each organiser was designated a particular area for which he or she would be responsible. This resembled the strategy that Collins had adopted in the Dail Loan in Ireland, where one sub-organiser was designated each of the four traditional provinces of Ireland, but of course O Mara was implementing this on a wider geographical scale. The organisers would appoint local fundraising groups within "their" area, and would report back to O Mara in New York, either via the Chicago sub-headquarters or direct to him, in New York.

At several locations, O Mara implemented short training sessions to selected individuals, where they were given a thorough grounding in approaching potential investors and selling the product; they were also given training in how to pass on what they had learned to small groups of others, which they did. This "training the trainers" initiative resulted in its cascading form, not only in more successful selling of the bonds to subscribers, but also in establishing a smaller pool of mobile part-time trainers, who could quickly be deployed to other locations or areas to exploit any sudden increased demand for subscriptions. In one location O Mara selected a small group of sympathisers who had been trained by a particularly active local Methodist church, in concentrating on and obtaining small scale contributions – about $20 or less – from many, rather than larger contributions from a few. Their effort proved extremely successful[13] and this fundraising strategy – with the suitably trained collectors – was adopted in other locations. The effectiveness of this could be witnessed in New York, where over 100,000 individuals purchased certificates up to the value of $25; this was an average individual subscription of $10. Small contributions they may have been, but the total revenue gained in New York was $1 million.[14]

The Loan was closed on 23 September 1920, having raised $5,123,640,[15] a tremendous achievement, and thanks to O Mara's organisation and financial sense. Over half what was collected was sent to Ireland. De Valera appeared hesitant about sending all the monies, and on one occasion he raised with Collins – significantly, writing via Harry Boland – his concerns about how secure would be the storage arrangements in Ireland if the monies were sent. Collins had tartly replied that it would not be stored it would be used and spent (the IRA were in constant need of ready funding). One historian has pointed out that Collins' ruthlessness in dealing with Alan Bell was more than enough sufficient reassurance that any Loan funds would be safeguarded.[16] However, de Valera did not release up to $3 million which remained in the United States.[17]

The monies destined from Ireland were placed in bank accounts and then transferred to accounts in New York,[18] including the Guaranty Trust,[19] for whom Collins had worked when in London and knew its potential for fund transfers. Some managers of New York branches were hesitant about accepting deposits of issuing draft, but O Mara and the Loan had an ally in a one particularly sympathetic manager of Irish descent. He came out fully in support of O Mara, and made his feelings of contempt known to the more hesitant fellow bankers.[20] The majority of the funds went through three separate banks,[21] before drafts were issued for sums, usually between £10,000 and £30,000. These were made payable to sympathetic – but obscure – Irish individuals, lists of such names having been provided from Ireland to Harry Boland. The drafts were then physically couriered by trusted messengers on passenger ships sailing from New York to Ireland. O Mara and colleagues were constantly vigilant about recruiting and retaining trusted messengers, who were vital to the whole transfer process. Some of the monies were also used to purchase US Liberty Bonds, which were couriered by a carefully selected special messenger.[22]

His financial work completed, O Mara was anxious to leave and go back to Ireland. He was not a young man and the journey from Ireland to the United States had been arduous. Harry Boland had made the journey by being disguised as a stoker, and working his passage; this was hard work but at least he was mobile and had some freedom of movement.[23] O Mara could not possibly pass as a member of the crew, and therefore was smuggled on board and stowed away throughout the voyage in a cramped space underneath life-saving equipment, and later hidden in a small lifeboat, and meals were secretly passed to him by two colluding crew members.[24] Then, on arriving in the United States, he had been pitched straight into the exhausting work of the raising of the Loan throughout the whole of the United States. He was missing his family, and anxious to get back to running his business in Ireland, of which he was kept informed by his loyal employees. In fact, once the organisation was set up and the funds were clearly being collected without much difficulty, O Mara requested de Valera, as early as March 1920, to be relieved of his duties as organiser of the Loan and as a Dail trustee. De Valera replied, asking O Mara to stay at least another two months until the main part of the Loan was gathered in. O Mara accepted this, and replied stating that he repeated his resignation, and – conscientiously – requested that he be given reassurance that by June, when his resignation became effective, another Dail trustee to the Loan would be found. De Valera then prevailed upon O Mara to stay, invoking his extreme need for his, O Mara's, services and also that his fellow trustee Bishop Fogarty valued his services.[25] O Mara shelved his resignation, and his enforced stay was relieved by a visit of his family to him in New York, followed by himself and his family staying and sightseeing for a fortnight in Washington and Baltimore.

However, relations between O Mara and de Valera rapidly deteriorated,[26] with O Mara increasingly concerned about the finances and de Valera's judgement.

O Mara's concern about de Valera's financial sense would have been further increased had he known of another activity of de Valera and Boland. Boland, following de Valera's focussed objective of gaining international recognition for the Irish republic, was always on the alert for would be "allies" of Ireland. This coincided with the new Soviet government in Russia also searching on the diplomatic level for allies and recognition.[27] The Soviets were establishing a self-styled legation or embassy in Washington (though totally devoid of official warmth and accreditation or recognition from the United States). In establishing and maintaining these Washington premises they ran into financial difficulties. De Valera, through Boland, secretly authorised a loan, and $20,000 was lent to the Soviets, who gave as collateral the crown jewels of the former imperial royal family of Russia. Boland forwarded Collins documentation from the Soviets acknowledging receipt of the loan, which Collins duly recorded, and meticulously issued a receipt of the Soviet receipt back to Boland.

In fact, the Russian régime lost interest in friendship with the would-be Irish republic.[28] It had adopted a policy of friendship and reconciliation with Britain, signing an Anglo-Russian trade deal in March 1921. The imperial Russian crown jewels remained in the possession of the Irish Free State (subsequently the Irish Republic) until 1949. It was a curious, somewhat quaint affair. However, at the time $20,000 outgoings from Irish funds to provide a loan was diverting $20,000 which was badly needed for the struggle occurring back in Ireland. O Mara, already conscious of the

$3 million being held back in the United States by de Valera, would have been further exasperated.

By November 1920 de Valera was frustrated with Cohalan and the Friends of Irish Freedom and founded his own Irish–American organisation, the American Association for the Recognition of the Irish Republic (AARIR). O Mara was instructed to build up the organisation. He loyally carried out this instruction, and the AARIR recruited many willing US citizens as helpers and officials. Two individuals, Joseph Hearn and a lawyer John F Finerty, became hard-working in this cause, and were to be staunch allies of de Valera in a later, darker stage of Irish history. In late December, de Valera left the United States and returned to Ireland, leaving Boland as his "Envoy" and O Mara to carry on working hard on the financial work, and on the AARIR. In March 1921, de Valera sent a request for O Mara's assistance in organising and raising a second Loan in the United States, and authorised a cheque to O Mara of £250,000 to cover expenses for this forthcoming second Loan campaign. At the same time, de Valera proposed that the New York offices which O Mara had set up for the first Loan be closed and then re-opened to house the AARIR staff. It seemed O Mara's offices were now changing from a financial establishment to those of a political propaganda movement.

The following month de Valera intervened in April 1921 at the Convention of the AARIR. De Valera sent a long telegram which was read out to the Convention. It stated the aim of raising $1 million every year, and asked for a $5 contribution from every member of the AARIR. O Mara's patience had reached its limits and the telegram to the AARIR may have proven the last straw. Whilst it was Griffith who officially had requested him to go to the United States and Michael Collins as Minister of Finance under whose official auspices he had been sent, de Valera had also specifically asked for O Mara to be sent and assist him.[29] O Mara had always been deferential to de Valera, and was always mindful of the latter's role as President. Yet de Valera had constantly taken him for granted. O Mara's frustration was complete, and he lost any faith in de Valera's judgement. De Valera, having initially completely side-lined the fundraising objective of his visit to the United States, in order to pursue the chimera of diplomatic recognition of the Irish Republic – and in doing so under-focussing on the fund potential of the United States – was now appearing to veer to the other extreme and over-fish the financial pond. There remained the issue of nearly half the monies from the first Loan still not having been sent back to Ireland, where funds were needed to keep the armed struggle continuing. Not only that, but now £250,000 of precious funds were actually leaving Ireland to the United States, and the United States was being asked to provide a further million dollars every year.

O Mara could no longer contain his frustration and he admonished de Valera in uncharacteristically harsh terms, writing a reply on 25 April 1921

My Dear de Valera,

A cable from you was read to the American Association of Recognition of the Irish Republic asking for a guarantee of a million dollars a year into action by a levy of 5 dollars a member on every member of the association.

There are nearly three million dollars lying idle here to the credit of the American trustees and at the disposal of your government. It is somewhat unworthy of our country to be always holding out its hat, but to hold out two hats at once is stupid....

to use your own words when we last discussed the matter "crops will not grow over trampled ground".[30]

O Mara had been kept up to date with news of Collins.[31] Some weeks before writing the reply to de Valera, O Mara had written discreetly to Collins voicing frustration and desperation in that he simply could not keep going indefinitely and heartily wished to finish. He confirmed his resignation of his Dail Loan trusteeship to Collins, effective within two months. At least Collins would heed him.

At the same time as his harsh reply to de Valera, O Mara wrote to Boland, still active in the United States, stating that de Valera's instructions in money matters "renders too remote the issue of a loan". He returned the cheque for £250,000 and instructed Boland to acknowledge receipt of the returned cheque to himself and fellow Dail trustees. Boland quickly replied, conciliatory in tone, but at the same time emphasising his, Boland's, role as "Envoy". He refused to receive the cheque and requested O Mara to continue his work. De Valera, through Boland, offered O Mara the post of de facto Irish ambassador to the United States.[32] O Mara was stung by Boland's outright refusal of his instructions regarding the cheque (a matter of finance, and therefore within his, O Mara's, remit and decision) and was thoroughly disillusioned with de Valera's conduct and his inept financial judgement.

He refused the post outright, stating in his rely to Boland that he could not take this or any position

under the government of the Irish Republic whose resident claims such arbitrary executive authority and in whose judgement of American affairs I no longer have any confidence.[33]

He sent his resignation letter to de Valera, for placing before the Dail. De Valera immediately sent O Mara a short, discourteous telegram, stating to O Mara that he was fired.[34]

It had been shabby treatment of an individual who had selflessly dedicated himself to hard work, unpaid – his personal expenses and outlay were estimated to amount to £10,000 – and whose business had suffered whilst he was absent. De Valera was to further downplay O Mara's part in fundraising in the United States. He did mention O Mara, but in conjunction with Frank P Walsh, the Chairman of the American Delegation for Irish Independence and he slanted success in the United States as mainly due to Walsh.[36] However, Collins from whose initiative and under whose authority as Minister of Finance O Mara[37] had been sent to the United States to assist de Valera, paid full and due respect to O Mara's achievements when he gave an account of fundraising to the Dail. In this account on 26 August 1921 Collins singled out O Mara and acknowledged

> But for the pioneering work done by Mr James O Mara, they would not have been nearly so successful in raising the monies abroad ... he *(Collins)* only voiced the feelings of everyone who worked with him, as he had done, that they would ever feel grateful to Mr James O Mara for the work he had done.[38]

The monies raised in the United States exceeded the $5 million target by the time of its closure in September 1920. In 1921 A second Loan was floated in the United States, between October 1921 and closing in December 1921, when the Anglo-Irish Treaty was signed; this netted a considerably smaller amount than the first, but it may have been implemented to show to the British during the negotiation period that support in the United States for Ireland was still vibrant. The total of funds raised in the United States amounted to $5,746,360.

That it was a success and an achievement for de Valera cannot be denied. However, whatever the motivation, de Valera deliberately prevented over half of these vitally needed funds from being sent to Ireland to support the struggle. During the vital years it was Collins, as clandestine Minister of Finance, who raised the funds, it was Collins who managed the funds and it was Collins who ensured – just – the financial survival of the Irish during the Anglo-Irish War.

Notes

1 Coogan *Michael Collins – a biography* p. 102, cited in Mackay *Michael Collins* p. 116
2 Dwyer *Big Fellow, Long Fellow* p. 93; Lavelle *James O Mara – a staunch Sinn Feiner* p. 141
3 Ibid.; ibid.
4 Lavelle *James O Mara – a staunch Sinn Feiner* p. 142
5 S Kelly "The Sinn Fein Millionaire – James O Mara and the first American bond-certificate drive" in *New Hibernia Review* vol 15 no 4 Winter 2011; Dwyer *Big Fellow, Long Fellow* p. 93
6 Dwyer *Big Fellow Long Shadow* p. 93
7 Ibid.
8 *Wall Street Journal* 5 February 1920
9 Announcement in evening edition of New York newspaper(s) 2 December 1919, cited by Lavelle *James O Mara – a staunch Sinn Feiner* p. 142

10 Promotional Material for the Sale of Bond-Certificates in the United States Frank Walsh Chairman American Commission on Irish Independence, cited in Carroll *Money for Ireland – finance, diplomacy, politics and the First Dail Eireann 1919–1936* Appendix II p. 103

11 P McCartan *With de Valera in America* (Brentano New York 1931) p. 154, cited by Coogan in *De Valera – long fellow, long shadow* p. 159

12 Lavelle *James O Mara – a staunch Sinn Feiner* pp. 141, 150, 153

13 Ibid. p. 153

14 J Humphreys "Millionaire helped finance the War of Independence" *Irish Times* 23 May 2013

15 D McCardle *The Irish Republic* (Gollancz 1937)

16 Coogan *The Man Who Made Ireland* p. 188

17 See Appendix I

18 S Munan, Witness Statement 1.774 24 November 1958 BMH Dublin p. 18

19 Hart *Mick – the real Michael Collins* p. 76

20 Lavelle *James O Mara – a staunch Sinn Feiner* p. 153

21 Humphreys "Millionaire helped finance the War of Independence" *Irish Times* 23 May 2013

22 Lavelle *James O Mara – a staunch Sinn Feiner* pp. 185–186, 190

23 Beaslai *Michael Collins* vol I pp. 307–308

24 Lavelle *James O Mara – a staunch Sinn Feiner* pp. 139–140

25 Ibid. pp. 154–156

26 Hannigan, in his *De Valera in America*, disputes that an irreconcilable rift occurred between O Mara and de Valera, and even questions whether there was a loss of friendship. However, even Hannigan criticises de Valera for refusing what he views as a perfectly reasonable wish, indeed right, of O Mara, to leave the US and return to Ireland p. 188.

27 National Archives of Ireland Documents on Irish Foreign Policy "Draft of Proposed Treaty between the Russian Socialist Federative Soviet Republics and the Republic of Ireland" May 1921 NAI DE2/245

28 Dwyer *Big Fellow, Long Fellow* pp. 159–160

29 BMH WS 837/file S.2140

30 Lavelle *James O Mara – a staunch Sinn Feiner* p. 245

31 Ibid. pp. 235–236

32 Ibid. pp. 245–248

33 Ibid. p. 248

34 Dwyer *Big Fellow, Long Shadow* p. 163; the telegram consisted of one line; Lavelle *James O Mara – a staunch Sinn Feiner* p. 249

35 Humphreys "Millionaire helped finance the War of Independence" *Irish Times* 23 May 2013

36 De Valera's speech to the Dail, 17 August 1921, cited by Lavelle *James O Mara-a staunch Sinn Feiner* pp. 267–268

37 Hart, in his comprehensive work on Collins, *Mick – the real Michael Collins*, having extensively researched into all aspects of Collins' life and characteristics, an objective work – and by no means totally sympathetic to Collins – states that credit should be given to de Valera for raising the $5 million Dail Loan in the United States, and further states that Collins had little to do with this.

However, he appears to ignore the essential role of O Mara who was sent under the authority of Collins' Ministry of Finance and who kept in touch with Collins. Also, Hart does qualify his praise of de Valera by stating that de Valera exercised poor judgement which caused fundraising opportunities to be missed in the United States. Hart also points to the failure of de Valera to send half of the monies raised in the United States back to Ireland, especially when needed during the vital period of the Anglo-Irish War. In pp. 190–191, and in the concluding chapter he does acknowledge de Valera's poor judgement in overstaying in the United States p. 423. See also Appendix I.

38 Dwyer *Big Fellow, Long Shadow* p. 185 and Lavelle *James O Mara – a staunch Sinn Feiner* p. 269.

12 Collins, Minister of Finance

The functioning of the clandestine departments of state was always difficult during the Anglo-Irish War. The clandestine ministries, particularly Collins' Ministry of Finance, was always under threat of discovery and raid by British forces. One prominent worker in the Local Government ministry wrote of conditions when working in 1920

> persons were appointed to ministerial positions and staff appointed to help them, it was impossible to have permanent or continuous locations ... during the entire period everyone connected with the Dail and its servants was hunted down by the British government; consequently all offices and office equipment had to be of the most portable character, capable of instantaneous removal at the sound of the approach of the British Black and Tans or Military. An entire department might find it necessary to make a hurried removal through a skylight, or down a drainpipe at a moment's notice.[1]

Clandestine ministries were the subject of repeated raids. After one ministry had been raided and moved premises to another discreet location, an office in the Dublin County Council complex, they were raided yet again. The workers were located on the top floor of the building which was used to archive the rents and rates of the entire city; the walls were lined with shelves on which were endless lines of massive hard bound tomes of rate records. Quickly, whilst the raiding party was mounting the stairs the workers "distributed" and interweaved within the huge volumes all their incriminating Ministry correspondence and papers. The raiders departed empty-handed.[2]

All told, it could be argued that the achievement was that the various Dail Ministries functioned at all. However, the Dail government was hampered by some of the individuals in charge of the differing Ministries and departments.[3]

Count Plunkett, the father of the executed leader of the 1916 Rising was nominally Foreign Minister; however this role was dominated by de Valera who was constantly seeking opportunities – generally unsuccessfully – for international recognition, and who tended to regard foreign affairs as primarily concerned with propaganda.[4] Under the Foreign Ministry the de facto Irish consuls in various locations abroad were more involved and preoccupied with publicity work and unsuccessfully assisting in facilitating arms deals for Collins and the IRA. The Ministry of Home Affairs was under Austin Stack. He carried out valuable work in scoping and developing the "Republican court" system but this was in a consultative capacity by presenting papers to the Dail; the Republican court system and "Republican Police" forces were operated on the ground by the local IRA commanders and local officials. In terms of running the Home Affairs department, as a Minister leading and overseeing policy, Stack was somewhat lax, indeed inefficient and he and his department were subject of complaints.[5] MacNeill, as Minister of Industry, never established any departments or attempted any form of organisation.[6] Robert Barton, in charge of the Ministry of Agriculture and the Land Bank, pursued his work with quiet competence. William Cosgrave was extremely able and hardworking, and his Ministry of Local Government was considerably assisted in its activities by Sinn Fein having effective control over local government councils.[7] The Ministry of Defence was under the fighting stalwart, Cathal Brugha. However, with characteristic sincerity, Brugha refused his ministerial salary and title of Minister of Defence, and continued working fulltime as a director of LALORs, a manufacturing and retail business in candles. Sincere and unostentatious, but he was also accused for this of not taking his role as Minister of Defence sufficiently seriously.[8] One historian of the Anglo-Irish War makes the telling point that the British were never interested in Brugha.[9]

Liam Lynch, commander of Cork No. 2 Brigade IRA and later commander of the IRA 1 Southern Division stated carefully of the clandestine Irish civil service

> We must admit that all civil organisations ... were an absolute failure during the last phase of hostilities. If anything they were a burden on the army – why even the civilian government failed.

whilst Mulcahy scathingly stated

> No single government department has been the slightest assistance to the Army.... The plain fact is that our civil services have simply played at governing the Republic whilst the soldiers have not played at dying for it.[10]

However, none quibbled about Collins and his Ministry of Finance.[11] Collins' energy and drive were undisputed. Dan Breen and Tom Barry, both hardened IRA combat operatives, generally unsympathetic and contemptuous towards IRA headquarters and central government, both commented that no job was too big or too small for Collins and if anyone wanted a job or task to be done Collins was the person to see.[12] A solicitor, discreet legal adviser to Collins and Griffith throughout the struggle stated afterwards of Collins

The word "cannot" did not figure in his vocabulary.[13]

P S O Hegarty, a former British civil servant who became a high-ranking Irish civil servant,[14] reflectively asserted – with a certain practitioner expertise – that Collins' Ministry of Finance was the only clandestine department that functioned.[15]

The different clandestine Ministries were scattered about in Dublin in various premises, some discreet, some not so discreet. De Valera operated his Foreign Ministry from a private residence, Brugha operated his Defence Ministry from his business premises at LALORs and Ernest Blythe operated his Ministry of Trade and Commerce out of premises in Fleet Street, Dublin under the guise of a front company, the Irish and Overseas Shipping and Trade Company. Each ministry had its own clearing house for correspondence and general registry in different premises. Later in 1920 Collins organised a central clearing house for all Dail correspondence and for all departments at a set of business premises in Church Street, Dublin. Every Minister was allocated a courier or runner for communications between Ministers and the Dail and for delivering other important messages and documents. Collins had two couriers, the faithful Joe O Reilly for him as Director of Intelligence, and Bob Conlan for him as Minister of Finance.[16]

As we have seen, there were many locations in Dublin which were used by Collins' intelligence organisation for meeting places, safe houses and live and dead letter boxes. Collins also had several premises during various periods where his Ministry of Finance operated. The first premises were those at 6 Harcourt Street, a three-storey building which housed the Sinn Fein Bank. However, this was deemed too high profile – it had been raided in September 1919[17] – so Collins moved the Finance Ministry to premises further along the street, at 72 Harcourt Street. This house was registered as owned and occupied by "The Irish Club", a designation that fooled no-one, least of all the British authorities, who placed it under surveillance by the DMP G Division.[18] (And Collins from time to time deployed counter watchers to identify the surveillance team, for future intelligence use.) No. 76 Harcourt Street had been purchased by Batt O Connor. O Connor was a Volunteer who had fought in the 1916 Rising and was a builder by trade. O Connor was invaluable to Collins and the Irish cabinet; it was he who had ensured the gold contributions to the National Loan collection had been securely hidden, he had professional knowledge of types of housing in and around Dublin and ability to discreetly facilitate renting of properties. The renting was arranged by a sympathetic solicitor, who used the names of sympathetic front men as the "tenants" and soothed any doubts from the owners by arranging, if necessary, for six months' rent to be paid in advance.[19] After the Ministry of Finance moved to 76 Harcourt Street, O Connor constructed hiding place for Collins; financial records and paperwork, portioning off a section of a wardrobe which could only be opened by a secret spring.[20] Most of the other premises which were acquired by the Ministry of Finance had hiding places for the increasingly large amounts of financial papers and records, all constructed by O Connor. When some were discovered in raids, the British investigators were impressed with the skill and dexterity with which they had been constructed.[21]

Some weeks after moving into 76 Harcourt St the premises were raided. Collins and O Connor had made arrangements whereby an escape could be made up a ladder and through the skylight, where Collins quickly went up and through, then along and entered the skylight of another building further along the street, the Standard Hotel, and then jumped down across the stairwell, made his way down and unobtrusively went out of the exit of the Standard Hotel. After this raid it was decided that new premises should be found. Temporary space was found for the clandestine War Office at Crow Street,[22] whilst the Ministry of Finance moved on a temporary basis to office space in the Land Bank.[23] Then the War Office moved to 5 Mespil Road, whilst the Finance Department moved to offices at 22 Henry Street[24] which was the main finance office, with other Finance Ministry offices at 22 Mary Street and 3 St Andrew Street.[25] No. 3 St Andrew Street, although smaller than the other Ministry of Finance premises, was a particularly important address, containing sensitive correspondence and working there were George McGrath, an accountant and future Accountant General of the Free State and Daithi O Donnchada, the Secretary to the Trustees of the Dail Loan.[26] In May 1921 the Mespil Road War Office was raided, and Collins moved the War Office and temporarily "shared" War Office premises with those of the Finance Ministry that were at 22 Mary Street.[27] When 22 Mary Street was raided in 1921 Collins escaped capture by bluff, casually walking down the stairs as the raiding party rushed passed him on the way up.[28] After this raid the Finance Office at 22 Mary Street moved to premises further up the street at 28 Mary Street. This was a draper's shop, which had a section of it between numbers 28 and 29 portioned off and concealed; this hidden space housed the Finance Ministry.[29] In Dublin, Collins' "normal" daily routine was divided between working on intelligence at the Ministry of War in 5 Mespil Street, then onto the Ministry of Finance at Mary Street.[30]

Due to the fluctuations in the conflict and working under the constant threat of raids, seizures and arrest, it took time for Collins to establish a fully operating clandestine Ministry of Finance. However, he accomplished this during the period of the Anglo-Irish War. Collins held several positions of responsibility – and intense workload – including IRA Director of

Intelligence, Adjutant General of the IRA, and IRA Director of Organisation. Some issues involving these differing functions would at times cross over, and be dealt with simultaneously, or in shared paperwork and files. However, on matters financial he always sent letters, reports or indeed any communication concerning finances entirely separate from other subjects of other departments,[31] and was conscious of the vital need for the Ministry of Finance to have primacy over other departments and ministries.[32]

Much of Collins' organisation and implementing practices of government finances was influenced by his period of working in London, where he appreciated the merits of the British financial system.[33] The Dail had set up 13 different departments and ministries, and as we have seen they operated with varying degrees of activity and efficiency.[34] With the passage of time the Ministry of Finance soon gained primacy.[35] In April 1919 Collins had secured, with Dail authority, the appointment of an official auditor of the accounts of the National Loan. In late February 1920 Collins moved that any cabinet business involving transfer of monies or funds should be discussed first on the agenda of the meeting of Ministers. In September 1921, it was decided that any financial proposal to be brought up at a forthcoming cabinet meeting should be sent, in advance, to the Ministry of Finance.[36] In June 1920 Collins secured the appointment of the Accountant General to the Ministry of Finance. This individual had charge of all departmental and ministerial accounts, except that of the Ministry of Defence. With this appointment the procedure was inaugurated whereby the Accountant General and his section would audit on a monthly basis all the departmental and ministerial accounts. Forms, receipt books, record books, and vouchers were standardised by the Ministry of Finance for use in all departments and ministries. The post of Accountant General to the Ministry of Finance would become that of Comptroller and Auditor General of the Free State, wielding a wider remit and powers of auditing accounts and monitoring expenditure of government ministries and departments. On the last day of every month, each department or ministry submitted an estimate to Collins' Ministry of Finance, giving the amount of monies that particular department needed to continue for the following month. The Ministry of Finance then calculated the total expenditure of all departments in an overall financial statement. Any surplus revenue of an individual department was calculated and included in the total statement (i.e. the department did not get that incoming revenue credited to it on the monthly basis). These estimates and the overall statement were then submitted to the Dail fund trustees, together with Collins' proposed allocation of funds to the departments and Ministries.[37]

Payment of clandestine Ministry employees was in many cases made in cash. Collins, on receipt of the estimate of the amount needed for the following month from the particular Ministry, would draw enough cash to cover payment to the employees of that Ministry and other expenses, record it, and give to a trusted individual at the Ministry of Finance, known as *Banc ar Siubpal* or "Walking Bank". This individual would then carry the cash to the address where the clandestine Ministry was located, give it over to a senior official in that Ministry, who would sign an official receipt, later to be handed over by "Walking Bank" to Collins. The senior official would then distribute the cash salary payments to the staff and dispense the remainder for the department or Ministry's work.[38] As with all other aspects, Collins paid close attention to payment of staff. In December 1921, even though preoccupied with the intense Dail debate over the Anglo-Irish Treaty, he found time to remind the Accountant General to ensure Ministry staff received that month's pay before Christmas.[39]

The Ministry of Finance compiled update reports, showing the position of departments and Ministries in terms of outgoings, expenditure and revenues received. (Though, as Collins pointed out to de Valera, few departments actually received revenues.) Later, during the Truce period, Collins pushed and persuaded the Dail to appoint a registrar of companies as the first step in company regulation in the new state. This was to counter a sudden proliferation of "corporate ventures" in the aftermath of the conflict. These companies all offered glittering investment opportunities to the Irish populace, ventures which were often risky, and Collins was concerned about the shaky financial basis on which they had been formed.[40] Collins' keen eye fixed on expenditures – together with the success of receipts from the National Loan – resulted in the Irish government enjoying an initial surplus. From the period 1 May 1920 to 31 December 1920, total incoming receipts were £335,150-15, whilst expenditure was £51,905-17, a surplus of £283,210-73. However, two ministries in particular had dramatically increasing costs. These were Defence and Foreign Affairs.

Defence costs – fighting the Anglo-Irish War – spiralled. Between June to December 1920 Defence expenditure was £16,000; between January to June 1921 Defence expenditure rose to £39,350; in the following six-month period between June to December 1921 Defence expenditure rose to £98,133.

Foreign Affairs and the nascent diplomatic service accounted for a significant part of expenditure. These activities involved attempts at gaining recognition for the Irish Republic. Two of the earliest decisions of the Dail were to establish an Irish representative in the United States with an "embassy" and another in France. The latter representative, based in Paris, was Gavan Duffy, some two years later to be one of the Irish negotiating team in the Anglo-Irish Treaty. De facto Irish consuls and representatives and agents were appointed in various European cities, and even in Buenos Aires[41] to take care of Irish trade interests.[42] One such city was Genoa in Italy, where Donal Hales, a teacher at Genoa University and who enjoyed contacts with Mussolini and the Italian poet, writer and adventurer d'Annunzio[43] was later to act in a more clandestine capacity. Another representative, Maire O Brien, acted as Dail publicity agent in Spain. (Spain was perceived by the Foreign Affairs Ministry as having much potential for recognition of the Irish cause, and it was important for its influence in South American countries where other representatives were making efforts.[44]) Maire O Brien struggled on her own, in poor accommodation and against a male-dominated populace, and manage to produce regular bulletins and propaganda material on behalf of Ireland. Similar ground-breaking work was carried out in Argentina, where Anita Bulfin, the sister of the Irish representative in Buenos Ayres carried out initiatives and pro-duced publications.[45] All such consuls, agents and representatives generally paid their own way in good faith with little or no formal salaries, but nonetheless some required funding and various expenses – even when some waived part of their expenses on occasions[46] – all of which had to be pro-vided for from Collins' Ministry of Finance.

The representatives were all full of initiatives to further the possibility of Ireland gaining international recognition, but some were careless or ineffi-cient when it came to funds. Art O Brien in London was eventually in trouble with the Free State government over his financial ineptitude and woeful record keeping. The Irish de facto representative in Germany,[47] on being re-deployed to assist colleagues in the United States appeared to have left behind in Berlin £7,500, monies allocated by the Ministry of Finance; Collins had to spend time and effort requesting the various representatives in the United States to ensure these monies were retrieved.[48] The Foreign Affairs Ministry proved lax at keeping proper accounts, and funds flow granted by the Dail had to be kept firmly under the allocation control of the Ministry of Finance.[49]

If the individual personnel of the nascent Irish diplomatic service largely functioned on goodwill, peripheral diplomatic operating costs still required expenditure. The upkeep of the premises of the de facto Irish consuls and representatives was expensive.[50] It was also realised that representatives themselves, if they managed to gain admittance and attendance at official diplomatic gatherings or meetings, would have to be dressed accordingly. A minimum amount of formal wardrobe attire was necessary for each rep-resentative, for which everyone would be granted an allowance of £100 Sterling.[51] In 1921 an individual allowance was granted to the representa-tive in the UK, Art O Brien, to enable him to carry out his many duties and tasks throughout the UK without him being constantly hindered by the expense, amounting to £4,000 per annum.[52] Also, Maire O Brien in Madrid was granted a salary of £250 per annum to enable her to continue her valuable work as a publicity agent in Madrid.[53]

By this time a Propaganda Department (which eventually became a Ministry) had been set up with publicity agents in the differing countries being paid a regular salary; the Ministry of Propaganda paid a contribu-tion towards the printing costs of the publications but most of these costs were provided by the Ministry of Finance, which also paid all the sal-aries.[54] In the first six months of 1921 Collins increased the overall budget for propaganda from just over £400 to an estimated £4,000 Sterling.[55]

It was all extra outgoings for the Ministry of Finance. Under the Minister for Propaganda, first Laurence Ginnell then after his arrest, Desmond Fitzgerald, the Ministry of Propaganda functioned efficiently. A Bulletin was produced for Ireland and Britain, and individual publications were produced abroad in several countries. Fitzgerald used his contacts with British and European press and ensured that full accounts of events, restrained and impartial in tone, were publicised. All this was effected within the modest budget allocated by the Ministry of Finance. However in the later stages of the Anglo-Irish War Erskine Childers pressed for a more strident form of propaganda. He put forward more bullish initiatives to gain wider publicity for the cause, which included paying correspondents and agents, all of which would require a large increase in budget, ultimately coming from the Ministry of Finance. De Valera fully approved of these proposals and sought to replace Fitzgerald with Childers as Minister of Propaganda. Griffith refused point blank to Childers being so appointed, and after heated discussions with de Valera Fitzgerald remained Minister of Propaganda. The communiqués and information disseminated continued to be restrained and effective, and Collins and his Ministry were saved additional expenditure.[56]

Any attempts or initiatives to gain any sort of diplomatic or international recognition of the nascent Irish state required expenditure. De Valera's visit to the United States with its main priority of securing United States' recognition, required a certain level of extravagant expenditure (see also Appendix I).

During January and February 1919 two Dail appointed individuals were sent to Paris to attempt to gain the nascent self-styled Irish state a hearing – and recognition – at the international peace conference attended by all the great powers. It ultimately failed, and little sympathy for the Irish cause was gained amongst the French press who were careful not to upset Britain, their staunch ally in the recent conflict. Collins had authorised the delegates a sum of £2,000 and £2,000 worth of gold coins. Their efforts were unsuccessful and no "official" report was sent by them.[57] Collins, despite extensive efforts, failed to establish precisely what became of the granted monies. However, cultivating influence to obtain openings to the massive peace conference, and cultivating influence amongst the literally hundreds of French journalists covering the conference dissipated funds quickly. One delegate wrote back from Paris, pleadingly

> What I want is a few more thousand pounds – don't be too greatly shocked by the light way I speak of it – for the purpose of smoothing a passage to the ears of great men-and securing the ear of the press. *You can get nothing done whatsoever otherwise.* They all expect it ...[58]
> (italics those of delegate).

In Italy the Irish trade consul in Genoa, Donal Hales, attended an official Catholic religious service at the Cathedral in Bobbio in north Italy, presided over by various church dignitaries. At the nearby Church of Columbanus (an Irish saint) a section of a large mosaic flooring was recently discovered during construction. Hales was there as representative of Ireland and, amongst the other official flags, managed to ensure that Sinn Fein's flag was also flying at the Cathedral. In the Church, the excavation and uncovering of the whole mosaic flooring were being delayed due to costs. Hales saw an opportunity for a step towards Irish recognition. He proposed that the Dail and Ministry of Finance allocate foreign aid to Italy to complete these works, and make up the shortfall in construction costs by giving them £450, thus giving a great and famous "son of Ireland" a suitable tomb. It was a timely initiative and proposal; however, it was like so many proposed initiatives helping the search of recognition, an initiative that could cost money.[59]

All these initiatives for some sort of diplomatic recognition involved much initial expenditure, with uncertain and intangible results. After Defence, overall Foreign Affairs spending was the major part of the Dail budget. Between June to December 1920 Foreign Affairs expenditure was £6,406; between January to June 1921 Foreign Affairs expenditure rose to £12,082; in the following six-month period between June and December 1921 Foreign Affairs expenditure further rose to £18,041. The high spending of Defence and Foreign Affairs contrasted with the Ministries of Agriculture, Education and Local Government, each of these spending an overage of £4,000 per year.[60]

Apart from the standing funds of the Loans, what other incomes were available to the Ministry of Finance? In short, comparatively few.

In June 1920 Collins had proposed to the cabinet that the Dail government collected the income tax, diverting it from the British administration coffers. However, he was forced to abandon this proposal due to the initial indicators of large-scale opposition from farmers and businessmen. These, although fully sympathetic to Sinn Fein and Irish freedom, either feared financial reprisal from the British if they withheld their taxes, or if they did actually withhold from paying the British authorities revealed themselves unwilling to pay the Dail government.[61]

Incomes from Sinn Fein-dominated local government authorities were available, but as the Anglo-Irish conflict intensified and British authorities reasserted control these rapidly diminished. By late 1920 Collins regretfully observed that the Republican courts in some areas had been unable to convene for over eight months. Also, his plan to collect some form of taxes or duties from these areas had totally failed.[62]

Incomes were possible from investments. Collins and his Ministry invested some of the Loan funds abroad both to conceal the funds and to gain a small safe return. However, Collins always ensured the investment was minimum risk. One potential foreign investment was a result of the (unsuccessful) attempt to gain Irish representation at the Versailles international peace settlement after the First World War. The would-be Irish delegate, Sean O Kelly, brought back a possible opportunity for investing in a French radio and telegraphic agency. Collins insisted to de Valera that sufficient time be given to analyse and reflect upon the proposal. He reviewed the whole projected deal, analysed the complexities and produced report which showed that, whilst the Irish would be investing the equivalent of five million French Francs, when other costs and immobilisations were factored in, the Irish would be in effect giving just over £3,700,000 for a doubtful opportunity or venture, and still not having full control of the enterprise. Collins judged the whole venture to be financially unsound and recommended no further action. None was taken. With Collins as Minister of Finance careful stewarding of the Dail funds was the priority.[63]

Trade initiatives were attempted. Blythe's Ministry of Commerce and Barton's Ministry of Agriculture both organised a co-operative fund of local famers and tradesmen and, together with financial support from both ministries, built a meat processing factory in Waterford. This expanded a similar business established in Wexford, and started small-scale exports to Britain.[64] Collins, always conscious of Ireland's economic dependence – or more emotionally economic slavery – on Britain, constantly exhorted and encouraged the nascent Irish government's de facto consuls and representative abroad to facilitate trade deals with their host countries. One Irish representative went to Russia and tried to persuade business representatives of the Bolshevik government to sign a trade deal with Ireland. Russian furs, hemp, flax and hides would be available to Irish buyers, whilst Ireland could export to Russia manufactured agricultural goods such as tractors, farming implements and working shoes, as well as evaporated milk and rope. A contact in New York was to engage the services of a US shipping company which could transport the cargoes both ways. The Russians showed initial interest, but then sheered off, having signed a trade deal with Britain which they were unwilling to jeopardise by any commercial dealings with Ireland. Also, members of the Irish cabinet had been concerned about the possible detrimental effect dealing with Soviet Russia would have on their ongoing negotiating attempts with France, Belgium and Switzerland.[65] In 1919 there had been attempts at trading with the new Austrian Republic, but this appeared to peter out.[66] South American countries appeared to have trade some potential. Eamon Bulfin was appointed as one of three Irish representatives to Argentina. Bulfin was born in Argentina and when a child his family had moved back to Ireland. He took part in the 1916 Rising, and was the Volunteer carrying out Connolly's order to hoist the flag of the Irish Republic from the top of the GPO. He was court martialled by the British and sentenced to death, but reprieved due to his nationality, his passport being produced in evidence. He had returned to Argentina.[67] After an inauspicious start as an Irish representative (shortly after his arrival, as an Argentinian national, he was conscripted into the Argentinian Army under national service regulations; he eventually managed to extricate himself,) he raised £1,600 from donations in Argentina for the Dail Loan. Then he identified trade potential. Large-scale nitrate works in Argentina had been closed down due to competition and a near-monopoly of a local British owned company, causing large unemployment. It was suggested that Ireland should buy up the nitrates from revitalised nitrate works and Irish businesses could act as the distributors and middlemen both the for Argentinian domestic market and outlets abroad. An Irish Bank being set up in Buenos Aires was mooted. Also, Argentina as a possible export market for Irish goods was considered, but the protectionist tariffs were high, and the rate of exchange ran heavily in the favour of Argentinian enterprises. Fact-finding missions in Uruguay, Peru and Paraguay were made, but was concluded by the three Irish representatives that it would be better to concentrate on Argentina and, later, Chile in terms of possible trade.[68]

Another and more reliable source of revenue was that of the Self-Determination Fund. In 1919 the Dail had made arrangements through Collins as Minister of Finance to solicit simple cash contributions to the Irish cause. This appeal was directed both at home in Ireland, in Britain and abroad. In Britain, Art O Brien, in the Irish de facto representative office in London, organised the appeal, particularly amongst the Irish living in Britain. The appeal stayed open throughout 1919 to 1921 and, whilst naturally less popular than a Loan scheme, did raise by late 1921, £35,709 from donations within Ireland and £53,343 from abroad. These funds were placed into the general funds.

Sinn Fein clubs were useful centres for fundraising and income through social functions and collections. During the Anglo-Irish War, most IRA commanders had little time for the debating activities and political discussions of the Sinn Fein clubs but did acknowledge their usefulness as a means for raising illicit funds. One IRA commander, however, did have reservations about how much of the precious funds raised in this way was spent on propaganda postcards, banners and tricolour belts, instead of being directly channelled to spending on arms.[69] The Glasgow branch of the Irish Volunteers complained to Collins that the Sinn Fein club was

only good for singing and dancing.

Collins made a conciliatory reply stating that he had received similar complaints from all over Ireland.[70]

However, Collins' initial reservations about Sinn Fein had all but disappeared. He had acquired respect for Sinn Fein, especially in the person of Arthur Griffith who had created and steered this organisation in its vital catalyst role of Irish nationalism since the mid-1900s. With the departure of de Valera to the United States, Collins and Griffith had become more in direct contact with each other, and this engendered mutual respect and confidence in each other[71] which was to be vital in future times of crisis. Also, by April 1919 the numbers of Sinn Fein Clubs in Ireland alone had risen to 1025, with a membership of over 81,000.[72] This was a potential fundraising source of which Collins could not be too dismissive, and he valued the small flow of funds from the Sinn Fein clubs, however irregular. Every little helped.

But expanding and keeping the IRA in the field to pursue the conflict called for other varied methods of financing. Often finances were raised by local initiatives and many methods – like all illicit fundraising for territorial liberationist struggles – were ad hoc and pragmatic. Arms were always in short supply. British soldiers were approached on an individual basis and offered to sell their "lost" rifle(s); in late 1920 the IRA had individuals in Glasgow attempting to approach selected British soldiers to purchase arms and ammunition.[73] But this meant spending, however small the amounts. Easier simply to take small arms by force. This was the original sole objective of attacking small police barracks; it was only at a comparatively later stage of the Anglo-Irish War that the strategic opportunity was seized, of advancing into areas of abandoned police barracks and rendering the territory under IRA control and de facto jurisdiction.

A major proportion of the funds to IRA units were raised from local activity. In 1918 there was inaugurated an Anti-Conscription fund in the southwest area where donations were solicited for the Cork units of the Volunteers, with blatant intimidation used against those wealthy enough to pay yet foolish enough to refuse outright to contribute.[74] During the Anglo-Irish conflict local fundraising continued, mainly according to the commanding officers' individual initiative.[75] In some units of the IRA there was a Battalion Levy,[76] where IRA fighters contributed to the costs of their arms, sometimes 2d or 3d from each man per week;[77] other units also accepted – or imposed – "donations" from the largely sympathetic local populations. In at least one area the local IRA "adopted" the assessment rates of property tax imposed by the local council on businesses and residences and imposed these for their funding.[78] In other areas there was imposed locally the "Arms Fund", with some cases of extreme intimidation used against non-contributors.[79] Sums gained varied from £33 to £180 from units of Volunteers collecting amongst themselves,[80] to one of the Cork IRA Brigades holding a levy on local businesses and residents which raised over £100,000 in a seven-month period.[81] There was even a hold-up and robbery of a British Army vehicle transporting cash for payment of civilians working at an army depot, which gained £300 in cash.[82] Small sums or large, it was all grist to the freedom-struggle mill, in terms of saving Collins' Ministry of Finance expenditure. In most areas of Ireland, the local population provided at short notice overnight shelter, food and changes of clothing to IRA men operating in flying columns. IRA fighters on the run were paid a small amount, a few pounds a week, from the Ministry of Finance, in order to prevent such valuable men from being captured, to keep them in the field and to ensure those with families would have some support. However, this central fund amount to men on the run had to be supplemented by, again, the local sympathetic population providing food and shelter.[83] In the later stages of the war some units of the IRA, short of men, press ganged local youth into joining. Cases were reported where unwilling "volunteers" could avoid such service by giving monies.[84] Therefore a form of local extortion in a few – and exceptional – cases became an ad hoc method of fundraising.

In many areas after hostilities ceased and the Truce came into effect the local levies and dues for the fighting units were still being exacted from and paid by the local population. During the Truce period, de Valera suggested to Collins that these local levies and dues for the fighters should be replaced by direct government funding to the IRA. Collins rejected this idea. This was not due to him begrudging the IRA funding, indeed quite the reverse. The reason was that by this time de Valera was becoming both powerful and manipulative, and political manoeuvrings within the Cabinet were in full play. De Valera's suggestion was motivated less by concern for the IRA and more for himself and the extreme republican elements within the cabinet – Stack, Brugha and Mellowes – to gain direct control over the IRA.[85]

On a still less-sophisticated level, revenues could be gained during the struggle by simple robbery. In Cork, robberies of businesses, defined as banks, post offices and shops, rose from seven in 1919, to 47 in 1920 and to 41 in the first six months of 1921.[86] Mail trains were held up and robbed frequently; in mid-August 1920 mail trains were being held up almost daily in Ireland.[87] As with all militant groups engaged in political violence and liberationist struggles, bank robberies were a potentially lucrative – and to the IRA particularly welcome – source of funds. As has been seen in the action of Lynch and his Cork No. 2 Brigade, the IRA ensured as far as possible that robberies for purely criminal profit were not permitted. Bank robberies occurred for the purpose of seizing funds for the IRA, as in October 1920, when Sterling was seized, from the Provincial Bank in Dublin and in May 1921, when a loose haul of notes and silver was carried off from the National Bank.[88] There were other smaller-scale raids on post offices netting small amounts of cash.[89] Significantly of all the banks robbed, the Hibernian Bank was never targeted. This was the known favoured bank of Sinn Fein and Republican sympathisers.[90]

But by the later stages of the Anglo-Irish War finances and resources of the Irish were under extreme strain. By November 1920, wanted IRA fighters on the run had their subsistence from the central finances reduced to £3 a week, and Dail funds in general were running short.[91] In April 1921, despite successful actions by the IRA in Sligo and Mayo, one of Collins' main comments in his communication with Mulcahy on these actions was

"… the great pity that arms were not captured."[92]

In May 1921, Collins stated that there would be no funds available for legal defence expenses for republican prisoners, even those accused of capital offences.[93] In the much-vaunted Customs House raid of May 1921 (which Collins vehemently opposed) the IRA was so short of money that some volunteers went into the building with only four rounds of ammunition.[94] By June 1921 one battalion of the Cork No. 1 Brigade was reporting that it had only ten rounds of ammunition for its 70 revolvers.[95]

By the time of the Truce the IRA guerrillas were at the end of their tether in terms of arms shortages and not being adequately fed.[96] In terms of sustaining the struggle, Collins managed to ensure that finances were there, but only just. This had been mainly due to his herculean efforts on raising, and managing the National Loan in Ireland.[97]

Collins was imaginative and often unorthodox in handling finances, but always, where at all possible, kept records. These could be somewhat unorthodox, as with various ad hoc handwritten audit lists and audits which he carried about with him, a precaution taken against the constant threat of raid on the various premises of the clandestine Ministry of Finance. However, keeping on his person too had its risks. On yet another occasion, Collins and his IRA colleagues were dining well in the Gresham Hotel. The hotel was raided by Auxiliaries who searched all diners present. Collins' correspondence – in cryptic handwritten form – contained papers with various itemised lists. One Auxiliary spotted the entry *"Rifles"* which aroused the suspicions of him and his colleagues, and he looked closer at Collins, comparing him to a photograph of wanted individuals issued to security forces. Collins quickly – but compliantly – replied that the entry was for stationery and that it read *"Refills"*. This genial bluff, together with his willingness to permit the Auxiliaries to drink from the bottle of whiskey they also found in Collins' jacket, together with his largesse in ordering a second bottle of whiskey for loyal toasts all round, convinced the Auxiliaries. After more drinks, Collins and his associates left for home, worse for wear but free and above suspicion.

He used his initiative and judgement in flexible decisions. One of the British informants, the porter at the Wicklow Hotel was shot by the IRA. His widow, who had always assumed her husband was pro IRA and had been killed by undercover British troops, applied to Sinn Fein for assistance as a widow. Her claim should have been rejected, but Collins learned that she had three children, and ordered that the true circumstances of her husband's death be withheld and that she be granted a pension. Strictly speaking, within Sinn Fein he had no such authority to action, but he went ahead, and ensured it was recorded.[98]

To Cathal Brugha such disregard for procedure, combined with Collins' natural flair for taking the initiative, was an anathema. In Brugha's view, Collins' disregarding procedure was typical of the flamboyant and independent-minded Collins who – to Brugha's loathing – was acquiring a widespread respect and popularity in Ireland. Brugha disliked Collins to a point of near hatred. Even his jealousy was noted, with regret, by de Valera.[99] As clandestine Minister of Defence he was Collins' immediate superior with regard to Collins' duties as Director of Intelligence. As we have seen Brugha did not devote all, or even a major part of his time, to his role as clandestine Minister of Defence. Due to his business commitments, he could give comparatively little time to his clandestine ministerial role. Given Collin's energy and resourcefulness – and the prime importance of intelligence in the Anglo-Irish war – it was inevitable that Collins would be more involved in running the war than Brugha. From Brugha's sedentary business viewpoint, Collins, with his constant movements and his packed and peripatetic schedule, would inevitably be careless, even cavalier in his role as Minister of Finance and careless in dealing with funds.

Brugha could never understand that Collins had years of training, working and experience in financial procedures. He never realised that, however busy, however rushed, and however much on the move, and however and on whatever ad hoc basis certain financial actions were made, Collins meticulously recorded transactions and where appropriate issued receipts and any other covering documentation. In the early days when he was secretary of the Irish National Aid and Volunteer Dependents Fund, when socialising and drinking with friends and associates, whichever person present bought a round of drinks, Collins would, in true flamboyant style, seize the change and pocket it for the Fund, and meticulously make out a receipt to the fellow drinking "donor."[100] Later, when managing the finances as Director of Organisation of the Volunteers or later IRA, he pursued his tasks with single-minded efficiency. Part of his remit was the circulation of, and collecting the funds from, the production of the Volunteer publication *An-t-Oglach*. In late 1918, he pursued the Limerick brigade of the Volunteers for the outstanding sum of 16 shillings and 8 pence, sending three reminders in a fortnight, then the final demand

I do not request, I insist.[101]

Later still, when de Valera was in the United States, Collins insisted that de Valera be regularly paid his salary, and Collins personally delivered it in cash to de Valera's wife Sinead at their Dublin home.[102] When de Valera arrived back from the United States, Collins updated him, but also recorded the £224 de Valera brought back with him – loose change compared to sums de Valera had been raising – and meticulously itemised this this as "remittances from the United States."[103]

Brugha had already complained about Collins to de Valera in January 1921, alleging that Collins and his Ministry of Finance had withheld £500 which he had requested and had been granted from the Dail to the Ministry of Defence. In fact, no-one at the clandestine Ministry of Defence – least of all Brugha – had had the courtesy and professionalism to inform Collins that the money had been granted; neither Collins nor any of his colleagues at the Ministry of Finance had been notified, and therefore did not release the funds.[104]

In March 1921, Brugha seized on an opportunity[105] to criticise and attack Collins following the appointment of Liam Mellowes – a political ally of Brugha's – as Director of Purchasing, a sub-department under Collins' Ministry of Finance. In front of Cabinet colleagues, with de Valera presiding, Brugha loudly and pompously demanded Collins give a full account of where the monies had been sent regarding projected arms purchases from sources in Scotland. The arms deal was ongoing and, like many, was faltering. Given the amounts of monies Collins was handling and the pressures he, Collins, was under, ensuring the overall financial survival of the nascent Irish state, the amounts of which Brugha was making an issue were insignificant;[106] even Mellowes was later to complain frequently about Brugha's rigidity and his stinginess with regard to official funds.[107] Brugha pressed home his attack stating that he would not be satisfied until he was given assurances that the accounts had been kept in a fully fit and proper manner. This caused Collins much trouble and time[108] in making inquiries and asking the head of the Volunteers in Glasgow, Joe Vize, for information and documents. The end result was that there was a discrepancy. Collins was visibly upset by the proceedings, by the nature of the accusation and mistrust (and possibly frustration with himself for not being so meticulous in financial documentation on this occasion). Given the strains he was under, this occurring at the height of the Anglo-Irish War, his reaction was understandable. De Valera dismissed Brugha's allegations in a single sentence, describing the charges as groundless[109] and ended the matter. Brugha, to the distaste of all present, refused to shake hands with Collins and stormed out of the room,[110] vowing to eventually expose Collins.

Brugha's implacable hostility towards Collins blinded him to Collins' absolute financial integrity. Collins' former employers in London unreservedly praised his integrity and after his death stated that

> the staff who were privileged to know him will never believe that he could do an unworthy act.[111]

Brugha was to show that he too was no respecter of procedures. During the Truce period, he attempted to curry favour with IRA senior commanders, and on one occasion gave a cheque for £1,000 direct to the Commander of the First Western Division so that they could purchase and replenish their arms stocks.[112] No consultation or reference was made to IRA GHQ or to the Ministry of Finance. (Ironically it did Brugha's long-term aims little good; the first Western Division stayed loyal to, and fought as part of, the Free State Army in the Civil War.)

Regarding the arms deal which formed the core of Brugha's unsubstantiated allegations, Collins was actually unable to recover some of the documentation involved in the projected arms deal. However, the true situation was that procuring arms for the IRA by arms deals was at best uncertain and at worst likely to lose valuable funds in return for nothing. Arms, or rather their procurement, was a constant problem to the IRA and potentially an expensive outlay for Collins and his Ministry of Finance. Collins ruefully informed one IRA commander,

> the question of armaments and of course ammunition for the same is a chancy business. Purchase of arms is difficult and also dangerous to those engaged in this vital task.[113]

There were three main potential source flows for gaining or purchasing arms; the United States, Europe via Scotland and from Scotland itself.

The Scottish branches of Sinn Fein and the IRA were flourishing. By 1919 Sinn Fein clubs in Glasgow alone had reached 75, whilst Scotland furnished three battalions of the IRA, recruiting from Glasgow, Edinburgh and Lanarkshire. In the mining areas of Lanarkshire, Irish immigrants set up clandestine IRA companies in their local towns and sourced gelignite and gunpowder from quarries, coal pits and shale mines, which were then ferried cross the Irish sea by trusted couriers. On eight separate occasions raiding parties broke in and robbed the Glasgow munitions works.[114]

Collins' chief agent in Scotland was Joe Vize, an Irish born ex-merchant seaman, who in 1915 had been commended by one of the ships officers for his steadfast behaviour when the vessel sank in the high seas. The following year Vize left the merchant navy, and in 1916 fought in the 1916 Rising. In Scotland, Vize was responsible for two raids on Hamilton Barracks in June and in August 1920, in which 40 rifles were seized and ferried cross the Irish sea by trusted couriers. Vize put together a small network for small-scale arms importation. Guns came by ship from Hamburg and were landed at Leith. The deals were arranged by two individuals acting as middlemen, a merchant and a Glasgow-based retailer. The guns, on their arrival, were received by a Glasgow shopkeeper, named "Gordon", who had funds available to pay for the arms. They were collected and then stored at Gordon and his wife's premises. Neither "Gordon" nor his wife were either IRB members or sworn IRA. Utilising them was a conscious decision of Vize, due to a certain amount of infighting amongst certain members and units of the Volunteers in Scotland.

The flow of arms from Scotland, under Joe Vize, was arguably one of the most successful in procuring arms for the IRA. Part of its success was because it constituted a small flow and was not concerned with attempting comparatively large-scale importations. However, the Scottish connection was not more successful and was hindered due to two reasons. First, there was the unreliability of some units of the IRA in Scotland, particularly the 1 Battalion Glasgow IRA.[115] Such units were more concerned with political socialism – there were significant remnants of Connelly's Citizen Army amongst the ranks[116] – and even with issues of Scottish nationalism. The second reason was the ever-present hostility of Brugha towards Collins.

Collins appointed Vize as Director of Purchasing and set him up in a clandestine office in Dublin.[117] However, when the "Cairo Gang" of British agents had begun their activities, in a September 1920 raid, Joe Vize was one of the key IRA men taken. Brugha ensured that the absent Vize was replaced as Director of Purchasing by Liam Mellowes, now returned from the United States. Mellowes – no ally of Collins – was tasked by Brugha to research the finances of various arms purchasing, including the Scottish connection. Mellowes spent more of his time when in Scotland interviewing, speaking with various IRA individuals,[118] investigating and intriguing, with little effort in maintaining the arms flow.

In the United States during the first two months of 1920 Harry Boland negotiated an arms deal with a salesman from the US Auto Ordnance Company for a consignment of Thompson sub-machine guns. Auto Ordnance was backed and financially supported by a business millionaire, Thomas Ryan, a contributor to the American Committee for the Relief in Ireland (the so-called "White Cross Fund") and sympathetic to Irish nationalism. Ryan had been in contact with Collins[119] prior to Boland's contacts with the Auto Ordnance salesman. The purchase was for a total of just over 650 guns at $220 each, Boland having managed to obtain a substantial discount. The deal was settled in late March 1920.

Meanwhile a small amount of Thompson guns – about 30 – were landed in Queenstown, Cork. The following month Collins and other senior IRA officers were given a demonstration at a concealed firing range in the outskirts of Dublin. All were impressed and realised the potential of this weapon.

Preparations were made to receive a larger consignment of 500 Thompson guns from the ship, the M/V *East Side,* which would sail from New York with the concealed weapons. A coastal area of Baltimore, near Cork was designated for the landing and would be would be sealed off by a unit of the East Cork Brigade IRA under Tom Barry. Funds to pay for the consignment were channelled through a former Wexford journalist and longstanding IRB member, Larry Delacy, who had joined Boland in the United States. From Boland, the funds were passed direct to Ryan. The *East Side* was due to set sail on 17 June 1921.The night before, however, the *East Side* was raided by officers of the US Customs and the entire consignment of 500 guns was seized. Although smaller numbers of Thompson guns had got through and would later get through, the *East Side* seizure was a significant blow, and a costly one. The purchasing of the consignment of 500 guns would have been just over £71,000[120] (over three times the amount the British in Winter's initiative had managed to seize from the National Loan).

In Italy the energetic Donal Hales, de facto Irish consul in Genoa, cultivated his association with Gabriel d'Annunzio. D'Annunzio, a pre-1914 eminent Italian poet and writer, gave much-vaunted military service to his country during the First World War against the Austrians, first in an élite infantry regiment, then in the Italian Air Force. After the First World War, his Italian patriotism outraged by what he conceived to be Italy being deprived of territory in the north-east, he led a group of independent Italian paramilitaries and seized the port of Fiume for Italy. The Italian government disowned this action, so d'Annunzio set up a short-lived independent statelet of the "Regency of Carnaro" around the port of Fiume, which was also rejected by the Italian government. He continued to be active on the fringes of Italian politics. It was almost inevitable, given his ethos as a writer and poet and his zeal to liberate occupied territory, that he would have a strong empathy with Donal Hales, the academic at Genoa University and representative of a nation struggling to gain recognition and independence. D'Annunzio also had useful contacts with sympathetic Italian politicians and military officers. An arms deal was projected whereby d'Annunzio would procure arms for the IRA. The consignment was a projected 20,000 rifles.[121] Collins was cautious. He wrote to Hales in August 1920, favouring the enterprise in principle, but also stating

> ... although finances are not exactly limited, yet a loss would render further dealings uninviting.[122]

Colleagues pointed out that d'Annunzio and his associates would be asking a considerable price for the arms. In late 1920 preliminary arrangements started. Plans were made to receive the shipment of arms.[123] A landing site was identified in the southwest, in the Skibbereen area. Containers were prepared suitable to offload the arms from the ship, and routes to the landing site were to be guarded by specific IRA units. An officer from Cork No. 1 Brigade was briefed in Dublin, then travelled overland on the continent, entering Italy via the Swiss border. In Italy, he was met by Donal Hales. Hales had already met and negotiated with d'Annunzio, who in turn had shown Hales the armaments and the ship that would transport them. Then the deal faltered. There were delays and no monies came through from the Irish side. Then in March 1920 Collins decided to change the method of payment transfer in an attempt to ensure that no individual could be identified as being involved. In June 1920 Sean T O Kelly, the Dail representative in Rome, sent a despatch to Griffith. (Hales was a consul in Genoa; Kelly had been re-deployed from Paris where he was Irish representative to France, to being Irish representative to Italy, based in Rome.) Kelly's despatch to Griffith cast doubt on whether d'Annunzio would or could deliver, and earnestlyhe entreated Collins' opinion on this project, stating that his, Collins' judgement on the deal would be the most important.[124] Then finally in July 1920 the deal was aborted.[125] Meticulous in the monies, Collins sent Donal Hales a cheque for expenses incurred, but also wrote that he had had reservations about the messenger or go-between, and ordered Hales not to make mention of the affair again.[126] It appeared that the security of the deal had been compromised and it was known to British intelligence.

Thus, the main amounts of arms purchased for the IRA were small amounts in ad hoc flows. According to one senior IRA commander, there was no successful large-scale importation of arms-sub-machine guns, or indeed any weapons during the Anglo-Irish War.[127] Well might Collins have emphatically stated to an IRA commander

> the question of armaments and of course ammunition for the same is a chancy business. Purchase of arms is difficult and also dangerous to those engaged in this vital task.[128]

To him, as Minister of Finance, large-scale arms deals were an expensive, and unpredictable risk.

Notes

1 Hugh Kennedy, later to become Ireland's Attorney-General, cited in Fanning *The Irish Department of Finance, 1922–58* (Dublin Institute of Public Administration 1978) pp. 16–17
2 BMH WS 889/file S.2180
3 In the clandestine Irish government, most of the functions were designated Ministries.There were some departments which eventually were designated ministries, such as the Department of Trade and Commerce. The Department of Propaganda was formed under the Foreign Ministry, but then as its role and importance increased became a Ministry. All departments and ministries had their budget scrutinised and monitored by Collins' Ministry of Finance.
4 Dwyer *Big Fellow, Long Fellow* p. 160
5 C Osborne *Michael Collins – himself* (Mercier Press 2003) p. 61; Dwyer *Big Fellow, Long Fellow* pp. 151–152
6 BMH WS 939/file S.66
7 BMH WS 939/file S.66. In the local government elections of January 1920, of the 206 local councils contested Sinn Fein gained control of 172; most of the remaining 34 were in Ulster. Sinn Fein's control included 11 out of the 12 cities in Ireland.
8 MacDowell *Michael Collins and the Irish Republican Brotherhood* p. 44. In fairness to Brugha, MacDowell's work is extremely partisan towards the IRB and its role in the struggle for Irish independence. Brugha broke with the IRB, holding that it had outlived its usefulness and its influence as a secret society within the IRA was unhealthy and divisive. On the other hand, in Coogan's researches, in his *Ireland in the Twentieth Century* p. 92, he cites an IRA individual Sean Dowling, in Unsean Maceowan *Survivors* (Argenta Press 1987) as stating starkly, "Brugha was Minister of Defence, but never did anything", and then goes on to further cite "... Collins was so energetic that he usurped many of Brugha's functions; he was sure hated by him."
9 Townsend *The Republic- the fight for Irish independence* p. 87
10 Cited by Hopkinson *Green against Green – history of the Irish civil war* p. 8
11 Brugha's various attacks were made on Collins personally and his alleged actions, not against the running and operating of the clandestine Ministry of Finance.
12 Dwyer *Big Fellow, Long Fellow* p. 151
13 BMS WS, WM707 /file S.602
14 P S Hegarty, a member of Sinn Fein in London worked as a British civil servant in the Post Office in London from 1902 to 1913, studying and passing

exams at Kings College London which enabled him to be promoted to the Secretary's Office. He joined the Irish Volunteers, but in the aftermath of the 1916 Rising he opposed physical force. He subsequently resigned from the British civil service. When the Free State came into being after the Treaty he became Secretary to the Irish Posts and Telegraph Ministry, serving continuously from 1922 to 1945

15 Hopkinson *Green against Green* p. 8
16 BMH WS WM 817/ file S.2115
17 M Forester *Michael Collins – the lost leader* (Sphere Books 1971) p. 109
18 Dwyer *Big Fellow, Long Fellow* p. 119
19 BMH WSWM707/ file S.602
20 O Conner *With Michael Collins* p. 130
21 Hart *Mick – the real Michael Collins* p. 247
22 Ibid.
23 Beaslai *Michael Collins* vol I p. 351
24 Ibid.
25 O Conner *With Michael Collins* p. 130
26 BMH WM707/ file S.602
27 Dwyer *Big Fellow, Long Fellow* p. 158
28 Ibid.
29 Hart *Mick – the real Michael Collins* p. 247; Costello *Michael Collins – in his own words* p. 50
30 Beaslai *Michael Collins* vol I p. 347, vol II p. 163
31 Dwyer *Big Fellow, Long Fellow* p. 150
32 R Fanning's work *The Irish Department of Finance, 1922–58* (Institute of Public Administration Ireland 1978) although primarily concerned with the period after the establishment of the Free State, does emphasise the legacy Collins left of the importance and primacy within Irish government financing the Ministry of Finance.
33 J Consedine "Michael Collins and the roots of Irish public finance", paper Department of Economics, University College Cork, found on www.ucc..ie/en/media/academic/economics/documents/research/michaelcollins0403.pdf
34 A McCarthy "Michael Collins, Minister of Finance 1919–22" in G Doherty and D Keogh (eds) *Michael Collins and the Making of the Irish State* pp. 54–70
35 Fanning *The Irish Department of Finance 1922–1958* p. 25
36 Ibid. pp. 25–27
37 Costello *Michael Collins – in his own words* p. 51, citing an explanatory memo from Collins to de Valera of 7 January 1921, Dail Eireann Files Public Record Office Dublin.
38 BMH WS889/ file S.2180
39 Collins to Accountant General 21 December 1921 Kathleen McKenna Napoli Papers National Library of Ireland NLI MS 22, 771
40 Dail Debates 18 August 1921
41 Hart *Mick – the real Michael Collins* p. 194
42 Beaslai *Michael Collins* pp. 297, 345; BMH WS 1769/ file S.96
43 Coogan *The Man Who Made Ireland* p. 171
44 Department of Foreign Affairs Report 10 August 1921 Documents on Irish Foreign Policy National Archives of Ireland DE4/4/2
45 Despatch from Buenos Ayres to Robert Brennan 4 December 1921 National Archives of Ireland NFA ES Box 32 file 216(4); Department of Foreign Affairs Report 18 August 1921 National Archives of Ireland DE 4/4/2; BMH WS 1769/file S.96
46 Donal Hales despatch from Genoa to Michael Collins 5 May 1920 Documents on Irish Foreign Policy National Archives of Ireland DE5/56

47 Germany was one of the countries with which the Dail government attempted to establish formal relations. However, its post First World War government of the early 1920s was naturally anxious not to be on bad terms with Britain.

48 Collins to Dail representative in the United States Smiddy, 8 June 1922, National Library of Ireland Joe McGarrity Papers NLI MS 17458/65

49 Accountant General to Gavan Duffy 29 April 1922 Documents on Irish Foreign Policy National Archives of Ireland DE5/19; Department of Foreign Affairs Standing Orders July 1921 Documents on Irish Foreign Policy National Archives of Ireland DFA ES Box 14 file 96

50 Accountant General Ministry of Finance to Gavan Duffy 13 July 1922, Documents on Irish Foreign Policy National Archives of Ireland DE5/19

51 Memorandum of Irish Foreign Minister Robert Brennan on diplomatic dress, 29 October 1921 Documents on Irish Foreign Policy National Archives of Ireland DFA ES Box 17 file 109

52 Report by Department of Foreign Affairs 21 August 1921 National Archives of Ireland DE 4/4/2

53 Documents on Irish Foreign Policy National Archives of Ireland Duffy to Brennan March 1921 DFA ES SPAIN; Memorandum on Ireland and Spain September 1921 DFA ES SPAIN; Brennan to Maire O Brien 10 October 1921 DFA ES SPAIN

54 National Archives of Ireland DE2/10 Dail Report on Foreign Affairs January 1920

55 F Costello *The Irish Revolution and Its Aftermath 1916–1923 – years of revolt* (Irish Academic Press 2003) p. 54

56 BMH WS 939/file S.66

57 Mackay *Michael Collins* vol I p. 108

58 M Walsh *The News from Ireland – foreign correspondents and the Irish Revolution* (I B Tauris) 2008 p. 107 citing R Fanning, M Kennedy, D Keogh and E O Halpin (eds) *Documents on Irish Foreign Policy 1919–1922* vol I p. 9

59 Donal Hales despatch to Michael Collins 27 May 1921 National Archives of Ireland NE5/52

60 Costello *Michael Collins in his own words* p. 51; J Consedine "Michael Collins and the roots of Irish public finance" Department of Economics, University College Cork p. 4 found on www.ucc..ie/en/media/academic/economics/documents/research/michaelcollins0403.pdf; F M Carroll *Money for Ireland – finance diplomacy and politics and the First Dail Eireann Loans 1919–1936* (Praeger Studies 2002) p. 11, citing Dail Eireann Self Determination Fund and Trustees Accounts 1/5/1920 to 31/12/1920, Dail Eireann Trustees Accounts for Half Year end 30/6/1921, Dail Eireann Trustees Accounts for Half Year end 30/12/1921 in Dail Eireann Files DE2/9 National Library of Ireland

61 Kostick *Revolution in Ireland – popular militancy 1917 to 1923* p. 99

62 Hopkinson *Green against Green – a history of the Irish Civil War* p. 7

63 Costello *Michael Collins – in his own words* pp. 42–43

64 BMH WS 939/ file S.66

65 McCarten's communiqué to Weinstein Moscow 13 May 1921 and McCarten's Memo to Dail of May 1921 Documents on Irish Foreign Policy National Archives of Ireland DFA ES Box file 32, file 228; National Archives of Ireland Gavan Duffy Papers 1125/7

66 Dail Report on Foreign Policy Documents on Irish Foreign Policy National Archives of Ireland DE2/269

67 Dail Report on Foreign Policy June 1920 Documents on Irish Foreign Policy National Archives of Ireland DE4/1/3; E Murray "Eamon Bulfin" Society for Latin American Studies – Dictionary of Irish–Latin-American Biography, found on www.irlandeses.org/dilab_bulfin.htm

68 Despatch of Irish representative in Argentina to Irish Foreign Minister October 1921 and 4 December 1921 National Archives of Ireland DE5/21, DFA ES Box 32 file 16 and DFA ES Box 32 file 216(4); BMH WS 769/file S.96
69 Hart *The IRA and Its Enemies* pp. 238–239
70 Joe Vize to Michael Collins 6 June 1919 *Mulcahy Papers* P7/A/7
71 Beaslai *Michael Collins* vol I p. 328
72 Dangerfield *The Damnable Question* p. 266. Contrast this with the situation a decade previously. As per the researches of Davis *Arthur Griffith and Non-violent Sinn Fein* p. 83, when Sinn Fein branches in Ireland, spread over 23 counties, numbered only 90. The affiliation fee, branch contribution to Sinn Fein central funds was ten shillings; no less than 29 of the 90 branches could not afford, or did not contribute.
73 *Annual Register* 1920 p. 141
74 Hart *The IRA and Its Enemies* p. 70
75 BMH WS 1439/file S.2737; BMH WS 792/file S.1769; BMH WS 1478/file S.906; BMH WS 1697/file S.2691; BMH WS 1539/file S.2860; BMH WS 1,121/file S.2421; BMH WS 927/file S.2236; BMH WS 1129/file S.2420
76 Taylor *Michael Collins* p. 108
77 BMH WS 42/file S.360; BMH WS 38/file S.354
78 South Roscommon Brigade IRA, BMH WS 691/file 1996; Tipperary No. 2 Brigade IRA, BMH WS 1486/file S.2813
79 Deasy *"Towards Ireland Free"* p. 211; Hart *The IRA and Its Enemies* pp. 101–102
80 BMH WS 1388/file 2713; BMH WS 1402
81 BMH WS 1478/file S906; BMH WS 792/fil S.1765
82 BMH WS 1399/file S.2722
83 BMH WS 358/file S.2689; BMH WS 437/file S.1553; BMH WS 439/file S.1554; BMH WS 823/file S.2087; BMH WS 927/file S.2236; BMH WS 980/file S.2305; BMH WS 1,263/file S.2569; BMH WS 1,121/file S.2421; BMH WS 1402 of 17/4/56; BMH WS 1255/file S.2560; BMH WS 1372/file S.2685; BMH WS 1323/file S.2652; BMH WS 1335/file S.2661; BMH 1336/file S.2673; BMH WS 1337/file 2663; BMH WS 1178/file S2460; BMH WS 1517/file S.2942: BMH WS 1388/file S.2713; BMH WS 1437/file S.2773; BMH WS 1313/file S.2637; BMH WS 1161/file S.2470; BMH WS 1486/file S.2813; BMH WS 1425/file S.2738
84 Hart *The IRA and Its Enemies* p. 260
85 Hopkinson *Green against Green* pp. 14–15
86 Hart *The IRA and Its Enemies* p. 81. Hart also points out that this was the tip of an iceberg. These figures only reflect robberies reported in the press, and raids on private houses and premises and highway robbery in the Cork area were also frequent.
87 Cabinet Papers 12 August 1920 CAB/24/11072
88 *Annual Register* 1920 p. 120; *Annual Register* 1921 p. 49
89 BMH WS 132/file S.2413; BMH WS 1023/file S.2323
90 Hart *Mick – the real Michael Collins* p. 196
91 Cited in Mark Sturgis' diaries entry 4 November 1920, Hopkinson *The Last Days of Dublin Castle* p. 65
92 Costello *Michael Collins – in his own words* p. 16, citing Collins despatch to Mulcahy of 15 April 1921, Mulcahy Papers University College Dublin
93 Mulcahy Papers University College Dublin, cited by Costello *The Irish Revolution and Its Aftermath* p. 143
94 Coogan, *Ireland in the Twentieth Century* p. 93; review of Hart's work, *Mick – the real Michael Collins* published in 20th-century/Contemporary History, Book Reviews, Issue 6 (November/December 2005), Reviews, Revolutionary

Period 1912–1923, Volume 13 and cited in *History Ireland – Ireland's History Magazine,* found on www.historyireland.com/category/20th-century-contemporary-history/

95 Hart *The IRA and Its Enemies* p. 107, citing report of O/C I Battalion Cork No. 1 Brigade to Adj of Cork No. 1 Brigade (Mulcahy Papers P7/A23)

96 Coogan *The IRA – a history* p. 21; Coogan *Ireland in the Twentieth Century* p. 111

97 Cited in Mark Sturgis' diaries entry 4 November 1920, Hopkinson *The Last Days of Dublin Castle* p. 65

98 Dwyer *Big Fellow, Long Fellow* p. 156

99 Ibid.

100 Mackay *Michael Collins* p. 79

101 Dwyer *Michael Collins – the man who won the war* (Mercier Press 2009) p. 50

102 T Ryle Dwyer *Michael Collins and the Treaty – his differences with de Valera* (Mercier Press 1981) p. 23

103 Costello *Michael Collins – in his own words* p. 52

104 Ibid.

105 Taylor *Michael Collins* p. 136

106 Dwyer *Big Fellow, Long Fellow* p. 156

107 BMH 939/file S.66

108 Beaslai Michael Collins vol II p. 362

109 Coogan *Ireland in the Twentieth Century* p. 92, citing O Donaghue *No Other Law*

110 Hart *Mick – the real Michael Collins* p. 263

111 Robert Mackey, Assistant Manager of Guarantee Trust London, cited by Coogan *The Man who made Ireland* p. 19

112 M G Valiulis *Portrait of a Revolutionary General – Richard Mulcahy and the founding of the Irish Free State* (University of Kentucky Press 1992) p. 102

113 Collins to O/C mid-Limerick Brigade 6 October 1919, Collins Papers National Library of Ireland, cited by Costello *Michael Collins – in his own words* p. 18

114 S McGinty "Scottish support of Irish independence in the 1920s" *The Scotsman* 29 June 2104 found on www.scotsman.com/lifestyle/culture/books/scottish-support-for-irish-independence-in-1920-s-1-3460189

115 M O Caithan "Michael Collins and Scotland" in *Ireland and Scotland in the Nineteenth Century* (Four Courts Press 2009). In this O Caithan also emphasises and gives full credit to the determination, energy and work of Joe Vize. However, he also points to errors made by both Vize and Collins, and censures Collins for complacency and being out of touch with the situation in Scotland. found on www.historyireland.com/20th-century-contemporary-history/the-tommy-gun-the-irish-connection/

116 B Hanley "The Irish Citizen Army after 1916" *Journal of Irish Labour History Society* cited in G Noonan *In the Heart of Enemy Lines – the IRA in Britain 1919–1923* (University of Liverpool Press 2014) p. 53. See also Appendix II

117 BMH WS 707/file S.602

118 Ibid. WS 993/file S.203

119 L Farrell "The Tommy Gun – the Irish connection" *History Ireland 20th-century Contemporary History* Issue 4 News Revolutionary Period 1912–23, vol 8 Winter 2000, found on www.historyireland.com/20th-century-contemporary-history/the-tommy-gun-the-irish-connection

120 The exchange rate of the pound to the dollar 1919–1925 fluctuated between 1:1.34 and 1:1.40

121 Barry *The Reality of the Anglo-Irish War* p. 48

122 Collins to Hales 13 August 1920, cited in Coogan *The Man Who Made Ireland* p. 170

123 BMH WS 1478/ file S.906
124 Despatch of O Ceallaigh in Rome to Arthur Griffith 18 June 1920 National Archives of Ireland Department of Foreign Affairs ES Paris 1920
125 BMH WS 292/file S.1407
126 Coogan *The Man Who Made Ireland* p. 171
127 Barry *The Reality of the Anglo-Irish War* p. 48
128 Collins to O/C mid-Limerick Brigade 6 October 1919 Collins Papers National Library of Ireland, cited by Costello *Michael Collins – in his own words* p. 18

13 The Anglo-Irish Treaty
Ireland's fiscal autonomy

As we have seen in the previous section, the Anglo-Irish Treaty negotiations concerned the main and highly contentious issues of Ulster and Dominion status within the Empire. However, there were other issues for discussion purposes. Sub-Conferences were set up where one or two of the principal delegates of "the big Four" on each side would attend, together with other experts and civil servants. A negotiating Financial Relations committee was formed by representatives on both sides for the issues of trade and financial settlements between Britain and the new Irish state, or Free State, and met on 19 October 1922, Collins representing the Irish delegation.

The British contended that Ireland should contribute to the war debt of the First World War, and were seeking an agreement of the amount of repayment. However, Collins contended that the Irish had been over-taxed during the nineteenth century, and perhaps a compromise would be a nullification of all debts and claims. The British rejected this premise, but Collins persisted and stated that, according to his calculations, the Irish claim stood at £3,940,000,000. The Chancellor of the Exchequer, Sir Robert Horne, was present on the British side during this meeting and asked incredulously if this was the figure of amounts dating back to Brian Boru.[1] Collins replied that it dated back only since the Act of Union, and included a projection based on the impact of British restrictions on Irish capital development. Whilst there was no question these financial matters would cause the Treaty negotiations to break down, there was a wide gap between the two sides. To resolve this, it was agreed that both sides would produce detailed memoranda. The British memoranda was to show the fair proportion which Great Britain and Ireland should pay towards debt and pensions, based upon the relative taxable revenue capacity of the two countries, and the Irish memoranda was to show the Irish financial claims against Britain.

The problem for the Irish was, that whilst Collins had both knowledge and experience of finances, neither he nor the Irish delegation had actual material either to produce an effective Irish memoranda or, more important, to contest the British memoranda. By contrast, the British attendees at this Sub-Conference were experienced in finance. Sir Robert Horne was Chancellor of the Exchequer, a former President of the Board of Trade and a Director of Lloyds Bank. Warren Fisher and Robert Hawtrey were senior officials at the Treasury. Sir Laming Worthington-Evans, although currently Secretary of State for War, had been a former Minister responsible for pensions and before entering politics had been a solicitor specialising in financial law. Worthington-Evans was known to be well-versed in the House of Commons Library and Westminster documentation, and could find data and material very quickly.[2] Horne and his fellow British representatives had at their disposal the data and records held by all the financial departments of the civil service and a small army of civil service researchers to produce material and supporting data. Collins, during one of his return visits to Dublin (the Irish delegation were returned to visit Dublin quite frequently during the negotiations) expressed his frustrations to one of the private secretaries to the Dail Cabinet. The private secretary suggested an approach to Joseph Brennan.

Joseph Brennan was a dedicated British civil servant. Educated at University College Dublin, then Christ's College Cambridge where he studied Mathematics, he then took and gained first class honours in Classics. After university he joined the British civil service, having passed the competitive exams to the first division grade of civil service. Posted to Dublin as part of the civil service, he served loyally in the Finance Department and in other legislative and finance departments. He had believed in Home Rule for Ireland (writing frequently in its favour in university publications whilst at Cambridge) but this was purely a political preference and choice. He never believed in direct action or any form of political violence. Once appointed as a civil servant, he never discussed politics with colleagues or engaged in political activity.[3] During the Easter Rising he was concerned, but mainly preoccupied in worrying about his brother, who was serving in the British Army. Throughout the Anglo-Irish War he remained a dedicated civil servant in Dublin. He was responsible for the drafting of the clauses concerning fiscal matters in the Government of Ireland Bill of 1920. Brennan was highly respected as an impartial civil servant, even gaining the praise of "Andy" Cope. Cope was a highly influential British civil servant and one of the main discreet intermediaries that ensured that negotiations for a truce between the IRA and British forces were successful and that a truce came into being, enabling the Treaty negotiations.

Collins contacted Brennan, met him discreetly at a safe house on 21 October 1922 and requested his assistance. Brennan, always correct and cautious, was sympathetic and promised to give his decision the following morning. He gave it some thought overnight, and concluded to himself that an official truce was in being and therefore he could assist the Irish negotiator, with whom he had much sympathy, by furnishing them with facts, figures and data which was strictly objective. He made it clear to Collins that, as a civil servant, he could offer no opinion on any matters under discussion or in dispute, but that he would research and find them data about the matters and explain accurately what the position was. He would leave Collins and his delegation to decide how they would use what he furnished them and what line of argument to follow.

Having established this, Brennan worked tirelessly to assist Collins. He was too scrupulous to use official work time, and also there was the risk that colleagues might inadvertently discover on what he was working. He worked at all hours in his spare time and, one by one, he produced informative papers on the potential revenues in Ireland, the Irish liability for the British imperial national debt, how a proposal would be implemented for the Irish to pay 3 per cent of the British imperial national debt, liabilities for pensions arising out of the War, the overall cost of the Royal Irish Constabulary and the DMP, and accompanying pensions, compensation for the Judiciary and functionaries of the legal system, public loan and the various categories, excess stock and bonus stock relating to the Land Act of 1903 and 1909.[4] Each paper, when completed, was delivered from Brennan to Collins through an intermediary.

In the midst of working out the amounts involved in one of the papers, Brennan received an urgent request from Collins regarding the potential Irish liability for pensions from the War and also police pensions from the two Irish forces, requiring the figures for the year 1920–1921 and projected figures for the year 1922–1923. Brennan worked quickly but carefully and answered these questions always sending the answers through intermediaries. He then reverted to and completed the remaining papers he was working on.

All the papers were finished by the first week in November 1921, a tremendous achievement, taking into account that it was all researched and written by Brennan in his spare time. Thanks to this mass of detailed research Collins was able cogently to discuss and at times rebut the British claims and contentions in the papers they submitted. In doing so he argued consistently for full control of every branch and category of Irish revenue to be handed over to the new Irish Free State. Significant progress was made and the Finance Relations Committee never had to meet again. Financial discussions were able to be finalised at a three-day Sub-Conference between 2 and 4 December 1921. The final outcome was encapsulated in the Treaty whereby the new Irish state gained full fiscal autonomy.

Collins did not let slip such a potentially valuable individual as Brennan to the future Irish state. The Anglo-Irish Treaty[5] transferred to the new Irish state all powers necessary for Ireland to establish its own local and national government. A civil service was set up, using for the most part the 21,000 government employees already in post.[6] Within this Collins personally ensured[7] the appointment of Joseph Brenan as the Irish Free State's first Comptroller and Auditor General from 1 April 1922. In keeping with the policy of allowing many former British government civil servants to retain their jobs, the First Secretary and head of the new Department of

Finance was William O Brien, who had been Chief Inspector of Taxes at the time of the Treaty changes. However, Brennan's job description and duties – and his knowledge – ensured that he, Brennan, as Auditor General had primacy over the First Secretary in the Department of Finance.

Notes

1 Dwyer *Big Fellow, Long Fellow* p. 198
2 Packenham *Peace by Ordeal* p. 109
3 L O Broin *No Man's Man – a biographical memoir of Joseph Brennan, civil servant and Governor of the Central Bank* (Institute of Public Administration 1982) p. 11
4 Ibid. pp. 100–101
5 Articles of Agreement for a Treaty between Great Britain and Ireland 6 December 1921, Article 17
6 Hart, in *Mick – the real Michael Collins* p. 364, cites this smooth establishment and civil service "handover" as one of Collins' successes
7 O Broin *No Man's Man – a biographical memoir of Joseph Brennan* p. 106

14 The North

During the early months of 1922, with Irish opinion divided over acceptance of the Treaty, and the IRA effectively splitting into pro- and anti-
Treaty sides, the situation became more complicated due to events in the
north. As we have seen, throughout the Anglo-Irish War, the Dail, in
establishing itself as the de facto government of Ireland, in reality established itself as the de facto government of the south. Within its inner work-
ings the issue of the north remained unspoken. In the north, IRA units
were relatively low key, operating in republican areas. There were eventually to be five Northern Divisions of the IRA operating in the north, but
their operations were restricted and the overall numbers were low; the
total strength of the IRA in the north, part-time and full-time fighters, was
less than 8,500.[1] However, within the largely loyalist areas, since early
1920, there were retaliation attacks, discriminatory policies and job expul-
sions against the Catholic minority as the northern entity felt increasingly
under threat due to what was occurring in the south. By August 1920 an
ad hoc welfare agency, the Catholic Protection Committee estimated that
just over 11,000 men and women in northern Ireland had been driven
from their jobs by sectarian violence and intimidation.[2]

The Treaty negotiations had resulted in an ambiguous compromise on
the north. A Boundary Commission was set up to examine and find on
which areas of the north could and should be transferred to the south.
Areas such as Tyrone and Fermanagh and parts of Armagh were obvious
areas for consideration due to their Catholic and nationalist majorities.
During the Treaty negotiations Prime Minister Lloyd George, canny as
ever, had given dual – and conflicting – assurances to both the Irish and to
the Unionists.[3] To Sir James Craig, Prime Minister of Northern Ireland,
Lloyd George assured that the integrity of the northern entity would
remain; to Collins, Lloyd George strongly hinted that, with the transfer of
large areas such as Fermanagh and Tyrone and other parts, the northern
state could be economically unviable, and eventually have to be absorbed
into the south.

After the Treaty was signed the Unionists in the north refused to accept
any alteration of the border, or any alteration of the status of the north.

The Unionists made extensive preparations. Sir James Craig had been granted a substantial sum of money from the British government, and the services of Brigadier General Sir Henry Wilson as military adviser. Military reinforcements were pledged as when necessary. The police force in northern Ireland was increased in numbers with "Specials" in three categories; the first two "A" and "B" were full-time and part time, both fully armed and with full powers at all times. Recruiting started in Belfast in November 1920 and was expanded. In County Fermanagh alone by early 1921 there were over 3,500 "A" and "B" Specials recruited and serving.[4] In Belfast over 750 "B" Specials were placed on full-time duties, in County Down over 800.[5] By the following year, in May 1922, the numbers in the province of "A" Specials under arms were 5,500 and the "B" Specials, 19,000 and five extra battalions of British troops were being sent from Britain.[6]

In the early months of 1922, in response to the intensifying sectarian violence, republican volunteers in Belfast were paid direct from funds of the Dublin pro-Treaty IRA units to defend certain Catholic areas against the pogroms. These volunteers were organised into a small, defensive paramilitary force, the Belfast Guard, a paramilitary force, and were clandestinely stationed and dispersed in Catholic districts in Belfast to counter Protestant Unionist sectarian attacks. Collins sent the small but regular flow of monies to pay the Belfast Guard through cash couriers.

Then in mid-1922 this defensive action was converted into an offensive by northern units of the IRA, following the escalation of the sectarian violence. Operations were planned by the northern units of the IRA, with the sanction of IRA GHQ-Officers from the 1 Southern Division who volunteered and were sent north to assist, and units from the IRA 1 Midland Division based in Longford and Westmeath counties were to cooperate in the attacks.

In order to confuse the British and make the operations deniable, Collins swapped some of the small arms he had received from the British with weapons from the anti-Treaty IRA. Rifles from Cork No. 1 Brigade IRA were sent to northern IRA units, and replaced with rifles handed over by the British after the Treaty. Most of the rifles sent to northern IRA units were from the 1 and 2 Southern Divisions IRA[7] (both of which were mainly anti-Treaty IRA). The arms were smuggled across the border through team of couriers. One of the couriers was Sean Haughey whose son, Charles Haughey, was to become an Irish cabinet Minister who was to be exposed as responsible for smuggling arms to the Provisional IRA in the north in the early 1970s when the Troubles erupted in Northern Ireland. Weapons and funds were transferred to IRA units in the north, irrespective of whether they were for, or against, the Treaty. Collins initially viewed this as a unifying factor in alleviating the growing split within the IRA during these months. In planning and supplying the attacks he was joined by, and cooperated with, Liam Lynch the commander of the anti-Treaty IRA I Southern Division.

However, Collins and his colleagues in the pro-Treaty IRA HQ at Beggars Bush Barracks were also careful to keep personal contact with units in the north who had declared for the Treaty, and to send them arms and funds direct.[8] Lynch, whose units were parties in the arms swap-overs, complained that, whilst his units had received the British originated rifles, a significant amount of the rifles from the 1 and 2 Southern Divisions IRA which units had sent to GHQ destined for the north, were being held back.[9] Perhaps Collins realised that with potential Civil War looming every weapon would be needed by the Provisional Government's pro-Treaty IRA.

To Collins this offensive was more than just a reaction to assisting persecuted Catholics and nationalists in the north. During the Treaty and in the debates and divisions afterwards the Republicans, including – or especially – de Valera, had concentrated upon the issues of the oath and being under the British Empire. The issue of Ulster tended to be overshadowed by this.[10] At one stage of the various exchanges and debates Mary MacSwiney, sister of the venerated IRA hunger striker Thomas MacSwiney and one of the die-hard anti-Treaty Republicans, told Griffith unequivocally

> ... take out the oath and the Governor-General and we'll all be with you.[11]

For Collins, the main overriding issue was Ulster, the occupied north. He was an Irish nationalist through and through. His ultimate objective was a united Ireland and the Treaty was a stage in achieving this. Once Ireland was independent and had its own finances and, more important, had its own army, the north could and would be retaken, by force if necessary. He had stated on one occasion during this period

> They (the British) broke the Treaty of Limerick and we'll break this treaty too, when it suits us and when we have our own army.[12]

The northern offensive was a possible opportunity to retake the north.

In doing this Collins was playing a dangerous game with skill. In the south he was, as a signatory to the Anglo-Irish Treaty and member of the Free State Provisional Government, working with the British to implement the Treaty and standing down the IRA whilst at the same time clandestinely providing arms and funding to the north for a campaign to IRA units set on acquiring by force British territory. Within Ireland, on the verge of Civil War, he was keeping in check the anti-Treaty units of the IRA, whilst at the same time clandestinely providing arms and funds to both pro-Treaty and anti-Treaty units, and in turn whilst simultaneously keeping close direct contact with the former.

As well as a military campaign in the north, Collins deployed and financed a subtler weapon. The role of the scholar and schoolteacher as a potential subversive force is well known and prominent in the twentieth century revival of Irish nationalism. The Irish Volunteers were the original initiative of a university professor (MacNeill); the 1916 rebellion numbered amongst its leaders a university lecturer (MacDonagh) and a barrister turned progressive schoolmaster (Pearse). The tough IRA fighter, Dan Breen (whose individual initiative in killing the two RIC officers escorting gelignite in Tipperary started the Anglo-Irish conflict) recalled in his memoirs his respect for, and being inspired by, Ireland's history taught by an Irish schoolmaster in Tipperary; other IRA fighters also acknowledged being so inspired when at school.[13] Collins himself was inspired with a patriotic fervour instilled by his primary school headmaster, who was a member of the IRB. The position of schoolteacher, in an age where children had no recourse and were never exposed to the ubiquitous worldwide web/internet/digital dimension – or even television – was that of one which wielded considerable influence.[14]

Collins fully realised this and initiated a scheme whereby teachers and school managers in the north who refused to recognise the authority of the Northern Ireland entity would be paid by the Provisional Government.[15] Lists were drawn up and some arrangements were made through banks in Ireland to have funds discreetly transferred into any bank accounts such schoolteachers would designate, as their account into which their "salaries" could be paid.

The military offensive by units of the IRA started in mid-May 1922, with the 3 Northern Division making a series of attacks on isolated military posts, blowing up blockhouses and fixed installations and cutting communications with the south. Units from the 3 and 4 Northern Divisions joined in a few days later and the small attacks were more coordinated. However, the security forces did not respond and kept within the confines of their strong barracks. When the attacks lessened then the police and army were deployed in overwhelming numbers in counter attacks in Tyrone, Antrim, Derry and Down. The counter-offensives hunted down IRA units, who took sanctuary over the border. These fugitive IRA, mainly from the 2 and 3 Northern Divisions were gathered within the Free State and sent to the Curragh military camp for initial rest, then intensive training and then would be sent back north. Funds were made available. These units were given an undertaking by Collins and Mulcahy that they would not be used or deployed in any fighting or conflict in the south. This promise was kept and on the abandonment of the Northern offensive and the outbreak of the Civil War the units and individuals at the Curragh were given a free choice of action. Some joined the Free State Army.[16]

The whole IRA offensive in the north was over by end of June. It had failed. In July 1920, the commander of the 3 Northern Division IRA informed GHQ that the northern Ireland authorities had beaten the IRA completely in Antrim and Down, and in Belfast the IRA were

... daily losing ground.... If they succeed elsewhere as they have succeeded in Belfast then it will not be long before the northern government have complete recognition from the population of the six
counties.[17]

Any success was unlikely, given the sheer firepower and numbers the
northern authorities could deploy against the smaller numbers of IRA[18]
who were fighting in an environment of a hostile population. The faltering
offensive was finally halted due to the murder of Brigadier General Wilson
in London. This focussed British hostility towards the worsening situation
in Dublin with the divided IRA and the anti-Treaty-ites becoming more
militant, and against Collins and the Provisional Government they were
eventually compelled to take action.

As a military campaign, the northern offensive had been unlikely to
succeed and was indeed a failure. However, it also showed Collins' absolute mastery in handling complex political manoeuvrings in a multi-conflict
situation, and in illicit transfer of monies in the clandestine funding of
political violence.

Notes

1 O Donaghue *No Other Law* p. 248
2 Kostick *Revolution in Ireland* pp. 155–156
3 A detailed and admirable account of the stages of Lloyd George's playing off
   Ulster against the Irish delegation during the Treaty negotiations is to be found
   in Dangerfield *The Damnable Question* pp. 331–338. Dangerfield ascribes
   much of the manoeuvring to the Assistant Secretary Tom Jones whose role is
   viewed as an *eminence grise*.
4 Kostick *Revolution in Ireland* p. 259
5 B A Follis *A State under Siege – establishment of Northern Ireland 1920–1925*
   (Clarendon Press 1995) p. 100
6 Ibid. p. 139
7 O Donaghue *No Other Law* p. 250
8 Ibid. pp. 250–251
9 Hopkinson *Green against Green* p. 84
10 English *Armed Struggle – the history of the IRA* p. 32
11 E Neeson *The Civil War* (Poolbeg 1989) p. 84. MacSwiney in the Treaty debates
   did indeed bemoan the lack of opposition being brought to bear against leaving
   the north in British hands. However, her most strident and frequent interventions
   were on the issue of what was perceived as abandoning the Republic.
12 Coogan *Ireland in the Twentieth Century* p. 127
13 D Breen *My Fight for Irish Freedom* (Tralee 1981) p. 21; BMH WS 1,121/file
   S.2421; BMH WS 1,263/file S.2569; WS 1,337/file S.2663
14 An incisive and highly informative analysis of the role of scholars and schoolteachers – and other occupations – in the rise of Irish nationalism is given in T
   Garvin "Great Hatred, Little Room – social background and political sentiment
   among revolutionary activity in Ireland 1890–1922" in D G Boyce (ed.) *The
   Revolution in Ireland 1879–1923* (Macmillan Education 1988) ch. 4
15 Minutes of Provisional Government 30 January 1922 Documents on Irish
   Foreign Policy National Archives of Ireland G1/1

16 ODonaghue *No Other Law* pp. 252–253; Hopkinson's researches, *Green against Green* p. 249, find that of the 525 Northern IRA men deployed to the Curragh, 243 were to join the Provisional Government, later Free State Army

17 O/C 3 Northern Division IRA despatch 27 July 1922 to GHQ University College Dublin Archives Department, P7/B/11/77

18 Hopkinson *Green against Green* p. 84; Coogan in *Ireland in the Twentieth Century* p. 132

15 The sinews of Civil War and the Republicans hamstrung

During the Civil War Collins found time to establish a civil police force, the Garda Siochana, and made a nationwide appeal for suitable men to join the new unarmed police force to serve the new state. The new force found recruits, however, resources were scarce. Uniforms were provided, training was given and new recruits were posted throughout the country, although in the conflict areas this was not always possible. Pay was usually seriously in arrears and police stations and accommodation was often makeshift.[1] Collins and the government had to allocate monies to the overriding priority of the Civil War, which cost £17 million to pursue.[2] By 1923, 30 per cent of all incoming revenues of the new state were spent on defence.

However, if revenue was tight for the Provisional Government, it was tighter still for the Republicans. This was the due to Collins and the Provisional Government interdicting potential Republican funds.

Collins had been appointed as Commander in Chief of the Free State Army, William Cosgrave taking over as head of the Provisional Government. Despite being fully occupied with the military situation he still took a role in government, still attending Cabinet meetings when he could and remaining Minister of Finance.[3] One important aspect was how to deprive the Republicans or Irregulars of funds. Initially in the Civil War the anti-Treaty or Republicans had the advantage in numbers over the Free State, but funds were becoming urgently needed to feed and supply the anti-Treaty IRA.[4]

There were two directions from which funds could be available for the Republicans, from the United States, where a large proportion of the Loan funds raised there remained, and from within Ireland and Britain.

With regard to the United States, there was little potential for the anti-Treaty Republicans for fundraising. United States opinion was unanimously relieved by and in favour of the Anglo-Irish Treaty which had brought peace. The reaction in the United States to de Valera's denouncing of the Treaty was that of surprise and shock. The subsequent reactions of the United States to the Irish divisions and to the Civil War was regret and a wish to avoid involvement, with little or no support for the anti-Treaty

Republicans.[5] Meetings in mid-1922 in the United States for fundraising held by the anti-Treaty-ites had raised mere hundreds of dollars, when hitherto such meetings during the Anglo-Irish War had fundraising potential of tens of thousands.[6] In late 1922 the Republicans sent Sean Moylan to the United States as their representative and to try and obtain funds. Moylan was commander of IRA Cork No. 1 Brigade and had been captured by the British during the Anglo-Irish War. At his court martial he was commended, and it was noted and taken into account, that he had intervened in the aftermath of a firefight against some of his own men, whereby he had prevented British wounded being finished off.[7] When the split came, he took the anti-Treaty IRA side, in charge of the newly formed Cork No. 4 Brigade IRA. In March 1922, he made mass raids on post offices, in common with his fellow anti-Treaty IRA commanders, raiding banks as well as requisitioning – or purloining – foodstuffs from local traders during this period.[8] He also imposed small extortionist "taxes" in localities in south-west Ireland to gather funds for the anti-Treaty IRA forces.[9] On his arriving in the United States, Moylan attempted fundraising. Moylan's expectations had been moderate; he had set himself a low target of $100,000 maximum.[10] But his attempt at fundraising was an overall failure.

Far more substantial – and available to the anti-Treaty Republicans – was the proportion of the funds of the Dail Loan still remaining in the United States. As we have seen, de Valera and James O Mara raised $5,123,644 worth of Irish Republican bond certificates. (A further Loan had been raised in the United States which was appealed for between October 1921 until the date of the Treaty being signed and brought the total of monies raised in the United States to $5,746,360.) As we have also seen, only approximately half of the monies raised in the United States were sent back to Ireland. De Valera kept the rest back, up to $3 million.[11]

When de Valera returned from the United States to Ireland, with O Mara still working there, de Valera and O Mara made arrangements for provisions for individuals to act for them in the safe keeping of the United States raised funds. These individuals were John Hearn, a US citizen and prominent figure in the AARIR, Sean Nunan, a former clerk to the Dail who accompanied de Valera to the United States and had remained there, still working on the Loan, and Joseph McGarrity, who had met de Valera on his arrival to the United States and facilitated the initial stages of his visit. These individuals could act on behalf of the three trustees. They also had safekeeping of half the United States raised funds which had been converted into US Liberty Bonds. These were kept in safety deposit boxes in banks in New York City, the Guaranty Safe Deposit Co., the Central Union Safe Deposit Co, the Garfield Safe Deposit Co., and the Harriman National Bank. The boxes in the banks were entrusted to combinations of pairs of these three individuals, either Hearn and Boland, or McGarrity and Noonan or Noonan and McGarrity. (The keys to all the safety deposit boxes were kept by James O Mara). These arrangements enabled de Valera to return to Ireland, enabled all three trustees to be in Ireland and any transactions concerning the funds in the United States to be carried out by individuals in situ. There had been a change in trustee. When James O Mara managed to extricate himself from working in the United States and returned to Ireland, grossly disillusioned with de Valera, he resigned his seat in the Dail and resigned his trusteeship, and his place as a trustee was taken by his brother Stephen.

Stephen O Mara worked with his brother in the O Mara family meat packing and bacon business in Ireland. Whilst his brother James O Mara had been elected to the Dail, Stephen pursued the path of local politics, becoming first an alderman then Lord Mayor of Limerick. When the Anglo-Irish Treaty was signed, James remained loyal to the Free State. Stephen, whilst stopping short of militancy or taking up arms, was a strong supporter of the Republican cause. As Lord Mayor of Limerick in March 1922, during the confused situation in the aftermath of the Treaty being signed when pro-Treaty and anti-Treaty IRA units were both present in Limerick taking up positions, he had assisted at defusing the situation and arranging a truce. Nonetheless he was unequivocally pro-Republican, to the extent that when Rory O Connor's anti-Treaty-ites occupied the Four Courts in Dublin, they also occupied the nearby Four Courts Hotel; then they evacuated it on realising that the hotel was owned by Stephen O Mara whom they did not wish to upset.[12]

Therefore, by January 1922, at the time of the intense debates and divisions in Ireland over the Treaty, two of the three trustees of the funds raised in the United States – de Valera and Stephen O Mara – were directly opposed to the Free State government and the Treaty, whilst the third, Bishop Fogarty, remained inactive regretfully observing events unfold. Also, the physical safeguarding of Irish bond revenues in the United States were away from the direct reach of the Dail, away from the direct reach of the original trustees, and fully accessible to United States citizens and one Irish individual (Boland) opposed to the new government.

In January 1922, as part of consolidating the funds held by the new Irish Free State, the Dail authorised Stephen O Mara, as trustee, to go to the United States to complete and terminate all Loan matters over there. In mid-February 1922 all three trustees (Stephen O Mara, de Valera and Bishop Fogarty) met with the Dail, which reiterated and confirmed that all funds and assets of the Loan held in various parts of the United States should be moved and consolidated into New York financial institutions, and that accounts be opened in Ireland in the names of the trustees, and that the Loans start to be repaid by the Dail. Both Collins and de Valera – at that time opposed to one another on the Treaty, but in the process of forming an electoral pact to head off total schism – agreed such funds returning to Ireland should not be used for any party-political purpose.

However, Collins was already concerned that two of the three trustees were opposed to the new Irish government. Less than a week after the meeting between the trustees and the Dail, Collins asked and authorised James O Mara to travel to the United States[13] as his representative. Collins' suspicions were further heightened in early March, when the Dail was informed that, two months previously in January, de Valera had withdrawn $250,000 from various banks in the United States. This may not have been untoward, in that it was part of the process of moving and consolidating United States funds; Bishop Fogarty willingly gave de Valera the benefit of the doubt. However, also in March James O Mara reported to Collins from the United States that an individual involved in the Loan was refusing to follow the Dail – and Collins' – instructions. The obdurate individual was Gilbert Ward, working in the New York offices of the Loan, and he had refused to release funds withdrawn from several banks across the United States. James O Mara, in direct communication with Collins, counselled that they seek an injunction, and also that his brother Stephen be required to resign as a trustee. Somewhat predictably, Stephen O Mara sent separate advice that Gilbert Ward was fully trustworthy and reliable, Bishop Fogarty, still trusting in Stephen, accepted this advice.

However, Collins remained suspicious and he sent Timothy Smiddy to the United States. James O Mara, after a brief period working with Smiddy, returned to Ireland. James O Mara was no doubt grateful to be out of an invidious position, but he held fast to his advice to Collins about Stephen O Mara. James O Mara had returned to Ireland deeply troubled and affected by the divisions and strife occurring there. He would be further saddened later when his brother returned to Ireland, and was arrested and placed in custody by Free State troops, at a period of the Civil War when draconian measures were being implemented and known Republicans and opponents of the Free State were being rounded up and incarcerated.

Timothy Smiddy had worked with Collins before. He was a distinguished Professor of Economics, having studied at several European universities and held the chair at University College, Cork and during the Anglo-Irish Treaty negotiations he was economic adviser to the Irish delegation. Courteous and professional, he had a full awareness of the wider picture and would eventually serve with distinction as Irish Minister to the United States, and then later in London as Irish representative to Britain. His official remit in going to the United States was to promote and protect Irish Free State interests. Having been sent as the representative of Collins as Minister of Finance, his mission was to find out the true and exact situation regarding the Loan funds located in the United States. Smiddy sent back information, confirming James O Mara's reports of the non-cooperation of Ward, (which he had initially doubted and disputed with O Mara[14]) and also, of further concern, that Ward had power of attorney over the all the Loan funds located in the United States.

Smiddy, as part of his official remit and duties was setting up an Irish diplomatic mission in the United States with consular offices in various cities. He sent a budget request for funds to Stephen O Mara as the trustee of the funds in the United States. O Mara refused this, revealingly stating that as a trustee he had to point out that the funds of the Republic could not be used in the service of the Provisional Government. As far as Stephen O Mara was concerned all Loan funds raised in the United States belonged to the anti-Treaty Republican side. Collins entered the fray, and in a confrontational despatch ordered the release of the funds requested by Smiddy, and advised O Mara that the Ministers, not the trustees, decided how the monies were to be spent. O Mara gave in and acquiesced to Collins' instructions as Minister of Finance, and released the funds for Smiddy's budget for Irish diplomatic missions in the United States. However, Collins did not relax his guard and or vigilance.

Smiddy pursued further inquiries. In April 1922 Gilbert Ward had been replaced by Gareth Healy who had worked on the Loan in the Chicago office, an office set up as part of James O Mara's Loan raising organisational structure. Healy moved and took over the main New York office. Smiddy made inquiries of Healy and received ambivalent and apparently evasive answers.[15] Moreover, Stephen O Mara, despite his climb down to Collins over Smiddy's budget funds, had not been idle. When Smiddy made further inquiries it was found that Stephen O Mara had managed, through lawyers, to advance de Valera's arrangements, and ensured that all Dail funds in the United States were in the names of Stephen O Mara, Ward and Healy, rather than the names of the original trustees. The three original trustees had lost control of the Loan funds in the United States, and this control and safekeeping was in the hands of individuals whose loyalty to the Free State was at best unknown, and in some cases unequivocally hostile. Even the good Bishop Fogarty was alarmed. He was later to state,

> ... it did make a strong impression on me that by accident or otherwise every penny of our money was in the hands of and controlled by people who were against what was the national will of the people and the government.[16]

Smiddy took in the situation and consulted lawyers. On 24 July 1922, he cabled Collins requesting authority to take legal action which would seek an injunction on behalf of the Irish Free State for possession of all funds and securities held in the New York financial institutions. Collins, equally alert to the situation replied within 48 hours on behalf of the Provisional Government of the Irish Free State and on behalf of Bishop Fogarty, as trustee of the funds. His reply authorised seeking court action against the New York banks which held the funds, to prevent any withdrawals, and against the named individuals de Valera, Stephen O Mara and their agents Gareth Healy and Gilbert Ward, to prevent them accessing any funds, any bank accounts, any securities (and any related safety deposit boxes).

Collins had accurately realised the situation. The anti-Treaty IRA and Republicans would need funds in any forthcoming struggle. He himself had maintained a continuous, albeit spasmodic armed struggle against British forces for three years and the funds had only just lasted out. He was reported to have told a senior British official when the Truce was called

> You had us dead beat – we couldn't have lasted more than three weeks.[17]

He realised that without funds time would rapidly run against the anti-Treaty-ites and Republicans. Therefore, the Free State eventually acquiring the funds was an objective, but not the priority. The overriding priority was to keep the United States funds out of reach of the Republicans. The injunction, once granted, had to remain and legal proceedings had to be as lengthy and protracted as possible.

In the New York Supreme Court legal proceedings commenced on 11 August 1922.[18] The injunction was granted on 21 August 1922. Two days later *The Times* in London effectively summed up the situation in stating that the New York Supreme Court injunction

> ... which restrains the Irregular leaders from drawing on funds collected in that country for the Republican cause, has struck directly at the most sensitive part of that organization.[19]

The lawyers representing the Irish Free State were of the same mind as Collins. They knew their brief, and made lengthy submissions and drew out the proceedings. The Republicans were represented by a team of able lawyers among whom was John F Finnerty, an ardent worker in setting up the AARIR, and a staunch supporter of de Valera. However, the arguments and submissions of Finnerty and his fellow lawyers, ably expounded, took from between September 1922 to June 1923. The lawyers representing the Free State continued to take testimony until February 1924.[20] By this time the Civil War had ended, the Republicans having given up in May 1923. The injunction had done its work well.

In countering potential funds to the anti-Treaty IRA coming from Ireland and Britain, Collins worked with the financial stalwart, Joseph Brennan. On 27 July 1922, the government requested all banks in Cork to withdraw facilities for any negotiable instruments. Then, in August, Collins received a report from General Dalton, Free State officer commanding the Free State Army front in the south-west, that the anti-Treaty IRA were financing themselves through the revenues of Cork, and through local traders. Then he received letters from the manager of the Hibernian Bank in Cork who was uncomfortable about transactions of paid vouchers on the Customs account of the local Bank of Ireland.[21] In a subsequent interview in Cork that Collins conducted with the manager, there was mention of transactions going through the Land Bank involving an officer of the First Southern Division, which had declared itself for the Republicans.

As we have seen, the Land Bank was established as part of the de facto Irish administration taking over the areas where the British had lost control. It was initially financed by the Dail, but it conducted business as an independent banking enterprise. Unlike the Sinn Fein Bank, it remained unsuspected by the British as having links to the Dail and Collin's ministry.[22] It could be and was used for pushing clandestine transactions through, and had substantial deposits available. However, it was one thing for the Land Bank to be unsuspected by the British, quite another for Collins not be aware of its potential. Moreover, the principal director of the Land Bank, Robert Barton, despite signing the Treaty and supporting the pro-Treaty-ites in the Dail debates, had just declared his allegiance to the anti-Treaty forces. Information from the Hibernian Bank manager included the Land Bank being in the chain of transactions resulting in a potential fund flow to the Republicans. Decisive action was needed.

Collins, preoccupied as he was with military matters, wrote to Cosgrave and stated that a first class official was needed in this[23] and recommended Joseph Brennan to deal. Brennan obtained a letter of authorisation from the Bank of Ireland which authorised – or rather instructed – on his, Brennan's request, the local manager(s) of the bank of Ireland to afford him access to all accounts, documentation of transaction records relating to any accounts handling government funds. Sure enough, when Brennan arrived in Cork in mid-August and made inquiries, it was found that since the first week in July the Republican officers had cajoled Customs officials to draw vouchers on the official Customs account at the Bank of Ireland, payable to headquarters Cork No. 1 Brigade (part of the First Southern Division). When they no longer could obtain the authorised signatures, they opened themselves a second Customs account and drew payments from this negotiating them through the local branch of the Land Bank. On one occasion £10,000 had been deposited in the account of a Republican officer in the local Munster and Leinster Bank and then withdrawals made days later, paying local tradesmen for supplies. An account was also uncovered in the name of a Quartermaster Sergeant at First Southern Division headquarters. Funds were also being transferred through the Land Bank to purchase drafts from a London bank, the London County Westminster and Parrs Bank, Holborn branch. This bank and branch was where Erskine Childers and his wife had several accounts.

In London, Art O Brien, the Irish representative, tried to carry on serving Ireland in his own way as best he could. However, the Treaty had come as a blow to him and he declared himself Republican, organising meetings and anti-Treaty publications and propaganda. He placed himself as answering to, and requested instructions from de Valera. He was believed to have been in contact with Rory O Connor in Dublin during the latter's take over and occupation of the Four Courts.[24] Both Barton and Childers had contacted and operated through Art O Brien during the period of the Anglo-Irish War; now, honest and sincere O Brien in London still maintained contact with Barton and Childers.

Brennan obtained from General Dalton a military Order freezing the accounts in question pending further instruction. He travelled to London where he interviewed the manager at head office of the London County Westminster and Parrs Bank, and received an assurance that any drafts already issued, if presented would be not be honoured. Brennan then returned to Cork and revisited the Land Bank. To guard against the Republicans going back to the Land Bank when they realised that their drafts were worthless and demanding restitution of the sums used to purchase the drafts, Brennan obtained a military Order and served it on the Land Bank, stipulating that these sums be frozen and placed in a holding account credited to the Free State government.[25]

The result of this speedy action by Collins and Brennan was that, of a potential £93,000 gained by the anti-Treaty-ites or Republicans, £38,300 was recovered; they had been deprived of over a third of their financial support.[26]

Funds in both the United States, and in Ireland and Britain, had effectively been closed off to the anti-Treaty IRA and Republicans. By September 1922 Liam Lynch, commander of the south and western Republican IRA was lamenting that

> we are very short of cash, as the enemy issued orders to banks to refuse to release funds they had discovered were ours.[27]

By November 1922 the fiery advocate of the Republicans, Mary Mac-Swiney, was voicing concern about the lack of funds and at the same time de Valera wrote that they were in severe need of funds, and by June 1923 de Valera regretfully acknowledged that, in stark terms, the Republican cause was broke.[28] The lack of funds was a major factor in the defeat of the Republicans.[29] One distinguished Irish historian, in a large work on Irish history, makes a summary of the causes of the defeat of the Republicans and of possible significance is that he cites the first reason to be lack of funds,

> The Irregulars on the other hand, *lacked the sinews of war*, lacked organization and even lacked credible policy (italics mine).[30]

This lack of funds was due to the vigilance and decisive action of Collins.

During the legal proceedings in the New York court and during Brennan's activities in Cork, Collins was killed. He was ambushed at Beal na mBath within a fortnight of interviewing the manager of the Hibernian Bank and directing Brennan to his inquiries, and the day after the injunction on the United States Loan funds was granted in the New York court. In keeping with Collins' character, the final moments of his life were in fighting and returning fire against the enemy. Also, fully appropriate, the final weeks of his life had been also occupied in safeguarding Ireland's finances.

Notes

1 Coogan in *Ireland in the Twentieth Century* pp. 146–147 gives an illustrative account of some conditions which epitomise the difficulties of the new force

2 Mackay *Michael Collins* p. 265

3 Hart *Mick – the real Michael Collins* p. 400

4 Deasy *Brother against Brother* p. 64

5 A full and comprehensive analysis of the reactions of the United States and US–Irish organisations based there towards the Anglo-Irish Treaty and the divisions within Ireland is to be found in Hopkinson *Green against Green* pp. 47–52, 253–256

6 Despatch of Smiddy to Michael Collins 5 April 1922 Documents on Irish Foreign Policy National Archives of Ireland DFA Box 30 file 99

7 *Irish Times* 6 June 1921

8 Coogan *Ireland since the Rising* p. 39; Coogan *Ireland in the Twentieth Century* p. 113; Hart *The IRA and Its Enemies* p. 116

9 Kee *The Green Flag* p. 737

10 Hopkinson *Green against Green* p. 254

11 See Appendix II

12 Hopkinson *Green against Green* p. 72

13 Collins to Diarmuid Lynch 22 March 1922 National Library of Ireland John Devoy Papers MS 18001/149

14 Despatch of Smiddy to Collins 10 April 1922 Documents on Irish Foreign Policy vol I 1919–1923 National Archives of Ireland DFA Box 30 file 99

15 Carroll, in his comprehensive *Money for Ireland* p. 35 is more sympathetic to Healy, pointing out that his inability to furnish certain information was due to Ward having taken with him account documentation and records when he vacated the New York offices

16 Defendants Commission, testimony of Bishop Fogarty Kennedy Papers P4/215 University College Dublin Archives, cited by Carroll *Money for Ireland* p. 47

17 L S Amery *My Political Life – Volume II war and peace* (Hutchinson 1953) p. 230; J J Lee *Ireland 1912–85 Politics and Society*, p. 91 cited by P Taylor, *Provos the IRA and Sinn Fein* p. 13

18 *Irish Free State et al. vs Guaranty Safety Deposit Co et al.* Civil Branch of the Supreme Court of the State of New York, New York County 222NYS182 May 1927

19 *The Times*, 23 August 1922

20 The New York Supreme Court eventually came to a decision and ruling in 1927, for the Republicans. A highly informative, scholarly and comprehensive account of the various legal proceedings regarding the Loan funds is contained in Carroll *Money for Ireland*. It recounts in full the legal events (whose period lies outside the scope of this book) and affords the reader differing legal opinions on the judgement and is valuable in placing the case within the context of the corpus of international law relating to recognition of states.

21 The Bank of Ireland was a private bank. Although it handled government funds, it was not and must not be confused with the central Bank of Ireland.

22 Beaslai *Michael Collins* vol I p. 345

23 C Younger *Ireland's Civil War* (Taplinger Publishing Company 1969) p. 423

24 National Library of Ireland Art O Brien Papers, 1922 MS 8460/8 and MS 8428/13

25 O Broin *No Man's Man – a biographical memoir of Joseph Brennan* pp. 114–117; A McCarthy "Michael Collins – Minister for Finance 1919–1921" in G Doherty and D Keogh (eds) *Michael Collins and the Making of the Irish State* pp. 54–70

26 O Broin *No Man's Man – a biographical memoir of Joseph Brennan* p. 117

27 Hopkinson *Green against Green* p. 131

28 Carroll *Money for Ireland* pp. 37–38

29 Ibid. p. xviii

30 F S L Lyons *Ireland since the Famine* (Fontana Press 2009) p. 463

Part IV

Later political violence and insurgency and their financing

Collins, Sinn Fein, the Dail and the IRA operated in an era when the main methods of communication were newspapers, and a somewhat basic telephone and telegraph system. With the advent first of television in the mid and late twentieth century, and then, in the later twentieth and early twenty-first centuries, rapid development and exponential increase of the worldwide web/internet/digital dimension, a totally different era has emerged. Therefore, any attempt to make direct analogies and parallels (anathema to historians) between illicit funding by Collins and those illicit fundings occurring in our modern era would be erroneous. However, it may be of benefit in this final part to consider, with regard to later militant groups, liberationist organisations and terrorist groups, aspects of their illicit finances and view how Collins' grasp and application of certain principles of *modus operandi* are still being used.

Organiser of insurgency

Collins' organisational abilities were both powerful and exceptional.[1] As we have seen, besides being clandestine Minister of Finance he was within the IRA Director of Intelligence and Adjutant General. He also held important responsibilities in Sinn Fein which took up yet more of his time, as well as his discreet work within the IRB, which he himself had reorganised after the 1916 Rising.[2] One historian, in a long-term work on Irish history since 1660, describes him as

... a 27 year-old guerrilla supremo in the making.[3]

Dan Breen and Tom Barry, both hardened IRA combat operatives, unsympathetic and contemptuous towards IRA headquarters and central government, both commented that no job was too big or too small for Collins and if anyone wanted a job or task to be done, Collins was the person to see.[4]

In terms of historical parallels, Collins' energy, drive and organisational abilities in his multi-functions and responsibilities – and his achievements –

are kin to those of Lazare Carnot during the French Revolution. Carnot was one of the Committee of Public Safety which governed France during the period late 1792–1794, a period during which the infant French Republic was threatened by war and invasion from a combination of several European powers, including Britain, Austria and Prussia. Thanks to Carnot's energy, drive and organisation[5] together with his superb grasp of long-term strategy,[6] the revolutionary committee were able to logistically concentrate the resources of France, raise and quickly train the manpower of France into mass armies and, by skilful strategic deploying of mass armies against their opponents, ensure the infant republic survived the three years of danger. The "Organiser of Victory" was assisted in economic mobilisation by his fellow member of the Committee, Robert Lindet, as was Collins by Robert Barton in the latter's quiet but long-lasting work in agricultural reform and the Land Bank.

However, a major difference between the challenges facing Carnot and those facing Collins was that Carnot was part of the state or régime and as such could draw upon the full resources of the state; ranged against Collins were the military and law enforcement forces of the state against which he was organising, raising and waging an insurgency and having to maintain underground state governing organisation.

In a later era in France, in an insurgency of three to four years, the French Resistance was facing similar challenges to the insurgents against the German occupying forces and the collaborationist Vichy regime. They experienced difficulties of organisation and coordination amongst the differing resistance groups and movements. However, the French Resistance groups were directly supported and supplied by the various British and United States intelligence services and the Free French organisation based in London. Moreover, and a most important difference, this support included substantial and near constant flow of funds; on one occasion the combat resistance group alone was offered ten million French Francs by the United States to cooperate in direct cooperation with the United States Office of Strategic Services (O.S.S.).[7]

Communications, timing and outreach to mass donors

In the raising of the National Loan Collins deliberately enlisted and involved as much as possible the Catholic Church in Ireland. Towards the end of the First World War when the British government attempted to extend conscription to Ireland, part of the mass opposition took the form of several organisations engaged in fundraising in an appeal for donations to an Anti-Conscription fund. Sinn Fein was involved. However, Sinn Fein raised but a small amount compared to the Catholic Church, to whom the general populace was more inclined to donate. The lesson was not lost on Collins, who deliberately and persistently appealed to the Irish Catholic hierarchy for support to the Loan campaign. Bishop Fogarty was a willing supporter of the Loan, as well as donating. Archbishop William Walsh of Dublin was another donor, making his donation public via the press in the United States. By contrast, Daniel Cohalan, Bishop of Cork, despite having several interviews with Richard Mulcahy, remained passive and decidedly unsympathetic to the Loan. However, the Irish born Archbishop Mannix of Melbourne, Australia, was an ardent international supporter (and indeed was to be one of the active intermediaries assisting in the tortuous and protracted negotiations in the Anglo-Irish War, which eventually resulted in the Truce) and within Ireland there were many of the lower Catholic Church hierarchy at parish level who spoke up for the Loan and accepted and forwarded donations on behalf of their parishioners. This continuous involving and inveigling of the Catholic Church to the raising of the Loan ensured the Loan gained widespread donations, and ensured that it transcended the traditional Republican base and outreached to the wider population.

In terms of communications, Collins' use of the film was ground-breaking. Collins use of the film and the (enforced) cooperation of the cinemas for promoting the National Loan was part of his awareness of developing mass media of the day for propaganda and illicit revenue raising purposes. Later, in July 1922, he was to compose memoranda assessing how Lloyd George used film and how the cinema was being exploited in Germany for propaganda and political messages.[8]

The communications strategy of timing and place in raising the National Loan, exerting special efforts and resources on Sundays and in the vicinity of churches, was deliberate. This care with timing and location was repli-cated in later years by the revolutionary activists carrying out the "Velvet Revolution" of 1989 in Czecho-Slovakia during the disintegration of the former Soviet Union and the central and eastern European totalitarian régimes. During this peaceful uprising, mass demonstrations were mobil-ised by groups of activists using the (then) new technology of Citizens Band (CB) radio to announce same day notice of locations of demonstra-tions and the routes to be followed, and the timings were scheduled for late afternoon, coinciding with the ending of the working day by many Prague workers, who would leave work, but delay going home, to demonstrate.

In terms of targeting critical mass, the later IRA in the 1990s in the Sinn Fein Lottery implemented a deliberate mass appeal, tapping in to multi small-scale income. The Sinn Fein Lottery became a success, by the early 2000s obtaining over £1 million a year and became a mainstay of Sinn Fein and Republican funding.[9]

In a later, more violent, horrific and fanatical conflict, Zarqawi in the Iraqi insurgency of post 2003 revealed the same skills in communications outreach to critical mass.

At this point clarification must be made. Collins in his intelligence war could be – and was – ruthless and unhesitating in the killing of the British opponents. However, it must be emphasised that there is no intention in this section to make any direct analogy between Collins and the fanatical, unhealthy and pathological Zarqawi. This section is comparing exploitation of *modus operandi*, not the individual leaders.

Zarqawi's overall strategy of division was horribly effective. The strategy was to perpetrate indiscriminate attacks on the Shia communities, which would provoke a violent reaction and counter atrocities, detaching them from their tacit alliance with the United States and coalition forces,[10] cause the polarisation of the Sunni communities into joining the insurgency and fan the flames of civil war. The end result would be the withdrawal of the coalition forces as soon as was politically expedient and leave the field clear for international intervention by Sunni dominated regimes.[11] When al Zarqawi was finally killed by coalition forces in mid-2006 it only temporarily abated the new levels of violence perpetrated by the insurgency.[12] His impact long outlasted his death.

Zarqawi's impact and success was due to communications strategy, his use of the Internet through the *al Ansar Web* forum propaganda. In the history of terrorists exploiting the world wide web/digital/Internet dimension, the repugnant and perverse genius of Zarqawi forms a major development. Operational information for would-be jihadists included planning an attack in six essential stages, constantly updating postings regarding the accessible routes to enter Iraq and names of mosques in Syria that could give "sympathetic support". Finances were also raised by "encouraging donations" on websites to small organisations, retail or philanthropic, established for short periods to collect, dispose of funds, then cease operating. These included posting appeals for donations, how to donate and where to physically take or place contributions, all short-term details whose location and logistics would change quickly. These short-term postings, carefully timed, worked well and raised revenues. Propaganda and operational logistics and small-scale finances were all successfully achieved by Zarqawi's use of the world wide web/internet/ digital dimension, and contributed to his phenomenal success as a terrorist insurgent group leader. Zarqawi as at the mid-2000s, was exceptional amongst terrorist groups in exploiting the world wide web/internet/digital dimension so completely. In 2005 experts were stating a future trend, in that

> Never before has a guerrilla organisation so successfully intertwined real time war on the ground with its electronic *jihad*, making Zarqawi's group of practitioners of what experts say will be the future of warfare.[13]

As with later insurgent leaders and movements in the twentieth and early twenty-first century, albeit on a different dimension, the realisation of the potential of mass communication, the sense of timing, the mass outreach, all exploited for insurgency and raising finances, were being perfected by Collins almost 100 years earlier.

State sponsorship of insurgency and terrorism

There is a significant contrast. This concerns the Volunteers of 1916 and the IRA and the Anglo-Irish War on the one hand and the later IRA or PIRA on the other, and the issue of state sponsorship or obtaining funds from the enemy of the opponent. In stark terms state sponsorship of terrorism is one country funding subversive or insurgent groups engaged in political against another country, that second country being the opponent or enemy of the sponsoring country.

The leaders of the 1916 Rising unequivocally sought military support from Germany. Despite Casement's efforts in his visits to Germany, no manpower was committed, but an arms shipment was sent on, to coincide with the scheduled start of the 1916 Rising. However, by a combination of ill-luck and miscommunication the arms cargo of the *Aud* never reached the insurgents. The limited German military support was acknowledged by the leaders of the 1916 Rising in their signed proclamation (and guaranteed them a death sentence under the treason statute). However, the 1916 insurgents neither asked for, nor were given, any financial support from Germany.

It was commonly held amongst the British military during and in the aftermath of the 1916 Rising that the insurgents were being paid at least in part, by Germany.[14] Pearse, in his court martial, made strenuous efforts to deny this, categorically stating that the Irish rebels neither asked for, nor received, any German finances.[15] Casement made failed attempts during his pre-1916 visits to Germany to turn and recruit British prisoners of Irish descent into an Irish unit fighting on the side of Germany, resulting in only a handful of volunteers, some of whom – as in the case of the later would-be informant Quinlisk – had mixed motives for joining. (So insignificant was the contingent of "volunteers" that at one stage the German High Command, desperate to find a use for them, contemplated arrangements for deploying them to assist Turkey in buttressing Turkey's eastern front.[16]) For his entire stay in Germany, Casement was given by the German government 8,000 marks for expenses, which he scrupulously accounted for, and never used nor retained any of this for any other purpose.[17] Just before and during the Anglo-Irish War, as has been seen, Collins and de Valera sought funds from the United States. However, the United States could not and would not be considered an enemy of Britain in the sense that it would be funding an insurgency against its enemy. Moreover, the donations were sought and came from popular sections, albeit widespread, of the population, not from the US government as an act of policy; indeed, President Wilson carefully – and publicly – ensured that he and the US government avoided any form of recognition of de Valera's cause. Furthermore, the nature of the funds was carefully considered by both Collins and de Valera. In early 1922 the AARIR offered $100,000 jointly to both sides in the pro- and anti-Treaty split to assist in convening a general election throughout

Ireland to settle the issue. Collins and de Valera both refused the funding, publicly stressing that it was entirely up to the Irish people to finance their own elections.

This can be contrasted with the later IRA, or PIRA, of the mid to late twentieth century. They unequivocally sought and gained state funding from what can safely described as an enemy of Britain at the time, i.e. the Libyan regime of Colonel Ghaddafi. This long-term state-sponsored financing arrived in three phases. These periods were 1972 to 1975, 1981 to 1984 and 1984 to 1987. Betwwen 1972 and 1975 there were several proposed projects and meetings in Libya. To facilitate, PIRA sent and Libya accepted and "accredited" a de facto permanent representative in Libya. This liaison eventually broke down due to the representative from PIRA acting too much on his own initiative (possibly with personal profit motives) which caused mutual distrust between IRA and the Libyan régime. However, during this three-year period the equivalent of $3.5 million in cash was sent from Libya to PIRA.

Contacts and liaison between PIRA and the Libyan régime were cautiously renewed in 1981. No arms deals were formulated, but over the following three years a series of payments were made to PIRA totalling the equivalent of $1.5 million.

Then in a two-year period between 1984 and 1986, UK-Libyan relations dramatically worsened. In 1984, following the killing of a British police officer in St James' Square, London from automatic fire from the Libyan Embassy during an anti-Ghaddafi demonstration, diplomatic relations between the two countries were broken off. Two years later, US service personnel were amongst the killed and injured in a discotheque bombing in Berlin. The Ghaddafi régime was blamed for planning the attack and sponsoring those responsible and the United States air force made retaliatory bombing raids on Tripoli and Benghazi. The planes took off from, and were serviced by, British RAF airfields.

PIRA-Libyan cooperation intensified and PIRA once again placed an "accredited" representative in Tripoli, "including the IRA" although by this time most foreign terrorist groups had established such an office in Tripoli "including the IRA".[18] Two arms consignments from Libya were successfully smuggled by sea to PIRA. The arms shipments sent were large, but the third, the main consignment consisting of 150 tonnes of armaments, was intercepted by the British navy in 1987. However, PIRA had already gained large amounts of small arms and, more important, the equivalent from Libya of $5 million as a "first instalment". (The second $5 million was withheld by the Libyan régime which was disappointed and suspicious of the failed arms shipment.)

In the 1970s and 1980s, in a period spanning 15 years, the equivalent of $10 million was given by the Ghaddafi Libyan régime direct to PIRA. During the interception and seizure of the third, unsuccessful arms consignment, one of the sailors on board the intercepted vessel threw a large sealed box overboard. The authorities immediately deployed navy divers, but they failed to recover the item. Unconfirmed reports stated that sometime later PIRA sent its own diver down, and recovered the sealed box. This apparently contained between £40,000 to £50,000 cash, thoughtfully included by the Ghaddafi régime in the consignment.

The overall result of this period of the 1970s and 1980s was a somewhat obvious contrast between the original IRA of Collins' era and PIRA. In the second decade of the twentieth century, the IRA of Collins and the Anglo-Irish War was under considerable strain and certainly not awash with funds. Collins expenditure on Defence in 1921 was £137,483,[19] monies which had to be found from his Ministry of Finance.

By contrast, in the later decades of the twentieth century, the massive funds to PIRA sent by their state sponsor, the Ghaddafi régime in Libya, meant that PIRA had substantial, even ample funding. The control of finances within PIRA was generally efficient, but somewhat ad hoc with records and accounting being somewhat disorganised.[20] One of the chief finance officers of PIRA during the 1980s was known to automatically state, when his opinion was sought during discussions regarding projected attacks or targeting

there's always a float, there's money available.[21]

Large cash reserves were stored in many guises. There was report of large cash reserves specially packed and hidden in plain sight in farm milk churns, one of which through genuine error was collected, transported and went missing.[22] It was careless, it was embarrassing and it was costly. However, it was not a financial disaster to PIRA. Irish insurgents frequently cited the maxim "the enemy of my enemy is my friend", and in the case of Ghaddafi's Libya in the late twentieth century, it was a wealthy friend to PIRA.

One financial aspect common to both the IRA of Collins and the later PIRA occurred in the late 1990s. As a result of developing a "long war" strategy since the end of the 1970s, illegal fundraising and clandestine transfers of monies were geared to the creation of a PIRA-controlled "parallel economy". This would produce a continuous source of funding – adding to the substantial assets from Libya – and also strengthening PIRA's economic and social integration within the nationalist communities. (This latter objective would also alleviate any desertions from PIRA to the breakaway groups, Real IRA and Continuity IRA.) In order to fulfil this, the leadership created a "Finance Department" to oversee PIRA's financial operations and subsequent handling, management and use of funds. This Finance Department imposed a system of strict discipline, and centralised control and accountability in the areas of criminal fundraising.[23] The departure from the comparatively ad hoc fund flow and management of PIRA in the 1980s, was PIRA adopting a more accountancy-based centralised control system. This was akin to government structure envisaged and established by Collins in 1919 where funding records of different departments went to, and financial authority to dispense funds originated from, the Ministry of Finance.

State response to insurgency: retaliation by economic warfare

During the Anglo-Irish War, de facto economic warfare was waged. In early April 1920, a series of raids on tax offices started, which eventually covered most of the 26 counties. The resulting destruction of tax records damaged the British administration's revenue raising by taxation, and forced them to heavily rely on Customs and Excise duties for revenue.[24] During the later stages it was waged by retaliation and depriving the enemy of resources. This took the form of organised arson, burning down residential houses and business premises. British destruction of property began in mid-1920 and was officially sanctioned in mid-1921. Field Marshal Montgomery, at the time a major in the British 17th Infantry Brigade later recalled

... it never bothered me how many houses were burnt.[25]

Liam Lynch, commander of the 1 Southern Division IRA pronounced in an official despatch that since the enemy was inclined to organise arson against the populace, the IRA might as well do its share.[26] To some extent it worked for both sides in terms of terror and intimidation and as a deterrent against cooperating with the enemy, but it inevitably resulted to the detriment of the Irish side in that the impacted populace had less available monies to contribute to the IRA.

A more modern – and perhaps more ruthless – form of state retaliation occurred in the mid-2000s during the increase by various Palestinian militant groups in recruiting and deploying suicide bombers targeting Israeli security forces. The Israelis, on learning that various militant groups laid aside and paid a form of pension to the bereaved families of those suicide bombers who had committed the final act, promptly deployed HGV building vehicles and machinery to pull down and destroy those family homes, nullifying any benefit such payments would bring and as a deterrent to any form of attacks.[27]

Phasing and grouping of accounts

This *modus operandi* of illicit monies transfer involves using multiple accounts and transferring over a period of time parts of the funds from one account to another, accounts either within the same bank or a different bank, and banks within the same jurisdiction or in other countries. Under the guise of individuals merely moving funds to another of their accounts, the monies are transferred through, the accounts are gradually emptied and eventually all monies have been funnelled out and are transferred to the next stage of the laundering, often in a different jurisdiction. This *modus operandi* is used successfully in several areas of financial crime, including terrorist financing. The number of accounts and periods of time for the differing transfers vary and it is difficult for law enforcement and bank compliance officers to detect indicators or patterns.

In terms of investigating Collin's bank account structures, the inquiry set up by Alan Bell was hampered through lack of investigative powers and sanctions which are available to modern anti-money laundering and anti-terrorist financing inquiries. Modern investigators have the benefit of obtaining bank account freezing orders, and production orders, effectively opening wide swathes of information contained in banks accounts. It appears that Bell was not even able to dismiss the witnesses and order them to reappear again before him, this time bringing bank documentation.

In the immediate post 2001 period a US senior prosecutor, seconded to a coordinated anti-terrorist financing Task Force, asserted that

> the ancient concept that bank secrecy must be prepared to keep a gentleman's financial affairs confidential – dating back to the days when only gentlemen had chequeing accounts and their servants did not – must give way to current reality.[28]

In the era during which the Irish struggle and conflict was occurring in the second decade of the twentieth century the heyday of domestic service was waning, but bank secrecy and the absolute confidentiality of client bank accounts were still held as indisputably paramount. At the start of Bell's ill-fated inquiry, the *Irish Independent* asserted that there was strong resentment by the public to the whole inquiry.[29] The *Freemans Journal* described the Bell inquiry as unprecedented and unethical, and that Dublin Castle was wrong to authorise any investigation which would result in bankers revealing information about client accounts. The inquiry was

> a sensational and far reaching encroachment of the ... Irish Executive on fundamental citizens' rights.

> ... to destroy the confidence of the public in the safety and secrecy of bankers' books is a matter which everyone ... must deeply deplore.

and declared itself totally opposed to the inquiry.[30]

Collins, in apparently opening an account in his own name in one of the Dublin banks, may have been somewhat careless. Whilst Bell did not obtain an actual admission that there was an account in this name from the bankers he interviewed, he gained enough from their evasive answers to be reasonably sure, and had he lived he would no doubt have vigorously pursued inquiries further. James O Mara in the situation of the United States Loan was more cautious. He monitored the bank draft payees, and counselled against using the same front names more than once, and certainly not using the same name more than twice.[31]

However, Collins skilfully used the accounts – of the ten Dublin branches of the three Dublin banks, and banks in the provinces together with the Sinn Fein bank and a London-based and a Paris-based bank – to skilfully transfer and conceal the funds by phasing and grouping of accounts.

In the late nineteenth and early twentieth century criminal groups and militant liberation movements engaged in political violence and terrorist groups used this technique.

In the 1990s the collapse of the Bank of Credit and Commerce International (BCCI) broke upon the international news. Long established as a combination of a quasi-philanthropic venture for international banking for comparatively underprivileged Third World peoples and a new venture in international banking, by the mid-1980s disquieting intelligence and reports had come to the attention of various US and criminal intelligence agencies of the vulnerability (and almost certain exploitation) of this international financial institution for money laundering. By 1986 it was "an open secret" amongst law enforcement agencies, financial regulatory bodies and financiers alike, that it was reputational bad news to be associated with BCCI.[32] Law enforcement authorities of several different countries, including the USA, Britain, Germany and Middle Eastern countries made lengthy investigations and some indicators linking the bank to international terrorism came to light. Follow-up investigations focussed on possible links to the Abu Nidal Organisation (ANO). Inquiries in Britain and Europe established seven international companies, either with the remit of import-export, or financial services, three were the principal companies and the other four were subsidiaries owned or joint owned by the other three. The seven companies had a total of 15 directors, some of whom were directors of more than one of the companies.

Tracing the transactions, the investigators found layering of the illicit funds carried out in one of two ways. Either by sending and receiving payments through several BCCI accounts held by one of the directors of one of the four subsidiary companies, transferring monies back and forward, but reducing the amounts in the accounts each time and eventually funnelling it through so it finally ended up in two of the accounts; or by sending and receiving funds to and from the corporate accounts of one of the three holding companies. Then the monies from these two flows were sent to a third individual who had four different accounts in BCCI. The monies would go into two of the four accounts, then be transferred in phases to the other two accounts. Then this third individual would arrange the transfer of the monies in the latter two accounts would be sent either to accounts in Syrian banks (whose account holders were linked to certain high profile figures in the then Syrian political régime), or onto two other international banks. If they went to the two international banks, the monies would then be transferred to the Syrian banks.

The whole illicit transfer process was a neo-classical example of phasing and grouping of accounts, executed in two stages. The first stage involved the moving of the funds either by the four director's accounts at BCCI and the large-scale deposits, then phased withdrawals, or the corporate accounts of the holding company, and then both streams onto the accounts of the third individual. The second stage was the accounts of the third individual, the inter transfers of his or her four BCCI accounts and then onto the two-way transfer to the Syrian-based accounts. Over two years, in five periods of intense transactional activity, $1,200,000 was clandestinely transferred to ANO-linked entities and individuals through the *modus operandi* of phasing and grouping of accounts.[33]

In 2000, partly by this *modus operandi*, funds were transferred through one of the largest banks in Jordan to HAMAS and HAMAS-affiliated groups. In 2015, the bank agreed to an out of court settlement against a civil action by US claimants who were victims of terrorist attacks, although maintaining that it did not knowingly facilitate terrorist financing.[34] Apparently some of the funds were transferred from a Saudi based fund though the bank accounts which transferred monies in timed amounts to other accounts within the bank, and then withdrawn in phases. The withdrawn funds were, per the plaintiffs, sent to families of deceased Palestinians, including HAMAS suicide bombers.[35]

In 2003 an international terrorist group used wire transfers to transfer illicit funds on an international basis. The monies were eventually used for paying rent for safe houses, buying and selling vehicles and purchasing electronic components with which to construct explosive devices. Part of the illicit transfer process, in order to conceal and confuse the movement of funds for the bank in the receiving country, having received the monies, was to transfer the monies to and from other bank accounts managed by the terrorist organisation's financial officer.[36]

Modern anti-money laundering and anti-terrorist financing have picked up on the phasing and grouping of accounts *modus* and issue red flag warnings to financial institutions[37] to be vigilant against this. In the early twentieth century Collins had grasped the principle and skilfully used it. As a *modus operandi* it is still used by those transferring illicit funds for political violence and conflict.

Bank robberies

From the very first period of this book, that is in the period of the anarchists of the pre-1914 era, bank robberies were a potential source of funding.

Often the anarchists were self-financing. This could be accomplished comfortably by such individuals as Prince Peter Kropotkin, born into the imperial Russian aristocracy and who had experience as a soldier, in travel and was a trained geographer, and much sought after in European academic and fashionable circles. He could rely on a fairly steady income from scholarly articles in a geographical journal and for the prestigious publication *Nineteenth Century*, as well as using his journalistic skills in producing polemical articles on the forthcoming war and revolution, which he endlessly prophesied. The French anarchist Grave also lived by writing on a more precarious basis. He earned meagrely by printing and typesetting, and also writing books and revolutionary tracts. He lived frugally in a single room which served as his home and workplace.

The Italian anarchist, Malatesta, having forsaken his well-to-do family and his university studies, learned an electrician's trade to provide for himself and some small surplus funds for the struggle. Later, as part of his escape from an Italian prison (to which he had been sentenced to five years for subversive activities) he stowed away in a packing case on a boat bound to Argentina. Part of his escape plan was to make for Argentina, and there, prospect for gold in Patagonia, which would be used to fund the struggle. He made Argentina, found gold in Patagonia and staked a claim, which the Argentine government promptly confiscated. The French anarchist Ravachol turned to criminal activity, perpetrating on an ad hoc basis fencing and exchanging counterfeit monies, petty theft and grave robbing, all of which kept him in funds whilst he engaged upon his serial murders in the name of anarchy.

However, in terms of more organised activity, bank robberies were a common *modus operandi* of raising funds amongst the anarchists. One Belgian-French anarchist cell, the Bonnot group, followed the teachings of Proudhon and Bakunin in the early twentieth century. The seven principal members perpetrated a series of bank robberies, expensive vehicle thefts and a robbery on a wealthy property. True to the anarchist creed they were indifferent to human life and during the course of these robberies they murdered cashiers, the householder and the domestic servant, an owner of one hijacked vehicle and a pursuing police officer, between November 1911 and mid-1912. They were apprehended in France after increased police resources and paramilitary units were deployed, with several of the group being imprisoned and two being executed. Their brief period of activity had netted over 70,000 French Francs to the cause.

During the same period a Polish-based group of Russian anarchists, the Grupa Rewolucjonistów Mścicieli, (Revolutionaries and Avengers Group) robbed shops and banks in the Lodz region on a regular basis in order to finance themselves for purchasing weapons, and to provide for families of members of the group who had been imprisoned, or killed by security forces. Probably the most famous or notorious anarchist revolutionary, Benevento Durrutti, active in anarchist circles in Spain at the same time as the Anglo-Irish War, and eventually to become leader of one of the principal republican militant groups in the Spanish Civil War in the 1930s, sustained his groups when under extreme pressure by fleeing to South America and carrying out multiple bank robberies in Chile and Argentina.[38]

Bank robberies, as has been seen, were a source of revenue during the Anglo-Irish War, although strenuous efforts were made by the IRA to ensure that exploitation of the situation in Ireland by criminal robbers targeting banks, was prevented. In future times PIRA in the 1970s engaged in bank robberies as part of their revenue raising activities.[39] An intelligence report by the British Army[40] cited this as a source of revenue. Raids occurred both in Ireland and in the UK. The raids on banks in London, carried out by a group of three individuals and a driver, netted in the early 1970s a few thousand pounds in cash. A small part of this was kept back to maintain the UK IRA cell(s); the rest, the bulk of the haul, was then physically couriered by train to Liverpool, then by ferry to Dublin and then to the offices of Provisional Sinn Fein, and eventually distributed to IRA cells in the north.[41] An Irish historian, quoting this report, states that it underestimates the revenue and places PIRA funds from bank robberies (the PIRA "... particular philosophy of banking, based on withdrawals only") as gaining £1 million by mid-1978.[42] In 1998 a criminologist specialising in terrorism assessed that 50 per cent of all bank robberies in the Republic of Ireland had PIRA involvement, and that bank robberies contributed the equivalent of £1,025,000 to their funds, although other *modus operandi* on fundraising were being developed and gaining more.[43] A confidential report to the Independent Monitoring Commission in northern Ireland of 2006, stated that PIRA engaged in bank robberies in the 1970s, but that in the late 1980s PIRA had adopted a long-term, sophisticated strategy of laundering large amounts of funds gained from other forms of crime which would ensure a long-term, steady flow of incoming funds, such as smuggling, counterfeiting and various types of fraud. However, that bank robberies had not been abandoned as form of raising large amounts of cash quickly.[44] In 2004, PIRA[45] attempted to establish a massive treasury by a single bank robbery which their Belfast and South Armagh brigades carried out in December. Two officials from the Northern Bank in Belfast were kidnapped and given instructions to cooperate with the robbery team the following morning, on threat of death to their families, who were also being held by PIRA. The two officials went to work at the bank the next day, and dutifully followed instructions, affording the robbery team access to and leading them to the vaults. In the evening, other members of the team drove a van to the bank and loaded it up with crates filled with cash, drove away, returned empty and filled the van up a second time. An estimated total of £26.5 million was taken, too much. Of the cash, £10.5 million was in new Northern banknotes; given the size of the amount, Northern Bank quickly decided and implemented an immediate change in the design of their banknotes rendering the stolen ones conspicuous and eventually unusable. PIRA encountered extreme difficulties in laundering the remainder. In the words of one former law enforcement officer at the time

> ... they took so much monies that they didn't know what to do with it so they tied to destroy the surplus.[46]

Less than three months later individuals were arrested by the Garda in Passage West, the authorities having been alerted by huge columns of smoke which turned out to be attempts to incinerate massive quantities of banknotes. These arrests led to other successful investigations. Paradoxically, PIRA in its largest ever bank robbery, had been too successful.[47]

Other domestic terrorist groups in the 1990s also targeted banks. In a 12-month period 1994 to1995, in the United States an extreme right organisation, the Aryan Republican Army stole over $200,000 from banks in four mid-western states. Funds were then channelled to other right wing militant groups in the United States.[48]

In the 1980s and 1990s, during what may be termed the heyday of increased public and private sector awareness of the threat of money laundering, the physical threat to banks and financial institutions – raids and robberies – was deemed to have diminished, certainly in relation to the other threats to such institutions. Lower level criminal groups and gangs tended to move away from bank robberies, "pavement artists" to the rapidly expanding high profit and comparatively low risk criminal activity of drug dealing. On a higher level of criminality, organised crime groups were contemptuous of such robberies, and held that banks were exploitable not for the assets they held but for the opportunities they offered for laundering and illicit transfer of funds already gained from drug trafficking, extortion, organised prostitution and in a later era, large-scale illegal immigration and human trafficking.

In the fight against crime during the 1990s, the resulting threat to banks was perceived as "fourfold", falling foul of the regulatory authorities, unwitting criminal involvement, physical impact and reputational damage.[49] The first two can be countered and prevented by banks improving and perfecting due diligence and compliance measures. The latter involves an efficient suspicious transaction reporting system and full cooperation with law enforcement. The third, the physical, was held to constitute the least important threat. The fourth – reputational damage – was perceived to be by far the greatest threat and could be caused by any, and even a single incident, of failure of compliance and regulatory procedures. In some more cynical law enforcement circles "reputational damage" was viewed as leverage which could be used as pressure against individual banks in investigations, should it be felt that a bank was not divulging enough information, or giving this information up too slowly.[50]

In the first decade of the twenty-first century, sanctions by regulatory authorities increased sharply against banks who had failed to meet with standards of compliance. Fines of millions were imposed upon errant banks. ABN AMRO in 2007 was fined €80 million for a genuine mistake[51] in a long transaction which included a beneficiary who was a national of, and residing in, a country which was then the subject of international sanctions. In 2008, Lloyds was fined £180 million for attempting to establish a business relationship with a financial institution based in a country which was at the time subject to international sanctions. In the second decade of the twenty-first century, fines imposed on errant banks ran into billions; Deutsche Bank in 2016 paid to the US regulatory authorities just over $7 billion, and that was a compromise settlement to the impending fine of over $12 billion;[52] in 2017 it had a further fine imposed upon it by US and UK regulatory authorities of $600 million for its involvement in money laundering. With such fines – irrespective of that the fined international banks had more than sufficient assets to be able to well afford to pay – it followed that the spectre or threat to the banks of "reputational damage" would be raised even higher on the fourfold list or scale of threat.

However, two trends disrupted and unhinged this perceived and established wisdom of the fourfold scale of threats.

The first trend was the disconnect between the increase in regulatory intervention and massive punitive fines and damage to banks' reputations. The post-2007 series of financial crises had already damaged trust and reputation in banks and the banking profession (as well as damaging trust in governments to avert and deal with such crises). In the words of one distinguished academic

> ... the public generally ceased to care about reputation ... also there is apparently little or no competition to which they can turn and transfer their assets and accounts ... all banks are held in contempt and are all in the naughty corner.[53]

International financial consultants are sceptical about how much a priority reputational damage remains to banks.[54] One representative of an international financial consultancy stated

> ... nowadays account holders large and small, household and corporate, on being informed of yet another banking scandal, or being informed that yet again a that bank has unwittingly facilitated money laundering accept that the bank has been found wanting in integrity- but customer service prevail, provided the accounts are secure, provided the transfer, deposit, withdrawal and credit facilities remain operating speedily and efficiently, life goes on.[55]

Another financial source opined

> Reputational damage was indeed a major threat in the age of the rise of the drug cartels and in the aftermath of the terrorist attacks of 9/11.

But now with all the scandals of banks, and the contempt in which banks and bankers are held for the financial crises reputational threat loses its sting. Banks co-operate because – sometimes – they want to do the right thing especially in terms of terrorism whose attacks and explosions impact on everyone, including banks and banking staff.[56]

Studies and monitoring by a Canadian university, the University of Manitoba, were made on four financial institutions subjected to heavy regulatory fines in the second decade of the twenty-first century. The financial institutions were Wachovia (now part of Wells Fargo, having been merged over a three-year period) fined $160 million in 2010; Standard Chartered, fined $220 million in 2012; HSBC, fined $1.9 billion in 2012; and BNP Paribas fined $8.9 billion in 2014. Analysis was carried out on the public reaction and the respective financial states of the four individual banks. In the case of one there was a temporary fall in share value in the first three-quarters after the fine was imposed and full details made public, but share prices afterwards recovered and substantially increased by the first quarter of the second year after the fine. However, apart from this there was little or no sign of financial depreciation, and public and customer awareness was that of quiet resignation and acceptance. Despite the high profile public fines there was, in summary

> ... no evidence of significant impact on reputational or financial factors of the four banks.[57]

The second trend which disrupts the fourfold scale of threats was the advent of international terrorism and the physical threat, hitherto deemed a poor fourth in the fourfold scale. This threat increased dramatically. The increase was due partly to the iconic and symbolic ethos of banks and financial institutions as soft targets for terrorist groups, and also the contents of the banks were an easy form of illicit revenue.

In Spain, between 1991 and 2002, Euskadi Ta Askatasuna (ETA) attacked no less than 2,120 financial premises, banks, insurance companies and investment firms. The object of this was summarised at an ETA leadership meeting in September 2002

> ... attack vital targets such as the Bank of Spain, the Madrid and Barcelona Stock Exchanges.

> I'm convinced that they *(Spanish government)* will sit down and negotiate.[58]

Another country, Greece, may serve as an example. In November 2000, CITIBANK premises in Athens were attacked by a left-wing group. Then in 2002, the Revolutionary Struggle came into being. It was formed from the remnants of the violent militant organisation N17 following the arrests of several of its prominent members by security forces in 2002, and it also took several ideological principles from another left-wing group, the Revolutionary People's Struggle. It engaged in a campaign of violence. In June 2007 it was designated by the European Union as a terrorist organisation and in 2009 the United States designated it as a Foreign Terrorist Organisation. When the financial crisis started to severely impact, throughout the 2009, the Revolutionary Struggle made banks their targets, by car bombing a branch in Athens of CITIBANK. In March of the same year another branch of CITIBANK in Athens was damaged by a car bomb, with Revolutionary Group claiming responsibility. Two months later it attacked a branch of EuroBank in Athens and in September of the same year bombed the Athens Stock Exchange. Later during the Greek financial crisis and the controversy with the European Union bailout, in April 2014 Revolutionary Struggle claimed responsibility for a car bombing on the Bank of Greece and Piraeus Bank. These attacks were targeting the symbols of financial repression.

However, there also occurred raids for terrorist revenue in Greece. In August 2016, Greek police arrested a known terrorist, a member of the small left-wing group Cells of Fire, together with a wanted bank robber, Marios Seisidis. Seisidis was wanted for over ten years as being one of the three bank robbers who robbed seven banks in the 2002–2006 period, taking a total of €700,000. The arrested terrorist, Costas Sakkas, denied formal links to the bank robbers but admitted being "on friendly terms" with them.[59] In September 2016, members of Revolutionary Struggle in Greece were suspected of robbing a bank in central Greece, gaining over €150,000. The *modus operandi* of the raid conformed to a pattern of similar robberies over the previous 12 months.[60]

In 2002, the Taliban, hastily fleeing Kabul during the United States' airstrikes and invasion, robbed the vaults of the Afghan Central Bank at gunpoint and seized $5.3 million in American dollar bills and about $330,000 in Pakistani rupees.[61] In another continent, during the post 9/11 period, and at the same year as the PIRA Northern Bank robbery, a further advancement was made by terrorist fundraising targeting banks. In 2004, Imam Samudra, one of the perpetrators of the 2002 Bali bombing, was in an Indonesian prison awaiting execution. In his cell, he conceived and perfected his *modus operandi* of internet bank fraud. Part of his online message and appeals to potential recruits for Jemmaah Islammiyah (by this time a disparate and multi-faction terrorist group) was exhorting followers to raise funds by online bank fraud, and he posted instructions on how to carry this out. He was executed in 2008 by an Indonesian firing squad (although his son continued the cause of jihad, eventually being killed fighting in Syria in 2015[62]). In 2011, Rizki Gunawan,[63] leader of the Sadar cell of a Jemmaah Islammiyah group in Medan was arrested. He had defrauded banks and savings institutions by online fraud, gaining the equivalent of over $500,000 to sustain his terrorist cell. His *modus operandi* corresponded to the detailed instructions and tuition posted by Imam Samudra.

With the rise of Islamic State and their sudden taking control of swathes of territory in Syria and Iraq in 2014, banks in the occupied territories were looted. A single raid alone on the central bank in Mosul immediately after the taking of the city, yielded ISIS $256 million in cash and some gold bullion.[64] During the looting of the banks in occupied territories Islamic State (IS) gained a further estimated $90 million from 60 branches of banks. IS then exploitated more revenue in an unorthodox way for a further limited period. Iraqi government employees in occupied territories were still paid. However, understandably, the Iraqi central bank ceased sending funds to banks in occupied areas. By an arrangement, the Iraqi government employees in occupied areas, still in post in the IS territory, travelled to unoccupied areas – mainly Kirkup – to collect salaries, and on their return paid a percentage to IS to continue residence with their families and their (repressed) lifestyle. This source of revenue to IS was reduced then stopped by the end of 2015 when the Iraqui Central Bank simply ceased paying the salaries.

The *modus operandi* of the IRA of the 1920s, that of raising illicit funds by robbing banks, however unsophisticated and basic in the modern era of the twenty-first century, is still perpetrated by groups engaged on political violence and terrorism.

Customs and "tolls" (extortion)

The anti-Treaty IRA or Republicans in the early stages of the Civil War tried to impose their own "income tax" on comparatively wealthy tradesmen and businesses in Cork; however sympathetic or otherwise such businesses were to the Republic, there was a surprisingly concerted and effective resistance to the income tax and the anti-Treaty IRA forces in Cork abandoned this attempt.[65] However, they managed to obtain some incoming revenues from Customs duties on imported goods and ad hoc tolls on the passage of goods through and into the port of Cork throughout the period they held Cork.[66] This simple, but effective *modus operandi* of financing was also used to good effect by the terrorist group al Shabaab. This group, in the lengthy struggle for control of Somalian territory, gained control of the ports of Gedo and Kismayo for a period of between 18 months and two years between 2010 and 2012 (before Ethiopian troops occupied one port and the Kenyan navy bombarded the other). It was only a short period, but the tolls gained on the export of charcoal from Somalia gave them a potential revenue of $15 million per year.[67] IS imposed such "tolls" in 2015, when their territorial gains through swathes of Iraq and Syria were at their largest extent. During the rise and expansion of IS in the region, which was comparatively sudden and swift, there was – inevitably – massive disruption of regional cross border trade. However, their remained some flows by road traffic. IS accordingly turned this to an ad hoc form of illicit revenue by imposing "tolls" of a $200 "road tax" on vehicles crossing IS territory from northern Iraq and an $800 per truck or lorry "customs duty" on trucks transiting IS territory along the Syrian–Jordanian border.

Cash couriers

Collins recognised the value of, and fully exploited, cash couriers. During the raising of the National Loan couriers came from the provinces discreetly carrying monies collected for the Loan. It could be a dangerous task. In late September 1920 one cash courier from Limerick, John Lynch, a Sinn Fein county councillor, arrived in Dublin couriering National Loan monies which he had arranged to hand over to Collins and his Loan workers in Dublin. Whilst at his hotel he was attacked and shot by two undercover British officers. His Sinn Fein political affiliation was the reason for his assassination.[68] The monies he was carrying apparently remained unseized. Collins often acted as his own cash courier. On one occasion in early 1921, when travelling around Dublin, he was stopped by two Black and Tans, whilst in possession of £16,000 of the National Loan. Fortunately, the two officers had been drinking and made a bungled pat-down search of Collins. The vital funds remained undiscovered.[69]

During the raising of the Loan and moving the monies, Collins valued Donnchadha's couriering activities so highly that he wished to raise Donnchadha's salary to £500 (the same as that of a Dail Cabinet Minister).[70] One of the major points of concern for the manager of the Hibernian Bank in 1922, when warning Collins of the funds vulnerable to anti-Treaty IRA seizure, was the hoard of £80,000 cash being held in the Cork branch of the National Bank of Ireland.[71]

Yet cash couriering as a *modus operandi* for illicit fund transfer for terrorism appeared to be a strategic intelligence blind spot, even after 9/11. These attacks resulted in a recognition of the increased importance of the financial dimension of terrorism and a spate of international anti-terrorist financing measures. But cash remained underfocussed.

After the attacks of 9/11, the UN Security Council passed resolution 1373, calling upon and exhorting (indeed, given the intense climate of the times, ordering) countries to combat terrorist financing; the Financial Action Task Force (FATF), within a month of 9/11, indicated in its Eight Special Recommendations for the guidance of countries on which areas and *modus operandi* of terrorist financing countries should focus. The Special Recommendations were comprehensive and covered the necessity for updating and ratifying of anti-terrorist financing Conventions. They called on states to criminalise the financing of terrorism; specified financial intelligence exchange and bank transaction reporting systems, and – radically – called for international freezing and seizing of suspected terrorist assets. They also focused attention on terrorist use of the formal and informal banking systems and methods of transferring monies, including wire transfer institutions. They omitted one basic method, namely, the use of cash couriers. It was only during the period from 2004 to 2005, with terrorist financing cases coming to light involving the use of cash couriers, that a Ninth Special Recommendation was formulated, and it was not until 2007 that it was ratified and that cash declaration reporting systems were uniformly in place within the EU.

And yet, in the 1990s in the case of al Qaeda, one courier alone, Jamal al Fadl, an al Qaeda defector, confessed that he was given over $100,000 to physically transport to Jordan and hand over to various individuals for operations.[72] During the period 1999–2000 a series of cash courier journeys and meetings occurred in hotels in south-east Asia, where cash couriers of al Qaeda and associated *jihadi* organisations handed over sums of monies and senior couriers attended meetings with operational teams and allocated certain sums for the operation, resulted in over $250,000 being cash couriered over three continents, and sums being allocated for direct involvement in the bombing of USS *Cole*, the 9/11 attacks in New York the Bali bombing of 2002 and the Djakarta hotel bombing of 2003.[73]

The tardiness in post 9/11 recognition of cash couriers was acknowledged by Jimmy Gurule, former head of anti-terrorist financing in the US Treasury from 2001 to 2003 and responsible for all intelligence, policy and training in anti-terrorist financing. He stated in 2005

> I really do not know why we were so late in recognizing the use of cash couriers for terrorist financing[74]

and three years later, in an authoritative work on legal responses against financing of terrorism, he went on to state

> Cash couriers are a major method to move funds globally.[75]

Between the Anglo-Irish War of the 1920s and attacks of 9/11 there had been a previous terrorist liberation struggle which was well known to historians, strategic intelligence analysts and reflective law enforcement officers alike. From 1956 to 1961 the Algerian War of Independence occurred, in which the Algerian National Liberation Front (FLN) militants fought an insurgent guerrilla war against France. As the war intensified, certain people in France became convinced that Algerian independence was both just and inevitable. One such individual was Francis Jeansen, an academic and editor of left-wing publications. He formed a small network which gave shelter and support to National Liberation Front (FLN) militants on the run. However, he also expanded his activities and smuggled funds out of the country that had been raised in France by sympathisers. The smuggling was carried out by cash couriers.[76] Jeanson's network grew to 40 full-time regular couriers smuggling cash in suitcases out of France, where the funds could be deposited for temporary storage in Swiss banks. The courier network covered the whole of France, with cash funds distributed in safe houses, ready for gathering together and collection for "runs" over the border. Jeanson carried out these activities without regular pay from the FLN and with neither initial approval nor regular orders from the FLN. The Jeanson network operated for just over three years, a vital period in the six-year struggle, and in one year alone was responsible for ten billion francs being made available to the FLN. (The modern equivalent is approximately £1 million at the post-2001 rate of exchange.)

After 9/11 it was not until 2007 that Europol, the EU law enforcement intelligence agency, in its annual terrorist threat assessment, mentioned cash couriers as a *modus operandi* for terrorist fund transfer;[77] later, in 2015, Europol produced a report emphasising that cash remained an essential *modus operandi* of money laundering by criminal groups.[78] In 2008 the FATF, in a report on terrorist financing, pointed out that cash couriers and the physical movement of cash was one way terrorists can move funds and circumvent anti-money laundering and counter-terrorist safeguards.[79] Later, in 2015, a FATF report on terrorist financing, which focussed on emerging risks and trends, stated the *prevalent nature* of cash continuing to be part of terrorist operations and the cross border cash couriering to be a *modus operandi* of illicit fund transfer,[80] and in the same year the FATF regional body for the Middle East and the Maghreb produced a report specifically on money laundering through the physical transportation of cash, stating that it was widely used by criminals and for the financing of terrorism.[81]

One terrorist movement, arguably underestimated, is heavily dependent upon cash couriers and has been since before 9/11 and remains so. Its fighters are the Naxalites, a rural Maoist Marxist guerrilla movement. Within India they impact upon a broad swathe of north-east, central and southern states. The Maoist groups, or the Naxalite movement, came into being in 1967 from violent and militant splinter groups of the Communist Party of India – Marxist Leninist CPI(ML) which was itself a splinter party, having broken away from the Communist Party of India – Leninist CPI(L) in 1964, which itself had broken away from the Communist Party of India (CPI). These political splits were as a result of the various developments the Communist Party in China, which the CPI, CPI(L) and CPI(ML) all claimed to have allegiance to and derive inspiration from. Thus, the origins of the Naxalites were and remain extreme Marxist. Starting in the late 1960s following an unsuccessful rebellion in the late 1960s Naxalite violence and attacks in India have been continuous. The essence of the struggle is that of agrarian redistribution of wealth, and the main protagonists are the agrarian populace. According to the CPI(ML)

The main force of the democratic revolution led by the working class is the peasantry and the means of struggle is solely violence and militarism.

Armed struggle has absolute primacy over other forms of struggle and there is no alternative to armed struggle – hence the continuation of the violence.[82]

Eleven states of India are affected by Maoist guerrilla groups.[83] The groups engage in open conflict in the field with both the Indian Army and Indian security forces. In 2008, the Prime Minister of India stated that the Maoist groups were "the single largest internal security threat to the Indian state".

For financial support, the Maoist groups rely on monetary contributions from the rural poor, usually given freely, or under a certain combination of empathy and peer pressure. In other cases, the support is that of simple foodstuffs and use of clandestine accommodation. Because of the vast size of the country, the Indian banking system has still not reached a large part of the population. (In 2007, it was estimated that between 60 and 70 per cent of the Indian population did not have any form of bank account.) To move monies, the Maoist or Naxalite groups have established networks of paid and trusted cash couriers, divided into two specialist functions:[84] one function involves couriers moving the funds and the other function is performed by individuals remaining in place, who are responsible for storing the funds. The latter have evolved sophisticated methods of concealing the funds for various periods of time, until collected by a travelling courier, and keep meticulous clandestine records of the funds coming in and out of their charge.

In West Africa, illicit cash couriers are an important component in terrorist fund transfer. Insurgent and terrorist groups fund themselves by varied and pragmatic[85] means. In 2015, Al Qaeda in the Islamic Maghreb (AQIM) were transferring proceeds gained by drug dealing, in large amounts of cash euro, from south Libya via Chad to their bases in Mali. In 2016 Boko Haram used cash couriers to transfer monies across the Chad–Niger border; one courier was intercepted by the authorities carrying the equivalent of $1.2 million in euro, US dollars and other currencies.[86]

Cash couriering is still, in the second decade of the twenty-first century, a principal *modus operandi* of terrorist fund transfer. And in the first decade of the twentieth century, Collins was masterly in its use.

Withholding funds from the central war chest

De Valera' s keeping back substantial amounts of funds raised in the United States intended to support the Dail and IRA struggle in Ireland is not the only time funds raised for insurgent groups have been withheld, or go astray. The FLN, successful in the Algerian War of Independence, mentioned above in the context of cash couriers, also experienced withholding or diversion of funds, although this occurred after the main struggle was over and independence secured. Mohammed Khider, one of the FLN leaders, quarrelled with the new head of state, Ben Bella, and resigned his post as FLN Secretary General in 1963. Khider went into voluntary exile in Spain, taking with him the FLN Treasury, of which as Secretary General of the FLN he had full access. This Treasury consisted of remaining large sum of monies collected from sympathisers in France during the struggle for independence. A year later there was an armed coup against Ben Bella led by one of the Algerian Army leaders, to which Khider and others pledged allegiance and support. The attempted coup was crushed but Ben Bella remained ousted from power. He was replaced by Colonel Boumedienne, the Army leader that had acted quickly and crushed the coup. Khider remained in exile in Spain, still controlling the equivalent of £6 million of FLN funds which he had discreetly deposited in Swiss bank accounts. However, the outcome was not as happy as that eventually experienced by de Valera. In early January 1967 Khider was gunned down in daylight in a Madrid street. The Algerian government took recourse to legal action before the Swiss courts to retrieve the funds. Unfortunately, after six years of legal proceedings, the Swiss courts rejected their claim on the basis that Khider was the real owner as he had opened personal accounts and had deposited the monies into these and that the entire funds may have been raised for the FLN but this at the time had no legal existence.

In south-east Asia in the first decade of the twenty-first century various groups of Jemaah Islamiyah were provided with funds by experienced and trusted cash couriers. Riduan Isamudin, better known as Hambali – eventually arrested and extradited and detained in Guantanamo – was the "travelling central banker"[87] who received large amounts of cash at various meetings throughout south-east Asia, for which he was responsible for distributing to various cells. However, in the half decade after 9/11, when he was providing these funds to the cells to facilitate their planned operations and attacks, on at least three occasions he did not give over all the total monies he had received, but stipulated a maximum amount to the cell leader for each operation, and withheld the rest. In acting thus, he was fully authorised to use his discretion; deciding to keep back part of funds was part of his remit as finance officer of the organisation.

Another example of terrorist leaders withholding funds from "their" organisation is that of al Zarqawi during the Iraqui insurgency of 2004–2009. Zarqawi through certain genius – perverted and horrific but nonetheless extremely able – rose to become effective leader of one of the principal anti-coalition insurgent groups in Iraq in 2004. His successful raising of finances for his group brought him to the attention of al Qaeda leadership which, in a secret communiqué to him sent in person by al Zawahiri, then al Qaeda's overall second in command, politely but firmly pointed out that the financial gains he and his group were accruing belonged to the al Qaeda movement and should be remitted to the central command. The communiqué, intercepted by coalition forces in late 2005, was mistakenly used by strategic analysts dealing with counter-terrorism to support the premise that al Qaeda was devoid of funds and financially finished. The overall premise of al Qaeda being being totally financially degraded was to be proven incorrect by later events.[88]

Irrespective of how al Zawahiri's communiqué to al Zarqawi was interpreted or misinterpreted, al Zarqawi refused point blank to render unto al Qaeda what were the financial gains earned by al Zarqawi and his group. Zarqawi was killed in 2006, but his legacy and strategy of fermenting insurgency and divisions within Iraq far outlasted his death. The funds gained by his group were withheld from the main organisation.

Thus, like the IRA of the Anglo-Irish War, later political violence groups and liberationist militants also experienced in various ways funds collected or allocated to their cause being held back. However, arguably, in none of any of these future occurrences were funds being withheld at such a crucial period in the conflict as those held back by de Valera in the Anglo-Irish War.

Notes

1 Kee *The Green Flag* p. 653
2 Coogan *Ireland since the Rising* p. 63
3 R E Foster *Modern Ireland 1600–1972* (Penguin 1989) p. 489. Even Hart in his candid biography of Collins, *Mick – the real Mick Collins*, in his concluding assessment fully acknowledges Collins' abilities as an organiser and builder of organisations and their invaluable contribution to the struggle in the years 1919–21 p. 423.
4 Dwyer *Big Fellow, Long Fellow* p. 151
5 C Hibbert *The French Revolution* (Penguin 1980) pp. 215–216; C Jones *The Great Nation – France from Louis XIV to Napoleon* (Penguin 1980) p. 483; S Schama *Citizens – a chronicle of the French Revolution* (Viking books 1989) p. 764
6 Schama *Citizens – a chronicle of the French Revolution* p. 592
7 M Cobb *The French Resistance* (Simon & Shuster 2009) p. 162
    The main differences and frustration between the differing IRA groups and Collins and those at Dublin HQ were, in the case of some of the IRA units, a lack of communications and HQ presence and visits to them, and a general complaint of HQ failure to supply them arms. By contrast the main differences between London and the differing French Resistance groups was not communications or the supplies, for which there was a near constant flow. The differences concerned the role envisaged for resistance groups and the supplies to carry this out. The British and Americans and Free French in London insisted the main role of the resistance was intelligence and ad hoc sabotage, hence the small planes flying secretly in and out of France containing despatches and explosives. The resistance argued for direct and semi-continuous military engagements and pleaded for supplies of light and heavy small arms.
8 Coogan *The Man who Made Ireland* p. 394
9 Dessie Makin, Sinn Fein Finance Director, on Joe Cahill as Treasurer of Sinn Fein in the 1980s in B Anderson *Joe Cahill – a life in the IRA* (O Brien Press 2002) p. 375
10 L Napoleoni *Insurgent Iraq: al Zarqawi and the new generation* (Constable 2005) p. 160
11 A A Allawi *The Occupation of Iraq – winning the war, losing the peace* (Yale University Press 2007) p. 234
12 P L Bergen *The Longest War – enduring conflict between America and al Qaeda* (Free Press Simon & Shuster 2011) pp. 161–162

13 S B Glasser and S Coll "The web as a weapon" *Washington Post* 9 August 2005 found on www.washingtonpost.com/wp-dyn/content/article/2005/08/08/AR2005080801018.html

14 Caulfield *The Easter Rebellion* p. 277

15 Ibid. p. 284; D Ryan *The Rising – the complete story of Easter Week* (Golden Eagle Books 1949) App I pp. 260–261

16 R R Doerries *Prelude to the Easter Rising – Roger Casement in Imperial Germany* (Frank Cass 2000) Document 114 correspondence of 3 December 1915

17 Ibid. Document 90 correspondence of 8 August 1915.

18 G Chadion and A Blis *The History of Terrorism from Antiquity to al Qaeda* (University of California Press 2007) p. 175

19 Carroll *Money for Ireland* p. 11

20 Dessie Makin, Sinn Fein Finance Director, on Joe Cahill as Treasurer of Sinn Fein in the 1980s, in Anderson *Joe Cahill – a life in the IRA* p. 372

21 Confidential source, ex-Gardai Special Branch, mid-2006

22 Ibid. early 2007

23 Confidential source, researchers, Independent Monitoring Commission for Northern Ireland, mid-2007

24 Dangerfield *The Damnable Question* p. 317

25 Major B L Montgomery to Major Percival 14 October 1921 A E Percival Papers Imperial War Museum

26 O/C 1 Southern Division to Chief of Staff 20 May 1920 Mulcahy Papers P7/A2

27 O Crowcroft "Jerusalem violence – why does Israel bulldoze the homes of terrorists?" *International Business Times* 6 October 2015, found on www.ibtimes.co.uk/jerusalem-violence-why-does-israel-bulldoze-homes-terrorists-1522716; S Rubin "When Israel demolishes a Palestinian home, does it really deter the attackers?" *Forward* 17 November 2015 found on http://forward.com/news/324677/is-demolishing-the-houses-of-terrorists-encouraging-terrorism-instead-of-de/

28 Confidential source, Prosecutor's Office New York County, mid-2002

29 *Irish Independent* 9 March 1920

30 *Freeman's Journal* 8, 9 March 1920

31 Lavelle *James O Mara – a staunch Sinn Feiner* p. 186

32 Confidential source, former undercover officers and financial crime specialist, in financial intelligence unit New Scotland Yard 1990 and follow-up interviews, with author mid-2009 and late 2015.

33 A more detailed description and account of these transfers and the BCCI affair – although with the individuals/suspects/perpetrators' identities withheld – is to be found in N Ridley *Terrorist Financing* (Edward Elgar 2012)

34 S Clifford "Arab Bank reaches a settlement in suit accusing it of financing terrorism" *New York Times* 4 August 2014, found on www.ny.times.com/2015/08/14/myregion/arab-bank-reaches-setlement-in-suit-accusing-it-f-financing-terrorism.html/r=0

35 *Al Jazeera* "Arab Bank settles US case over 'terrorist funding' – Jordanian Bank had been found liable by a US jury for financing terrorism for transferring funds to HAMAS members" 15 August 2015, found on www.alijazeera.com/news/2015/08/arab-bank-settles-case-terrorist-fnding-1508151470706.html

36 Financial Action Task Force Report "Terrorist Financing February 2008", case study, citing its own previous Typologies Report of 2003–2004, found on www.fatf-gafi.org/media/fatf/documents/reports/FATF%20Terrorist%20Financing%20Typologies%20Report.pdf

37 US Federal Financial Institutions Examinations Council – Bank Secrecy Act Anti-Money Laundering Examination Manual – *Appendix F Money Laundering and Terrorist Financing "red flags"*, section on *Activity inconsistent with*

customer accounts and section on *Funds transfers*, found on www.ffiec.gov/bsa_aml_infobase/pages_manual/olm_106.htm

38 A Paz *Durruti in the Spanish Revolution* (Oakland Press 2007)

39 P Taylor *Provos, the IRA and Sinn Fein* (Bloomsbury Publishing 1997) interview with Brendan Hughes, PIRA leader, p. 109

40 General Glover, Northern Ireland – future terrorist trends confidential briefing paper, 2 November 1978, cited by T P Coogan *The Troubles 1966–1996* (Arrow Books 1996) p. 248

41 K Conway *Southside Provisional – from freedom fighters to the Four Courts* (ORPEN Press 2014) pp. 41–43, 69

42 Coogan *The Troubles 1966–1996* p. 250

43 W A Tupman, "Where Has All The Money Gone – the IRA as a profit-making concern" *Journal of Money Laundering Control* vol 1 no 4 April 1998; W A Tupman "Violent Business – networking terrorism and organised crime" in L Mackenzie (ed.) *Law Justice and Power in England and Wales* (Praeager Press 1998)

44 Confidential source, 2015

45 Sir Hugh Orde, head of Police Service of Northern Ireland statement to BBC 7 January 2005 regarding PIRA involvement

46 Confidential source, Irish Gardai mid-2006

47 D Templeton "The Provos got so much from the heist, they could not handle it" *Belfast Telegraph* 19 December 2014, found on www.belfasttelegraph.co.uk/news/northern-ireland/theprovos-got-so-much-cash-from-northern-bank-heist-the-could-not-handle-it-30833641.html

48 A complete, if somewhat sensationalist profile of the Aryan Republican Army was outlined in the *Washington Post* 13 February 1997

49 Confidential sources, UK National Criminal Intelligence Service and New Scotland Yard early 1990s, compliance officers in banking institutions in the EU mid and late 1990s, Romanian banking sources May–June 1999, early 2001 and late 2003, Dutch criminal intelligence sources April 2004

50 Confidential sources UK and US law enforcement agencies mid-2007, Italian and French law enforcement agencies January 2008 and June 2010. In fairness other law enforcement sources during the same periods spoke to the author of the excellent working relationship their agency or squad or unit enjoyed with banks, where confidential information was shared formally and informally, in real time, as a result of urgent requests during investigations into both money laundering and terrorism. In such cases there was no need or question of leverage.

51 Confidential source European bank official mid-2008

52 *Reuters* "Deutsche Bank agrees to 7.2 billion US$ mortgage settlement to US" 23 December 2016, found on www.reauters.com/article/us-deutsche-bank-mortgages-settlement-idUSKBN14CO41

53 Former Professor of Commercial Law, South African University, now Professor of International Financial Studies, Asian University, interview with author September 2016

54 Confidential sources, CEO of international financial consultancy, and international lawyer specialising in compliance, interviews with author October 2016 and November 2016

55 Confidential source, managing director, transaction and business analytical services, interview with author late September 2016

56 Confidential source, senior EU banking executive interview late September 2016

57 Closed presentation from Professor, University of Manitoba, at Cambridge International Annual Symposium on Financial Crime, September 2016

58 Confidential source, EU law enforcement mid-2004
59 P Chrysopoulos "Greek police arrest wanted terrorist and bank robber" *Greek Reporter* 5 August 2016, found on http://greece.greekreporter.com/2016/08/05/greek-police-arrest-wanted-terrorist-and-bank-robber/ and www.keeptalking-greece.com/2016/08/05/greek-police-arrests-urban-guerilla-suspect-and-alleged-bank-robber/
60 P Chrysopoulos "Terrorist group members suspected in bank robbery in Greece" *Greek Reporter* 16 September 2016 found on, http://greece.greekreporter.com/2016/09/16/terrorist-group-members-suspected-in-bank-robbery-in-greece
61 J F Burns "Threats and responses – Kabul, for Afghan Central Bank, it's out with the old money and in with the new" *New York Times* 7 October 2002, found on www.nytimes.com/2002/10/07/world/threats-responses-kabul-for-afghan-central-bank-it-s-with-old-money-with-new.html?_r=0
62 D Koswarapure "Imam Samudra's son killed in Syria" *Jakarta Post* 16 October 2015, found on www.thejakartapost.com/news/2015/10/16/imam-samudra-s-son-killed-syria.html
63 H Y Prabowo "Terrorist financing, cybercrime and the underground economy" *Jakarta Post* 9 July 2012, found on www.thejakartapost.com/news/2012/07/09/terrorist-financing-cybercrime-and-underground-economy.htm
64 R Tait "ISIS' half-a-billion-dollar bank heist makes it world's richest terror group" *Daily Telegraph* 14 June 2014, found on www.telegraph.co.uk/news/worldnews/middleeast/iraq/10899995/ISIS-half-a-billion-dollar-bank-heist-makes-it-worlds-richest-terror-group.html
65 Kostick *Revolution in Ireland* p. 189
66 Mackay *Michael Collins* p. 27
67 *Al Qaeda in Yemen and Somalia – a ticking time bomb* Report to the US Senate Foreign Relations Committee 111th Congress Second Session, US Government Printing Office Washington DC 21 January 2010 p 18; L Fleming "Somalia – 10 things we've learned", point 4, BBC World Africa 19 October 2012 available at www.bbc.co.uk/news/world-africa-18916319
68 Dwyer *Big Fellow, Long Fellow* p. 136
69 Mackay *Michael Collins* p. 193
70 A McCarthy "Michael Collins – Minister for Finance 1919–1922" in G Doherty and D Keogh (eds) *Michael Collins and the Making of the Irish State* p. 59
71 Ibid. p. 57
72 Y Shahar *Bin Laden – marketing terrorism* International Policy Institute for Counter-Terrorism 2004, available at www.ict.org.il/articles/bin-ladn7.htm
73 A fuller account of these couriers and other instances in other theatres of terrorism during the period 2000 to 2005, and also examples of other terrorist groups utilising cash couriers is given in Ridley *Terrorist Financing – the failure of counter-measures* chapter 5
74 Anti-terrorist symposium, University Cattolica Milan January 2005
75 J Gurule *Unfunding Terror – International Legal Responses* (Edward Elgar Publishing) 2008
76 J Talbot *The War Without a Name – France in Algeria 1956–62* (Alfred Knof 1980) pp. 164–165; M Crenshaw *Revolutionary Terrorism – the FLN in Algeria 1956–62* (Stanford 1983) pp. 93, 98, 138
77 Europol TE-SAT 2007 (open source version)
78 Europol "Why is cash still a king? A strategic report on the use of cash by criminal groups as a facilitator for money laundering", October 2015, found on file:///C:/Users/Toshiba%20C70/Downloads/europolcik%20(1).pdf
79 Financial Action Task Force (FATF) "Typology Report on Terrorist Financing" 2008 p. 23, found on www.fatf-gafi.org/media/fatf/documents/reports/FATF%20Terrorist%20Financing%20Typologies%20Report.pdf

80 FATF Report "Emerging Terrorist Financing Risks" October 2015 p. 23, found onwww.fatf-gafi.org/media/fatf/documents/reports/Emerging-Terrorist-Financing-Risks.pdf
81 Middle East and North Africa FATF Report "Money-Laundering through the physical transportation of cash" 2015 p. 3, found on www.fatf-gafi.org/media/fatf/documents/reports/money-laundering-through-transportation-cash.pdf
82 B Dasgupta *The Naxalite Movement* (Allied Press 1975) pp. 26–127
83 R N Mishra and A Maitra "The Maoist menace in India" 20 January 2008, found on www.boloji.net./analysis2/0304.htm
84 confidential source, former senior Indian police officer September 2011
85 Agriculture is a major part of economies of many African states. Terrorist groups accordingly adapt and target agricultural activities as part of their *modus operandi*. Boko Haram, active in north-west Nigeria, Niger and Chad, engage in cattle and other livestock rustling and exploit "confiscated" or "requisitioned" farms to provide a small but regular, illicit flow of funds.
86 *Terrorist financing in Central and West Africa 2016* FATF/Intergovernmental Action Group on Money Laundering in West Africa/Groupe d'Action contre le Blanchiment d'argent en Afrique Centrale, found on www.fatf-gafi.org, under reports, report of October 2016
87 Confidential source, closed law enforcement anti-terrorist financing symposium, Djakarta mid-2004
88 Ridley *Terrorist Financing* pp. 195–207

Part V

Michael Collins

The raising of the National Loan was described by Arthur Griffith as

one of the most extraordinary feats in the country's history.[1]

But Collins himself was one of the most extraordinary individuals in the country's history. A historian of modern times, writing of a later era of resistance and popular insurgency,[2] defined the three essentials of successful popular resistance as, first the need for clear targets, second, a tangible hope of success, and third the acceptance by the population of lawlessness and killing for the higher good. Collins, by his focus, provided the first by targeting the RIC and then by eliminating the opposition intelligence; he ensured the second, both hope and indeed survival, by providing the financial means; the Irish populace in turn responded with the third.

By 1921, the IRA was desperately short of arms, dangerously overstretched and near breaking point. By this time the finances to the clandestine Irish state were dangerously diminished. Yet both lasted out the three-year war, only just. That they had lasted was due to the herculean preparations in intelligence set up and finances carried out by Collins in the previous two years of 1917–1919, and his brilliant organisation and improvisation in the intelligence war and somehow keeping the war financed. His work in the Anglo-Irish Treaty negotiations was vital in financial terms for the new state's fiscal autonomy. His laying the foundation principles of the Ministry of Finance ensured that, within that fiscal autonomy, Ireland's financial management was secure. His speedy action in depriving the anti-Treaty IRA of available funds was a major factor in the Free State victory in the Civil War.

Some historians have viewed the period of Irish history determination in the first two decades of the twentieth century and the result of Ireland gaining self-determination, as a revolution. In this historical perspective, if Carnot's crucial organisation enabled the survival of the first French Revolution and First Republic during the three years of peril 1792–1795 and earned for him posterity's accolade of the "Organiser of Victory", then Collin's work in finance and intelligence during three years of peril ensure his place in posterity as the individual who ensured the survival of the nascent Irish nation–state.

In the history of Ireland Collins is a major figure and made vital contributions to Irish independence and statehood in many areas. One of his greatest achievements, made in combination with mastery of clandestine intelligence, was in the "Sinews of War", the finances.

It was, and is, Ireland's good fortune to have had in Collins an individual of such patriotic integrity and of brilliance in clandestine finance. It is perhaps good fortune for all that not every militant insurgent group, past or currently engaged in political violence against us, possesses such an individual as Collins.

Notes

1 *Dail Debates* 28 July 1920 p. 171
2 R O Paxton *Vichy France – old guard and new order 1940–1944* (Barrie and Jenkins 1972) pp. 291–292

Appendix I

Historians and de Valera's United States funds

De Valera raised a lot of funds in the United States during his visit, funds which formed part of the National Loan. Given the amounts and how vital the National Loan was to the Irish struggle for independence, it may be instructive to view how various historians have described and dealt with this topic. The following review (outlined in chronological order of publishing) may be of interest to the reader.

Lord Longford, in his much-acclaimed account of the Anglo-Irish Treaty negotiations (F Packenham *Peace by Ordeal* Jonathan Cape 1935) gives a comprehensive account and analysis of the Treaty negotiations and as background gives a brief account of the Anglo-Irish struggle. In the latter, he mentions both Collins and de Valera as engaged in Dail fundraising and states that de Valera raised $6 million in America whilst Collins raised £380,000 in Ireland in order to provide the self-styled Irish government with finance (p. 41). He does not mention that de Valera failed to send up to $3 million of the monies he collected, to Ireland.

In a later work, Longford co-authored a biography with O Neill (Longford and O Neill *De Valera* Hutchinson 1970). In this he acknowledges O Mara and his crucial work in the US bond collection in that

> O Mara's arrival made an immense difference to the bond drive.

and points out that de Valera's collecting this was one of the positive actions of de Valera's visit, in that

> In spite of all disputes the bond drive had been a wonderful success; five times the amount initially contemplated by the Irish Cabinet had been collected,
>
> (pp. 102, 113)

but their work makes no mention of up to $3 million being kept back in the United States and not sent to Ireland.

M J McManus, like Longford writing in the first half of the twentieth century, less than 30 years after the 1916 rebellion, in a partisan work on de Valera (M J McManus *Eamon de Valera* Talbot Press 1944) covers most of de Valera's time in the United States by describing his struggles in the complex alignments of the differing American–Irish factions and associations, sympathetically following de Valera's progress, and blaming the implacable hostility of Devoy and Cohalan on de Valera's difficulties (pp. 105–108). On the fundraising of the Loan, it is stated that de Valera received massive popular acclaim, with the bond (certificate) drive

> ... a sensational success ... the Loan speedily out-topping the five million dollars mark.
>
> (p. 96)

However, there is no mention that up to $3 million were retained in the United States and not sent back to support the struggle in Ireland.

Rex Taylor, writing in the 1950s in a biography (*Michael Collins* Hutchinson Press 1958) states that Collins was responsible for raising the Loan and that the targets were, in Ireland, to raise £250,000, and in the United States where de Valera was to raise $5 million. Taylor dwells on de Valera quibbling in correspondence with Collins, and that de Valera

> ... succeeded in earning animosity of a section of Irish–American opinion.

However, he details the amounts that de Valera raised, or that up to half of this was not sent back from the United States to Ireland.

Bromagh, also writing in the 1950s (M G Bromagh *De Valera and the March of a Nation* Hutchinson 1956) in a partisan biography of de Valera, emphasises the hostility of Devoy and Cohalan towards de Valera and their intrigues (pp. 99–100). Bromagh, beyond describing Collins as Minister of Finance and that he was interested in American aid, does not mention Collins' massive work in raising the Loan in Ireland. However, the author states

> ... America held the promise of aid and nothing Collins could say any longer would deter de Valera from planning the journey that to him offered *the only promise left* of political *and financial* fortifications in the impending battle for nationhood.
>
> (p 89) (italics mine)

It appears that American financial aid was the only hope and source. On de Valera in the United States the author mentions the bond drive as a success of $6 million but,

> tangible assets that needed safeguarding ... the bond drive had put 6 million dollars in banks which Cohalan was manoeuvring to control
>
> (pp. 102–103)

the implication being that de Valera needed to keep a tight hold of these funds. (However, the necessity of keeping possession of the raised funds whilst they were in the United States does not follow or dictate that they should not be sent to Ireland for the struggle, the purpose for which the funds were raised.) The author does not mention that up to $3 million were held back by de Valera. Bromagh later deals with the allegations of the *Irish Press* acquisition, stating that the

> ... accusations of his being a controlling director of the *Irish Press* – a number of Americans had transferred their interest in the Republican bonds to him for his journal was known

and that de Valera refuted all allegations, and that

> ... in his complicated financial scheme he won.

(pp. 250–251)

However, the author does not make clear that the bonds being transferred and used for the Irish Press were the funds collected in the United States during the Anglo-Irish War (and had been kept back and remained there).

In the 1960s one of the doyennes amongst Irish historians, T P Coogan, in a comparatively early and wide scoping work (T P Coogan *Ireland since the Rising* Praeger 1966), in the section on the Anglo-Irish War and the struggle for independence, makes no mention of de Valera in the United States. It acknowledges Collins' achievement in raising the National Loan in Ireland of over £250,000 Sterling, this being carried out at the same time as he was conducting a guerrilla war with a price on his head (p. 26). However, as we shall see below, in later works Coogan specifically focusses on de Valera and the US fundraising.

Margery Forester, in her work (M Forester *Michael Collins – the lost leader* Sphere Books 1971) states that despite de Valera in the United States causing divisions among Irish–American societies and supporters he achieved good work in the cause. Forester acknowledges O Mara's organising role and that he, O Mara carried out "the bulk of the work" of Loan raising in the United States. The fundraising in the United States resulted in

> ... amounts running to thousands of pounds were constantly remitted to Collins,

(pp. 149–150)

but there is no mention of de Valera holding back up to $3 million.

Kee, also writing in the 1970s, in his incisive analysis of Irish history analysis (R Kee *The Green Flag – history of Irish nationalism* Penguin Books 1972) gives Collins full credit for raising the Loan in Ireland, and due to his exceptional administrative ability and organizational powers

the Loan was finished at more than £357,000 (p. 653). He describes de Valera's long visit to the United States in his return to Ireland in 1920, crediting him with raising the equivalent of £1 million (at the time the rate of exchange was one pound Sterling to approximately four dollars) for the Republican Loan, and also that his visit had not been a total success due to his being entangled in the quarrels of Irish–American groups and factions (p. 710). There is no mention of de Valera keeping funds he raised in the United States from being sent back to Ireland. However – and this is author speculation – perhaps he hinted at this by stating de Valera's contribution to the Loan being the equivalent of $4 million for the Republican Loan (not between $5–6 million as other historians cite) and also the phrase in describing Collins' total as

... 357,000 Sterling *for Ireland itself* (italics mine).

In a later biography of the 1990s Dr James Mackay (*Michael Collins* Mainstream Publications 1996) gives comparatively small coverage to de Valera in America, stating that he was treated like royalty and that he made a great impression, but does not detail de Valera's fundraising activities, nor that substantial amounts of funds raised there were kept back.

T Ryle Dwyer, in a short work on Collins and de Valera, focussing mainly on the Anglo-Irish Treaty (Dwyer *Michael Collins and the Treaty – his differences with de Valera* Mercier Press 1981) de Valera's fundraising in the United States is mentioned and is quite clearly stated to have the purpose of,

... calling for diplomatic recognition and gathering funds *for the struggle at home* (italics mine).

(p. 12)

T P Coogan in 1993 wrote a comprehensive biography of de Valera (*De Valera – long fellow long shadow* Hutchinson 1993) where he is unequivocally frank about de Valera's visit to the United States during the Anglo-Irish war. He gives full credit to the success of the bond-certificate drive in the United States being due to O Mara's organisational ability (p. 159). He points to the comparatively extravagant lifestyle enjoyed by de Valera and, as always with Coogan, deploys meticulous research and cites a British officer who was staying at New York's Waldorf Hotel the same time as de Valera, and who commented on de Valera's extravagant hospitality to many ex-pat and visiting Irish (citing Lt Col Thwaites' work, N Thwaites *Velvet and Vinegar* London 1932). Granted this could scarcely be regarded as a totally impartial source, but Coogan's researches also cite a note on de Valera's accounts which was the cost of £1,900 for de Valera's wife to visit him, de Valera buying lavish gold presents for individuals and a high dentist's bill.

On the monies raised Coogan is relentless in stating that millions were held back from the Irish struggle. He points out that whilst de Valera was in the United States he lost touch with the situation in Ireland, at a crucial period in the struggle, and then continues to state that three million worth of bond certificates raised in America

> ... which for some inexplicable reason he had not sent back to Ireland

and later repeats the same in

> Making allowances for the expenses incurred during his tour and that some monies were remitted to Ireland, he nevertheless left behind him something approaching 60 per cent of what was collected....

> he too collected some 5 million U$ but ordered about 3 million U$ to be retained in America even when he left the country

and

> ... for reasons best known to himself de Valera left in the New York bank some 3 million of the monies.

Also, Coogan again draws upon his meticulous and extensive research and cites Cork IRA unit leader Sean Moylan (Moylan, memoir composed and given to the Irish Bureau of Military History). In this Moylan emphases his combat role, expresses dissatisfaction in that

> What about the Dail Loan *and the generous subscription from the USA*? I can only go to say that, as far as my knowledge goes, not a cent of any of those funds was devoted to the organisation of the Irish Republican Army ... generous friends gave me food and shelter (italics mine).

From this Coogan concludes that Moylan's experiences were those of the average combat Volunteer, and that it

> ... indicates the relief which the millions de Valera left behind him could have brought to the ranks of the IRA.
>
> (pp. 181, 192, 193–194, 391)

Coogan in later chapters outlines how de Valera gained control of the Irish Press and the involvement of the US raised funds, including using a holding company in Delaware USA (an interesting location) and then in another chapter recounts how de Valera denied having a financial interest in the Irish Press, but in fact it was exposed in 1958 that he was indeed officially in control, and that the enterprise was worth £1 million (by 1950s value) (pp. 417–419, 67–677).

In 1996 Kostick, writing a left-wing version of the struggle for independence (C Kostick *Revolution in Ireland – popular militancy 1917 to 1923* Pluto Press 1996) mentions both de Valera's fundraising in the United States and the bond drive which resulted in the huge amount of $5,123,640 and Collins' fundraising activity in Ireland producing £380,000. In keeping with the left-wing interpretation of the book, it is pointed out that de Valera's contributions, were mainly on $10 donations, therefore,

> the self-sacrifice of the poorer Irish people ensured the bond drive was successful.

No mention is made of sending these sums back for the struggle in Ireland, or of keeping some of the funds back in the United States. Perhaps significantly, Collins' fundraising is described as "impressive", whilst de Valera's fundraising is described as taking place during an "*extravagant* and popular speaking tour" (p. 99) (italics mine).

In 1998, Fitzpatrick, in his chapter in a comprehensive history of Ireland (R Foster (ed.) *Oxford History of Ireland* OPUS 1998, chapter 5 D Fitzpatrick "Ireland since 1870") states that de Valera's extended visit to the United States gained $5 million in "republican bonds", and that this was despite opposition from the entrenched Irish–American organisation but makes no mention of the amounts actually sent to Ireland, and no mention of Collins' Loan raising achievement in Ireland itself.

T Ryle Dwyer in 1998 wrote a dual biography of Collins and de Valera (*Big Fellow, Long Fellow* St Martins Press 1998) in which he describes de Valera's fundraising visit to the United States.

There is an account of the quarrel with US–Irish factions under Devoy and Cohalan and O Mara's hard work, and subsequent disillusionment. Also, de Valera's personality and domineering is mentioned, with even Harry Boland concerned about his losing touch with reality. However, the monies raised by de Valera are dealt with as follows,

> However his mission had not been a total failure because he collected over 5 million U$ for the cause at home.
>
> (pp. 108–121)

There is no mention of a substantial part of, or indeed any part of, these funds being held back in the United States.

Carroll, writing in 2002 in his comprehensive and incisive study (*Money for Ireland Finance Diplomacy and Politics and the First Dail Eireann*

Loans 1919–1936 Praeger Studies 2002) acknowledges de Valera causing difficulties, animosities and divisions amongst the Irish–American societies and associations, but emphasises that de Valera's very presence generated the sale of Republican bond-certificates

> ... if he asked them to buy Irish Republican bond certificates they would; and they did, over 5 millions worth.

He also gives de Valera credit for insisting upon devising and using a financial instrument to raise the monies. (However, he does not credit James O Mara's hard work and cooperation with the US pro-Irish lawyers to ensure that the financial instrument did not fall foul of United States laws. Indeed, O Mara's entire – and invaluable – organisational work in selling the bond certificates and gathering the funds is not mentioned). Carroll states that de Valera raised over $5 million for the cause, and later brings this total up to $6 million, taking into account the later second smaller Loan in the United States. However, there is no mention of de Valera ensuring that up to $3 million was held back in the United States and was not sent to Ireland (pp. 22–23).

Later he goes into considerable detail as to how the monies which did remain in the United States were in danger of falling into the hands of the anti-Treaty IRA and Republicans, and Collins' activities and recourse to legal action in the United States courts. When dealing in a later period with the cases in international civil law of various parties trying to reclaim Loan funds, he states that a major element in the success of the Fianna Fail Party in 1934 was the influence of the newspaper the *Irish Press* and that this newspaper,

> had been founded in a large part by the bond-certificate money from the United States.
>
> (p. 84)

In a later academic paper by a Senior Lecturer in Economics, Dr John Considine, on Michael Collins laying the foundations of Irish finance, includes figures from Carroll's research (J Considine "Michael Collins and the roots of Irish Public Finance", Department of Economics University of Cork, found on www.ucc.ie/en/media/academic/economics/documents/research/michaelcollins04–03.pdf). The paper touches upon de Valera's fundraising as part of the National Loan, that this resulted in between $5–$6 million being raised, and he pointedly states that Collins in Ireland never received all the monies raised by de Valera and that

> Just over half the monies were returned to Ireland.... It was never clear why all the monies were not returned to Ireland immediately.
>
> (pp. 7–8)

In 1992 Coogan wrote a biography of Michael Collins and his achievements regarding Ireland gaining independence (*The Man Who Made
Ireland – the life and death of Michael Collins* Roberts Rhinehart 1992)
where he categorically states de Valera being responsible for withholding
funds raised in the United States, and that a significant part of those funds
held back were used later for his acquiring the newspaper,

> ... de Valera allowed something over half of this to come to Ireland-
> the rest remaining in American banks from which source he eventually
> succeeded in getting control of sufficient funds to found what was his
> family's press empire, *The Irish Press.*

He then raises the question as to why these funds were not sent where and
to whom they were originally agreed and intended

> Why he did not send *all the money* to the Ministry of Finance or pass
> it on to the American White Cross must remain a matter of conjecture
> (italics mine).
>
> (p. 188)

In 2003 Coogan wrote a comprehensive, large-scale general history of
Ireland (*Ireland in the Twentieth Century* Arrow Books 2003) in which the
Anglo-Irish War and the struggle for independence was an earlier part. In
this, he is quite specific about the possessive nature of de Valera to the
United States monies raised, and that he prevented half of these funds
being sent back to Ireland during the struggle. Coogan acknowledges de
Valera's success but then goes further,

> ... he certainly raised a lot of money ... a total of 5,123,640 U$ ... in
> the same manner in which de Valera saw the Irish cause being personi-
> fied and controlled by him, he seemed to regard this money as being
> his to direct. Only half of it was remitted to Ireland to help the war
> effort; the rest remained in New York banks and ... de Valera eventu-
> ally succeeded in getting control of enough of it to enable him to found
> a newspaper empire in Dublin.
>
> (pp. 86–87)

In 2005, P Hart wrote a biography of Collins which was by no means
totally sympathetic to its subject. (P Hart *Mick – the real Michael Collins*
Penguin Books 2005 and 2007) He, impartially, recounted Collins' more
aggressive and dominating personality and the negative impact it had on
working with fellow Irish nationalists and ministerial colleagues in the
clandestine Irish government. However, he gives full credit to Collins for
his success in Ireland in raising the National Loan, and in dealing with de
Valera in the United States points out that allegedly $1.5 million of the

monies raised were spent in the United States by de Valera and Boland on a high lifestyle, reiterating Coogan's point and also states

about half the US loan was sent to Ireland – mostly in 1921.

Due to this he continues, the Irish Republic had to rely upon the Irish-raised funds through 1919 and 1920, and concludes in favour of Collins that

it was Michael Collins' job to keep the revolution afloat.

In 2013, James O Mara's great-grandson wrote an article (J Humphreys "Millionaire helped finance war of independence", *Irish Times* 23 May 2013). Admittedly partisan, it pulls no punches regarding criticism of de Valera in his treatment of O Mara's tireless work in the United States fund-raising and then unequivocally states that $2.5 million of the funds raised were sent back to Ireland but the remainder, together with the smaller second Loan raised of $600,000 were held onto by de Valera. It later states that after the legal judgements finally made over ownership of the funds, that de Valera pulled off a memorable stroke in Irish politics. This was that he contacted the bondholders in the United States, asking them to sign over the bonds to him in order to set up the *Irish Press*, which many did. Then in 1933 when he gained power, he pushed through legislation in the Dail that all bondholders (including him) should be not just be paid the equivalent of 58 cents a share, but an additional 67 cents making each share worth $1.25. He used the increase in available cash to buy the Irish Press.

Townsend, writing in 2014 of Ireland's struggle (C Townsend *The Republic – the fight for Irish independence* Penguin 2014) states that de Valera raised in the United States over $5 million, amounts which made a highly significant contribution to the struggle, but he also states that much of the monies did not reach Ireland in time to help the struggle and also over half of this money remained in American banks during the 1920s (pp. 70–72). The author does not elaborate as to who was responsible for these monies not being sent back to Ireland.

Lynch, in a short partisan work in 2015 (R Lynch *Revolutionary Ireland 1912–1925* Bloomberg 2015) writing of de Valera in the United States, emphasises that de Valera failed to gain recognition of the Irish Republic, but due to a breathless round of fundraising raised almost $6 million and states that much of this would find its way back to Ireland to support to support the Dail government's establishing a revolutionary government (p. 63). However, the author does not elaborate on the other funds which did not find their way back.

For the purposes of this book – i.e. the funding of political violence during the Irish struggle for independence – from the above historians, it can be concluded that de Valera was indeed successful in the amounts he raised, i.e. between $5–6 million. Of this approximately half was sent back to assist the struggle. Up to $3 million was not sent to Ireland, but held back, deliberately, by de Valera. These monies were withheld from the Irish struggle at a vital stage of the armed conflict of the Anglo-Irish War. From this it can be extrapolated that the achievement of maintaining the armed conflict struggle was by far due to Michael Collins as Minister of Finance.

It is perhaps appropriate that the final word should be given to a doyen of Irish history, T P Coogan, with his meticulous and extensive researches. Coogan makes perhaps the most telling point of all. In giving the account of James O Mara's increasing disillusionment with de Valera during the fundraising in the United States he cites O Mara's opposition to de Valera's proposal of a starting an additional Loan, and O Mara drawing attention in a despatch that there was already $3 million worth of raised funds in US banks, Coogan points out,

> De Valera's ascendency was such that no one even thought of debating O Mara's point that 3 million U$ was lying unused in banks whilst further begging bowls were extended.
>
> (T P Coogan *De Valera – long fellow, long shadow* p. 212)

Appendix II
Collins and Connolly

Connolly, one of the leaders of the 1916 rebellion, was an international socialist whose dual political thinking also embraced Irish nationalism, but an objective of a socialist Ireland.

Born into a poor family in Edinburgh, he served in the British Army for seven years, before eking out a living as a political organiser, arriving in Dublin as an organiser of the Irish Transport Workers Union.

At this time, conditions of the Dublin urban poor were some of the worst in Britain and living and working conditions were dire. In 1912 the transport workers engaged in strike action, and during the course of the industrial dispute the Dublin police inflicted much violence and beatings on the strikers and passers-by. To counter this Connolly formed the Irish Citizen Army, a type of workers self-defence militia. The headquarters was Liberty Hall, the large Dublin building of offices of the Irish Transport and General Workers, which also housed somewhat ramshackle printing presses which Connolly used for his various socialist publications. A sympathetic British ex-officer, Captain Jack White, the son of a British Army general who was publicly revered for his defence of Ladysmith in the Boer War, organised the formation and drilled the recruits. His first action was perhaps symptomatic of the conditions of the Dublin poor; he set aside £50 of his own money to purchase for the recruits, pairs of shoes, on the basis that ill-shod men and women (Connollywas a staunch defender of equality for women) could not drill or march. The total number of the Irish Citizen Army never exceeded 300, but thanks to Connelly's writings and publications it was high profile and a potent symbol of the Irish freedom cause.

As an international socialist Connolly was profoundly shaken by the outbreak of the First World War and the apparent feebleness of international labour to prevent the conflict. Impatient as he was with nationalism, in 1914 he castigated Redmond's support for the war by advising in a speech of 30 August 1914 in Dublin

> If you are itching for a rifle ... itching to fight, then have a country of your own. Better to fight for your own country than to fight for the robber empire. If you ever shoulder a rifle, let it be for Ireland.[1]

Connolly's involvement as one of the leaders of the 1916 came late in the day. His articles became so strident and insistent on physical force to be carried out by the Citizen Army that by 1915 Pearse, Clarke and the other IRB leaders were alarmed that a precipitate rebellion by the tiny Citizen Army would be crushed and destroy all their careful preparations for the planned Easter rebellion. Accordingly, they took Connolly into their confidence and after lengthy discussions Connolly agreed to be part of their uprising.

Even after agreeing to join the Rising and add his Citizen Army contingent to the insurgents, Connollyremained steadfast to the long-term objective of socialism. The night before the Easter Monday Rising, he addressed the paraded Citizen Army in Liberty Hall and ordered,

> The odds against are a thousand to one. But if we should win hold on to your rifles, because the Volunteers may have a different goal. Remember we're not only out for political liberty but economic liberty as well. So hold on to your rifles.[2]

Members of Irish Citizen Army fought alongside the Volunteers in Dublin during the Easter Rising and in the aftermath Connolly and two of its commanders, Michael Mallin and Constance Markiewievicz, were court martialled and sentenced to death. Mallin, an ex British Army soldier, was shot, Markievicz was reprieved. After her release, she continued to campaign for Irish freedom alongside Kathleen, the widow of Tom Clarke and Mary, the sister of Pearse.

The remnants of the Citizen Army became assimilated into the reformed Irish Volunteers, soon to become the IRA. In Scotland they remained, often within the Volunteer organisations formed in that country, a tight knit independent-minded grouping.

Collins had little time for the international socialist tenets of Connolly, He personally respect Connolly's bravery and his practical approach to the 1916 conflict. Also, he did appear to have some common economic thinking with Connolly.

Connolly was adamant that the economic struggle was equally as important as the political. He wrote

> ... if you remove the English army tomorrow and hoist the green flag over Dublin, unless you set about the organization of the socialist republic, your efforts would be in vain ... England would still rule you to your ruin.[3]

Collins also realised the importance of the economic struggle. Describing the previous decades in Ireland, he stated

> our economic subjection was necessary that we might serve Britain's purposes.[4]

During the Treaty negotiations he made a priority of, and was successful in, gaining for the new Irish state full fiscal autonomy and unfettered and independent trade (as per article IX of the Treaty).

Both Collins and Connollyadvocated a fairer society in Ireland, and an Ireland that would look to its own resources and capital.

Connolly advocated

> Trade Union funds instead of being deposited in banks by those institutions to those capitalist exploiters could be placed to the credit of soundly run co-operative enterprises, developing the farmers development ... and aiding the toilers in town and country.[5]

Writing in the post Treaty period, Collins, in his view of a future Ireland, writes in a similar vein about Irish industry in that

> ... the system should be on co-operative lines, rather than the old commercial capitalist lines of huge joint stock companies

and, further, that in agriculture land should be made more freely available, and that cattle ranches should be broken up, in order that all agricultural workers have an opportunity to raise cattle.[6]

And Collins also writes in a similar vein regarding Irish capital being invested in Ireland

> Millions of Irish money are lying idle in Irish banks. The deposit in Irish joint stock bonds increased in the aggregate by 7,318,999 pounds during the half year ending 31 December 1021. At that date total deposits and cash balance in Irish banks was 194,391,000 pounds and 14,000 in Post Office Savings. If Irish money was invested in Irish industries there would be an enormous amount of development of Irish commerce.[7]

During the political upheaval in Ireland after the Treaty, Collins advanced the argument of the Treaty giving "the freedom to achieve further freedoms" and in this the Treaty gave Ireland economic autonomy and benefits which would ensure the whole of Ireland, i.e. the north as well, to come together. These arguments were rejected by the hard-line anti-Treaty IRA. These included Liam Mellowes, Connolly's follower and staunch advocate of egalitarianism and the rights of labour in the new Ireland. He, of all people, refuted the argument with the incredible outburst

> We do not seek to make this country a materially great country at the expense of its honour ... we would rather have the people of Ireland eking out a poor existence on the soil, as long as they possessed their souls....[8]

Perhaps Connolly would have responded more pragmatically and positively towards Collins' way to economic freedom.

Notes

1 Townshend *Easter 1916 – the Irish rebellion* p. 112; Ryan *The Rising – the complete story of Easter Week* Appendix II p. 261
2 Cited in Caulfield *The Easter Rebellion Dublin 1916* p. 24
3 C Desmond Greaves *The Life and Times of James Connolly* 1961 (Lawrence & Wishart, 1961) pp. 14–20
4 Collins *The Path to Freedom* p. 47
5 Connolly *Labour in Ireland* p. 323
6 Collins *The Path to Freedom* pp. 113, 115
7 Ibid. pp. 116–117
8 R Fanning *Independent Ireland* cited by F Costello *The Irish Revolution and Its Aftermath* p. 295

Bibliography

Official records

Annual Register, A Review of Public Events at Home and Abroad, 1919, 1920, 1921, Longmans Green & Co

Bureau of Military History Archives Cathal Brugha Barracks, Irish Department of Defence

National Archives of Ireland, Department of Foreign Affairs 1919–1921

National Library of Ireland, Michael Collins Papers

National Library of Ireland, Art O Brien Papers

UK Government National Archives, Cabinet Papers 1919–1921 and Colonial Office Papers 1921

University College Dublin, Richard Mulcahy Papers

Reports, articles and learned papers

Bowman-Grieve L and Conway M 2011 "Exploring the form and function of Dissident Irish Republican Online Discourses", found on http://doras.dcu.ie/1763/7/1/rish_republican_online_discourse_FINAL-NOT-PR-OOF.pdf

Considine J 2016 "Michael Collins and the roots of Irish Public Finance" Department of Economics University of Cork, found on www.ucc.ie/en/media/academic/economics/documents/research/michaelcollins04-03.pdf)

Coogan T P 2005 Book Review of P Hart "Mick – the real Mick Collins" *History Ireland*, found on www.historyireland.com/category/20th-century-contemporary-history/

Duff J B 1968 "Irish–America and the Versailles Treaty" *Journal of American History* 55(3) 1968

Europol October 2015 "Why is cash still a king? A strategic report on the use of cash by criminal groups as a facilitator for money laundering", found on file:///C:/Users/Toshiba%20C70/Downloads/europolcik%20(1).pdf

Farrel L 2000 "The Tommy Gun – the Irish connection" *History Ireland* and published in *20th-century Contemporary History*, Issue 4 News, Revolutionary Period 1912–23, Volume 8 Winter, found on www.historyireland.com/20th-century-contemporary-history/the-tommy-gun-the-irish-connection/

Fletcher H 2008 "IRA splinter groups", found on www.cfr.org/separatist-terrorism-ira-splinter-groups-uk-separatists-/p9239/

Financial Action Task Force 2008 "Typology Report on Terrorist Financing", found on www.fatf-gafi.org/media/fatf/documents/reports/FATF%20Terrorist%20Financing%20Typologies%20Report.pdf

Financial Action Task Force Report October 2015 "Emerging Terrorist Financing Risks", found on www.fatf-gafi.org/media/fatf/documents/reports/Emerging-Terrorist-Financing-Risks.pdf

Financial Action Task Force/Inter-Governmental Action Group Against Money Laundering in West Africa/Task Force on Money Laundering in Central Africa Report 2016 "Terrorist Financing in Central and West Africa", found on www.fatf.gafi.org/publictions.methodsandtrends/documents/terrorist-financing-west-central-africa.html

Humphreys J 2013 "Millionaire helped finance war of independence" *Irish Times* 23 May

Irish Department of Finance, Minister for Finance speech at Beal na mBlath 22 August 2010, found on www.finance.gov.ie/viewdoc.asp?DocID=6422

Lynch R 2006 "Donegal and the joint IRA Northern Offensive" *Irish Historical Studies* vol xxxv no 138 November

Mackenzie Institute 2016 "Provisional Irish Republican Army" in *Security Matters*, found on http://mackenzieinstitute.com/provisional-irish-republican-army-pira/

McGinty S 2014 "Scottish support of Irish independence in the 1920s" *The Scotsman* 29 June, found on www.scotsman.com/lifestyle/culture/books/scottish-support-for-irish-independence-in-1920-s-1-3460189

Morrough M 2000 "The Anglo-Irish Treaty of 1921" *History Today*, found on www.historytoday.com/michaelmorrough/ango-irish-treaty-1921

Murray E "Eamon Bulfin" Society for Latin American Studies-Dictionary of Irish–Latin-American Biography, 1 December 2003 found on www.irlandeses.org/dilab_bulfine.htm

Noonan G 2011 "Supplying an army; IRA gunrunning in Britain during the War of Independence" *History Studies University of Limerick History Society Journal* vol 12

O Caithan M 2009 "Michael Collins and Scotland" *Ireland and Scotland in the Nineteenth Century* Four Courts Press, found on www.historyireland.com/20th-century-contemporary-history/the-tommy-gun-the-irish-connection/

Shahar Y 2004 "Bin Laden – marketing terrorism" International Policy Institute for Counter-Terrorism, available at www.ict.org.il/articles/bin-ladn7.htm

Templeton D "The Provos got so much from the heist, they could not handle it" *Belfast Telegraph* 19 December 2014, found on www.belfasttelegraph.co.uk/news/northern-ireland/theprovos-got-so-much-cash-from-northern-bank-heist-the-could-not-handle-it-30833641.html

Books

Allawi A A 2007 *The Occupation of Iraq – winning the war losing the peace* Yale University Press

Barry T 1974 *The Reality of the Anglo-Irish War – refutations corrections and comments on Liam Deasy's "Towards Ireland Free"* Anvil Books

Beaslai P 1926 *Michael Collins and the Making of the New Ireland*, vol I, vol II Phoenix Publishing

Bergen P L 2011 *The Longest War – enduring conflict between America and al Qaeda* Free Press Simon & Shuster

Boyle A 1977 *The Riddle of Erskine Childers* Hutchinson

Bromagh M G 1956 *De Valera and the March of a Nation* Hutchinson

Caulfield M 1963 *The Easter Rebellion Dublin 1916* Roberts Rhinehart

Clark C 2013 *The Sleepwalkers – how Europe went to war in 1914* Penguin

Collins M 1968 *The Path to Freedom* Mercier Press

Connolly J 1917 *Labour in Ireland* Maunsel & Company

Conway K 2014 *Southside Provisional – from freedom fighters to the Four Courts* ORPEN Press

Coogan T P 1963 *De Valera – long fellow, long shadow* Hutchinson

Coogan T P 1966 *Ireland since the Rising* Praeger Press

Coogan T P 1992 *The Man Who Made Ireland – the life and death of Michael Collins* Roberts Rhinehart

Coogan T P 1993 *The IRA – a history* Roberts Rhinehart

Coogan T P 2003 *Ireland in the Twentieth Century* Arrow Books

Costello F 1997 *Michael Collins – in his own words* Gill & Macmillan

Costello F 2003 *The Irish Revolution and Its Aftermath 1916–1923 – years of revolt* Irish Academic Press

Crankshaw E 1981 *The Fall of the House of Hapsburg* Papermac

Crenshaw M 1983 *Revolutionary Terrorism – the FLN in Algeria* Stanford

Dangerfield G 1961 *The Strange Death of Liberal England 1910–1914* Capricorn Books

Dangerfield G 1976 *The Damnable Question – a study in Anglo-Irish relations* Constable

Dasgupta B 1975 *The Naxalite Movement* Allied Press

Davis R 1974 *Arthur Griffith and Non-violent Sinn Fein* The Kerryman Publications

Deacon R 1963 *A History of the British Secret Service* Grafton Books

Deasy L 1973 *Towards Ireland Free – the West Cork Brigade in the War of Independence 1917–1921* Mercier Press

Deasy L 1998 *Brother against Brother* Mercier Press

Doerries R R 2000 *Prelude to the Easter Rising – Roger Casement in Imperial Germany* Frank Cass

Doherty G and Keogh D (eds) 1998 *Michael Collins and the Making of the Irish State* Mercury Press

Dwyer T Ryle 1981 *Michael Collins and the Treaty – his differences with de Valera* Mercier Press

Dwyer T Ryle 1998 *Big Fellow, Long Fellow* St Martins Press

Dwyer T Ryle 2009 *Michael Collins – the man who won the war* Mercier Press

English R 2003 *Armed Struggle – the history of the IRA* OPUS

Fanning R 1978 *The Irish Department of Finance 1922–58* Institute of Public Administration Ireland

Foot M R D 1976 *Resistance – analysis of resistance to Nazism 1940–1945* Eyre Methuen

Forester M 1971 *Michael Collins – the lost leader* Sphere Books

Foster R (ed.) 1998 *Oxford History of Ireland* OPUS

Foster R E 1989 *Modern Ireland 1600–1972* Penguin

Gallagher F 1965 *The Anglo-Irish Treaty* Hutchinson

Greaves C D 1961 *The Life and Times of James Connolly* Lawrence & Wishart

Gurule J 2008 *Unfunding Terror – international legal responses* Edward Elgar Publishing

Hannigan D 2010 *De Valera in America – the rebel President and the making of Irish Independence* St Martins Press

Hart P 1998 *The IRA and Its Enemies – violence and community in Cork 1916–1923* Clarendon Press

Hart P 2005 *Mick – the real Michael Collins* Penguin Books

Henry R M 1920 *The Evolution of Sinn Fein* Talbot Press

Hopkinson M 1988 *Green against Green – a history of the Irish Civil War* Gill & Macmillan

Hopkinson M 1999 *The Last Days of Dublin Castle – diaries of Mark Sturgis* Irish Academic Press

Hopkinson M 2002 *The Irish War of Independence* McGill-Queens University Press

Hopkirk P 2006 *Setting the East Ablaze* John Murray

Horne A 1977 *A Savage War of Peace 1954–62* Macmillan

Jeanson F 1960 *Notre Guerre* Les Editions de Minuit

Jeanson F 1962 *La Revolution Algerienne – problemes et perspectives* Feltrinelli Editione

Jones C 1980 *The Great Nation – France from Louis XIV to Napoleon* Penguin

Jones T 1971 *Whitehall Diary* ed. K Middlemass Oxford University Press

Keagan J 1998 *The First World War* Hutchinson

Kee R 1972 *The Green Flag – a history of Irish nationalism* Penguin Books

Kochan L 1966 *Russia in Revolution 1890–1918* Paladin, Granada Publishing

Kostick C 1996 *Revolution in Ireland – popular militancy 1917 to 1923* Pluto Press

Lavelle P 1961 *James O Mara – a staunch Sinn Feiner* Clonmore & Reynolds

Lawrence T E 1938 *The Letters of T E Lawrence* ed. D Garnett Jonathan Cape

Lynch R 2015 *Revolutionary Ireland 1912–1925* Bloomberg

Lyons F S L 2009 *Ireland since the Famine* Fontana Press

MacDowell V 1997 *Michael Collins and the Irish Republican Brotherhood* Ashfield Press

Mackay J *Michael Collins – a life* Penguin Mainstream Publishing 1997

Mansergh N 1940 *Ireland in the Age of Reform and Revolution 1840–1921* George Allen & Unwin

Martin F X (ed.) 1966 *Leaders and Men of the Easter Rising* Dublin 1916 Methuen

Martin F X, Byrne F J, Vaughan W E *et al.* (eds) 1996 *A New History of Ireland – Volume VI Ireland under the Union* OPUS

McCarten P 1932 *With de Valera in America* Fitzpatrick Ltd

McManus M J 1944 *Eamon de Valera* Talbot Press

Mitchel A 1993 *Revolutionary Government in Ireland – Dail Eireann 1919–1922* Gill & Macmillan

Napoleoni L 2005 *Insurgent Iraq – al Zarqawi and the new generation* Constable

Neeson E 1989 *The Civil War* Poolbeg

Noonan G 2014 *In the heart of enemy lines – the IRA in Britain 1919–1923* University of Liverpool Press

O Broin L 1982 *No Man's Man – a biographical memoir of Joseph Brennan, civil servant and Governor of the Central Bank* Institute of Public Administration Dublin

O Connor B 1929 *With Michael Collins – in the struggle for Irish independence* Peter Davies

O Donohue F 1954 *No Other Law – the story of Liam Lynch and the Irish Republican Army* Irish Press

O Hegarty P S 1952 *History of Ireland under the Union 1801–1922* Methuen

Packenham F 1992 *Peace by Ordeal* Pimlico Books. Originally published 1935 Jonathan Cape

Pares B 1939 *The Fall of the Russian Monarchy* Cassell

Paxton R O 1972 *Vichy France – old guard and new order 1940–1944* Barrie & Jenkins

Paz A 2007 *Durruti in the Spanish Revolution.* Oakland Press

Ryan D 1949 *The Rising – the complete story of Easter Week* Golden Eagle Books

Schama S 1989 *Citizens – a chronicle of the French Revolution* Viking Books

Seton-Watson R W 1967 *The Russian Empire 1801–1917* OPUS

Talbot J 1980 *The War without a Name – France in Algeria 1956–62* Alfred Knof

Taylor P 1997 *Provos, the IRA and Sinn Fein* Bloomsbury Publishing

Thompson P 2005 *The Battle for Singapore* Portrait Books

Thornley D 1964 *Isaac Butt and Home Rule* McGibbon & Kee

Townsend C 2014 *The Republic – the fight for Irish independence* Penguin

Townshend C 2005 *Easter 1916* Allen Lane

Travers P 1998 *Settlements and Divisions – Ireland 1870–1922* Helicon

Tuchmann B 1966 *The Zimmerman Telegram* First Ballantine Books

Tuchmann B 1980 *The Guns of August* Macmillan Press

Valiulis M G 1992 *Portrait of a Revolutionary General – Richard Mulcahy and the founding of the Irish Free State* University of Kentucky Press

Walsh M 2008 *The News from Ireland – foreign correspondents and the Irish Revolution* IB Taurus

Winter O 1995 *Winter's Tale* London Richards Press

Younger C 1969 *Ireland's Civil War* Taplinger Publishing Company

Index